Bonds of Citizenship

America and the Long 19th Century

GENERAL EDITORS
David Kazanjian, Elizabeth McHenry, and Priscilla Wald

Black Frankenstein: The Making of an American Metaphor
Elizabeth Young

Neither Fugitive nor Free: Atlantic Slavery, Freedom Suits, and the Legal Culture of Travel
Edlie L. Wong

Shadowing the White Man's Burden: U.S. Imperialism and the Problem of the Color Line
Gretchen Murphy

Bodies of Reform: The Rhetoric of Character in Gilded Age America
James B. Salazar

Empire's Proxy: American Literature and U.S. Imperialism in the Philippines
Meg Wesling

Sites Unseen: Architecture, Race, and American Literature
William A. Gleason

Racial Innocence: Performing American Childhood from Slavery to Civil Rights
Robin Bernstein

American Arabesque: Arabs and Islam in the Nineteenth-Century Imaginary
Jacob Rama Berman

Racial Indigestion: Eating Bodies in the Nineteenth Century
Kyla Wazana Tompkins

Idle Threats: Men and the Limits of Productivity in Nineteenth-Century America
Andrew Lyndon Knighton

Tomorrow's Parties: Sex and the Untimely in Nineteenth-Century America
Peter Coviello

Bonds of Citizenship: Law and the Labors of Emancipation
Hoang Gia Phan

Bonds of Citizenship

Law and the Labors of Emancipation

Hoang Gia Phan

NEW YORK UNIVERSITY PRESS
New York and London

NEW YORK UNIVERSITY PRESS
New York and London
www.nyupress.org

© 2013 by New York University
All rights reserved

LIBRARY OF CONGRESS CATALOGING-IN-PUBLICATION DATA

Phan, Hoang Gia.
Bonds of citizenship : law and the labors of emancipation /
Hoang Gia Phan.
p. cm.—(America and the long 19th century)
Includes bibliographical references and index.
ISBN 978-0-8147-3847-4 (cl : alk. paper)
ISBN 978-0-8147-7170-9 (pb : alk. paper)
ISBN 978-0-8147-3893-1 (e)
ISBN 978-0-8147-7192-1 (e)
1. Slaves—Legal status, laws, etc.—United States—History.
2. Citizenship—United States—Philosophy. 3. Citizenship—United
States—History. 4. Slavery—United States—History. 5. Indentured
servants—Legal status, laws, etc.—United States—History. 6. Social
structure—United States—History. 7. Slavery in literature.
8. Citizenship in literature. 9. Master and servant in literature.
I. Title.
KF482.P49   2013
342.7308'7—dc23

2012035343

References to Internet Websites (URLs) were accurate at the time of
writing. Neither the author nor New York University Press is responsible
for URLs that may have expired or changed since the manuscript was
prepared.

New York University Press books are printed on acid-free paper, and
their binding materials are chosen for strength and durability. We
strive to use environmentally responsible suppliers and materials to the
greatest extent possible in publishing our books.

Manufactured in the United States of America
c 10 9 8 7 6 5 4 3 2 1
p 10 9 8 7 6 5 4 3 2 1

A book in the American Literatures Initiative (ALI), a collaborative
publishing project of NYU Press, Fordham University Press, Rutgers
University Press, Temple University Press, and the University of Virginia
Press. The Initiative is supported by The Andrew W. Mellon Foundation.
For more information, please visit www.americanliteratures.org.

For Tho and Lien Phan

Contents

	Acknowledgments	ix
	Introduction. "A Man from Another Country": Citizenship and the Bonds of Labor	1
1	Bound by Law: Apprenticeship and the Culture of "Free" Labor	24
2	Civic Virtues: Narrative Form and the Trial of Character in Early America	63
3	Fugitive Bonds: Contract and the Culture of Constitutionalism	107
4	Hereditary Bondsman: Frederick Douglass and the Spirit of the Law	142
5	"If Man Will Strike": *Moby-Dick* and the Letter of the Law	172
	Conclusion. The Labors of Emancipation: Founded Law and Freedom Defined	201
	Notes	211
	Index	249
	About the Author	257

Acknowledgments

This book has benefited from the intellectual and material support of many. At the University of California, Berkeley, I was fortunate to work closely with Stephen Best, Colleen Lye, and Samuel Otter. Individually and collectively they inspired and challenged me as this project first took shape. A special word of gratitude goes to Stephen for his invaluable support and encouragement of the project throughout its inception and writing. I am grateful also to Angela Harris for sharing her legal expertise as reader and interlocutor.

The University of California, Berkeley, and the Berkeley English Department provided much-needed institutional support for my research in its early stages. Over the course of the project, additional support was provided by the Doreen B. Townsend Center for the Humanities; the Andrew W. Mellon Foundation; Williams College; the University of Massachusetts, Amherst; and the Five Colleges, Incorporated. The Law and Humanities Junior Scholar Workshop held at Columbia Law School (2003) afforded me the opportunity to share my work with a brilliant grouping of scholars. I thank David Eng, Katherine Franke, Cheryl Harris, Daniel Hulsebosch, Teemu Ruskola, and Austin Sarat for their suggestions during discussion. Special thanks to Walter Johnson, whose illuminating commentary on my paper for the Workshop helped me to refine this book's historical arguments. Audiences at New York University, Williams College, and the Five Colleges also provided productive dialogue. At the University at Albany, SUNY, Bret Benjamin, Rosemary Hennessey, and Mike Hill encouraged and pushed my research further, while sharing their own work with me and giving generously of their time to mentor me as a junior colleague.

At the University of Massachusetts, Amherst, I am grateful to many English Department colleagues for their support and research stimulus: Nick Bromell, Suzanne Daly, Laura Doyle, Mason Lowance, Asha Nadkarni, Jordana Rosenberg, TreaAndrea Russworm, Joseph Skerrett, Jenny

Spencer, and Ron Welburn. I am especially grateful to Ruth Jennison, my comrade at Berkeley long before we became colleagues at UMass, for these many years of intellectual collaboration. I want to thank also my colleagues in the W. E. B. Du Bois Department of Afro-American Studies, whose work is a model of interdisciplinary scholarship: Amilcar Shabazz, Manisha Sinha, James Smethurst, and Steven Tracy. The following pages have also benefited immensely from the scrupulous attention of the readers for NYU Press. I am grateful for the support of my series editors, David Kazanjian, Elizabeth McHenry, and Priscilla Wald. NYU Press editor-in-chief Eric Zinner supported this book project from its very beginning. I thank him and assistant editor Ciara McLaughlin for guiding me through the publication process with such care and enthusiasm. I also thank Aaron Winslow for research assistance, as well as Tim Roberts and Susan Murray for assisting in preparation of the manuscript.

Finally, I thank my family for their unwavering support of my intellectual pursuits. My sisters, Dao and Loan, and my brother, Khai, encouraged these pursuits long before any of us imagined what might come of them, and cheered me along the way these many years. This book is dedicated to my parents, Tho Chanh Phan and Lien Diep Phan. To them I owe my greatest debts, and my deepest bonds.

Bonds of Citizenship

Introduction. "A Man from Another Country"

Citizenship and the Bonds of Labor

> What will the people of America a hundred years hence care about the intentions of the scriveners who wrote the Constitution?
> —Frederick Douglass, "The Constitution of the United States: Is it Pro-Slavery or Anti-Slavery?"

In 1849, as the Union crisis escalated over yet another likely compromise with American slavery, Frederick Douglass startled the antislavery movement with an unusually equivocal statement of his view of the Constitution as a slavery-sanctioning text: "On a close examination of the Constitution, I am satisfied that if 'strictly construed according to its reading' it is not a pro-slavery instrument.... I now hold that the original intent and meaning of the Constitution (the one given to it by the men who framed it, those who adopted it, and the one given to it by the Supreme Court of the United States) makes it a proslavery instrument."[1] Douglass's concluding claim that "the original intent and meaning of the Constitution" made it "a pro-slavery instrument" was uncontroversial, the reiteration of an interpretation widely accepted by abolitionists and slaveholders alike in antebellum America. Indeed, this view of the original Constitution as a slavery-sanctioning document remains accepted by most modern historians. What startled so many in 1849 was Douglass's first claim, one that seemed to contradict this interpretation of the Constitution. How could one hold the view that the "original intent and meaning" of the Constitution was to sanction and safeguard slavery, while simultaneously arguing that "if strictly construed," the Constitution was not a proslavery document? How could the meaning of this founding legal document be construed against that "intended" meaning "given to it by the men who framed it"? These were the central hermeneutic questions of the debate over what would come to be called the 1850 Compromise and its federal Fugitive Slave Act.

In his editorial entitled "The Address of Southern Delegates in Congress to their Constituents; or, the Address of John C. Calhoun and Forty Other Thieves," appearing in the same 9 February issue of the *North Star*, Douglass elaborated upon this distinction between the conception of a law's "original intent and meaning" based on the historical context of its framing and its *legislative intent*, based on the "strict construction" of its language. Douglass observed: "It will be seen that [Calhoun's] "Address" assumes a clear recognition of slavery in the United States Constitution, by the clause relating to taxation and representation—that relating to the return of fugitive slaves, and that respecting the importation of slaves."[2] The problem for these political representatives of the slaveholders, Douglass argued—and here we have the first articulation of the emerging shift in Douglass's interpretation of the Constitution—is that the so-called "slave clauses" contained no such clear recognition of slavery: "We deem it unfortunate for these honourable menstealers, that in no instances have they been able to find a word in either of these clauses which bears the definition of slaves or slavery. The word slave in all these references is the word of this conclave, and not the Constitution."[3] According to Douglass, slaveholders were confounded in their attempts to read the Constitution as a slavery-sanctioning document because, just as the word is absent from their own "Address," it is absent from that founding law whose legitimating authority they invoke. If slavery's political representatives avoided using the "gross form of the *word* slavery" to name that system they defended, the Constitution's framers also avoided this word, likewise referring to slavery and its subjects only through euphemism and indirection. As Douglass argued further: "The fact is, the framers of that cunning instrument were ashamed of the *name*, while they had not the honesty to renounce the *thing*, slavery; and it is the same sense of shame today which leads the friends and defenders of this inhuman system to use the term 'peculiar institution,' 'the relation existing between the European and African races' and the like."[4] In Douglass's reading, this shared "way of sliding over of the hateful word slavery" links the rhetorical practice of the slavery-defending southern delegates to the writing practice of the slavery-sanctioning constitutional framers.[5]

Douglass's reading practice thus extends beyond the "ambiguous terms" of Calhoun's "Address" to the "ambiguously worded" Constitution itself: "The language in each of the provisions to which the address refers, though doubtless *intended* to bolster up slavery and respect slave property, has been so ambiguously worded as to bear a very different construction; and taken in connection with the preamble of that instrument, the very opposite of the construction given it by this wily band of slaveholders."[6] Douglass is not arguing here that the framers' "original intent" was actually an antislavery Constitution. Instead, Douglass concedes throughout this 1849 editorial that the slave clauses were "doubtless intended to bolster up slavery and respect slave property," but argues that the ambiguous terms used in the final text of the Constitution leave its meaning open to a much more radical "construction."

Douglass elaborates upon this significant disjunction between the letter of the law and the "original intent" of the law by proposing a hypothetical scene of reading: "Suppose a man from another country should read that clause of the American Constitution which Calhoun alleges refers to fugitive slaves, with no other knowledge of the character of American institutions than what he derived from the reading of that instrument, will anyone pretend that the clause in question would be thought to apply to slaves? We think not."[7] On the one hand, Douglass extends his local critique of the proslavery interpretation of the Constitution to situate the founding document within an international context. Such contextualization was a popular rhetorical gesture; Douglass and other antislavery writers often alluded to the idea that slavery undermined the United States' reputation as an enlightened republic.[8] On the other hand, Douglass's hypothetical scene of reading is a provocatively decontextualized one: this "man from another country," unfamiliar with the peculiar context of the Constitution's inscription and the nation's history, would necessarily be a "strict constructionist." This "man from another country" could not imagine that the "fugitive slave clause" and its terms of labor subjection were intended to apply to slaves, "nor dream of such an outrage, such a savage monstrosity, on reading any other part of the Constitution."[9] In this hypothetical scene of reading, the true "spirit of the law" is to be located only through a reading of the letter of the law, regardless of its "original intent."

What is of further significance to our understanding of the constitutional debates of the Union crisis is that this "man from another country" interprets the Constitution the same way Douglass will throughout the next decade, after publishing his "Change of Opinion" in 1851. Douglass's "man from another country" is the figure for the type of reading practice modeled by Douglass himself in this critique. As a figure of reading, the trope allows Douglass to brush history against the grain, interpret the famous "slave clauses" otherwise, and thus conceive of an alternative spirit of the law. As Douglass concludes: "Blot slavery from existence, and the whole framework of the Constitution might remain unchanged."[10] In 1849, as the debates over yet another national compromise regarding slavery raged; and as the antislavery movement splintered into different factions, this experiment in reading against "original intent" signaled a radical transformation in Douglass's political perspective.

For cultural history, this "man from another country" provides a view into the ways in which antislavery politics led to transformations in "literary" and legal hermeneutics, as well as the "culture of Constitutionalism."[11] Reading the text of the Constitution against the grain of "original intent," Douglass's strategy is to focus on the elisions and ambiguities of reference within the very letter of the law. Douglass first zeroes in on what he calls the "ambiguous... inappropriate... and equivocal language" of the fugitive slave clause:

> If the provision in question refers to slaves escaping from slave States into free States, and was intended to define the right of masters to apprehend their slaves, and the duty of free States to deliver them up, the language used, is most ambiguous and inappropriate. The words "held to service and labor," for instance, does not necessarily imply the relation of "master and slave," and is rather a description of minors and apprentices, than of slaves.[12]

Douglass's use of the infamous fugitive slave clause as exemplary of the ambiguities and equivocations permeating the language of the Constitution is itself a significant decision, raising important questions regarding the conceptualizations of freedom, unfreedom, and citizenship in a slaveholding nation, which I will address in the second part of this introduction, and at greater length in chapter 3. Here I want to note that the point of Douglass's lesson in constitutional interpretation is not merely that the founding document does not contain the words "slave" or "slavery," a point made by many critics before and since Douglass's reading. As Eric Foner has described, it was this absence of direct references to slavery, color, or race in the text that reformers such as Salmon P. Chase, the architect of the moderate political abolitionist strategy, used to argue that the framers' shared "original intent" was the eventual disappearance of slavery from the Union, its withering away as a political-economic institution.[13] The more significant point is that Douglass goes beyond pointing to the absence of the words "slave" and "slavery" to posit two interdependent claims about the words that do appear in the letter of the law.

First, Douglass points out that there exists no necessary relation between the words used in the fugitive rendition clause ("held to service or labor") and "the thing" those words are "alleged" by Calhoun's *Address* to "name" (that is, "the relation of master and slave"). Further, Douglass posits that these very same words of the clause refer instead to a different type of labor bondage and other types of laboring subjects: indentured servitude and apprenticeship (and their subjects, "apprentices and minors"). Douglass's second, positive claim regarding the true referent of the phrase "held to service or labor" in the frequently cited fugitive rendition clause was in 1849 a counterintuitive one to say the least, running expressly counter to what was widely understood to be (and what Douglass concedes throughout this editorial to be) the "original intent" of the clause.

By 1849, indentured servitude had long declined as a dominant form of labor subjection, replaced by chattel slavery and wage labor, and few readers in 1849 could imagine the term "held to service or labor" in the fugitive rendition clause to be a description of such servitude. Throughout his ruling in the famous 1842 case of *Prigg v. Pennsylvania*, for example, Supreme Court Justice Joseph Story, maintaining the importance of the "original intent" of the "fugitive slave clause" and taking for granted its historical context, interpreted the term "person held to service or labor" to refer solely to the slave: "Historically, it is well known, that the object of this clause was to secure to the citizens of the slave-holding states the complete right and title of ownership in their slaves, as property, in every state in the Union into which they might escape from the state where they were held in servitude."[14] John Calhoun's "Southern Address," to which Douglass's 1849 editorial in the *North Star* was a response, began its argument for the rights of slaveholders by citing Justice Story's majority Opinion in *Prigg v. Pennsylvania* and its originalist view of slavery as the Constitution's historical "compromise." Douglass's interpretation is thus also counterintuitive because by 1849, indentured servants and apprentices have been erased from the horizon of signification as even implied referents of the phrase "person held to service or labor," and the "ambiguous" terms of this fugitive rendition clause immediately conjure only the figure of the runaway slave.

Ambiguous Identities and the Forms of Law

Douglass's counterintuitive construction of the fugitive labor clause provides insight into a broader historical and literary-critical argument, whose implications are developed throughout *Bonds of Citizenship*: the dominant historical conceptualizations of slavery and slave personhood (in this case, the critical commonplace that the fugitive labor rendition clause was "originally intended" to refer exclusively to fugitive slaves) are contingent, partial truths, whose very intelligibility is circumscribed by what Douglass calls "the *forms of law*"—and what Karl Marx, writing during the labor struggles of this period, would call their *forms of appearance* in the law.[15]

Marx uses "form of appearance" (*Erscheinungsform*, a term given special emphasis) throughout *Capital*, from his opening analyses of exchange-value (*Capital* 1: 127), the commodity-form (*Capital* 1: 165), and the money-form (*Capital* 1: 236), to his study of variable capital and simple reproduction (*Capital* 1: 714). For our present discussion of that repressed referent of the Constitution's fugitive *labor* rendition clause made visible by Douglass's "man from another country," Marx's dissection of the mystifications of the wage-form is most pertinent:

> The wage-form . . . extinguishes every trace of the division of the working day into necessary labour and surplus labour, into paid labour and unpaid labour. All labour appears as paid labour. . . . In slave labour, even the part of the working day in which the slave is only replacing the value of his own means of subsistence, in which he therefore actually works for himself alone, appears as labour for his master. All the labour appears as unpaid labour. In wage-labour, on the contrary, even surplus labour, or unpaid labour, appears as paid. In the one case, the property-relation conceals the slave's labour for himself; in the other case the money-relation conceals the uncompensated labour of the wage-labourer. . . . All the notions of justice held by both the worker and the capitalist, all the mystifications of the capitalist mode of production, all capitalism's illusions about freedom, all the apologetic tricks of vulgar economics, have as their basis [this] form of

appearance ... which makes the actual relation invisible, and indeed presents to the eye the precise opposite of that relation. (*Capital* 1: 680)

As with the hermeneutic of Douglass's "man from another country," this comparative analysis of slave labor and wage labor was tied directly to Marx's dialectical critique of "the forms of law" as the codification of economic relations. Against the bourgeois economists' "crude obsession with the material side [*Stoff*]," which thus led them to "ignore all differences of form" (682), and made them "unable to separate the *form of appearance* from the thing which appears within that form" (714), historical materialism distinguishes between those forms of appearance "reproduced directly and spontaneously, as current and usual modes of thought"—that is, through ideology in the narrow sense—and "the essential relation manifested in" (682) these forms.

As Louis Althusser and Etienne Balibar emphasize in *Reading Capital*, Marx's method is to "distinguish between the *relations of production* themselves ... and their 'legal expression,' which does not belong to the structure of production considered in its relative autonomy."[16] In analyzing the relations of production specific to the capitalist mode of production, therefore, "it is a question of distinguishing between the connection that we have called 'property' and the *law of property*."[17] This method "consists of looking for the relations of production *behind* the legal forms, or better: behind the secondary unity of production and law, which has to be disentangled. Only by this method will it eventually be possible to trace the theoretical boundary while still taking into account the ambivalent function that Marx assigns to legal forms: they are necessary yet 'irrational,' *expressing* and *codifying* the 'economic' reality which each mode of production defines in its own way, and yet simultaneously *masking* it."[18]

By focusing on the ambivalent function of what he called "the forms of law," Douglass's reading of the "fugitive slave clause" recovers its other referents, apprenticeship and indentured servitude, forms of bound labor sharing elements of both enslaved and "free" waged labor. Following Douglass and Marx in their shared focus on legal codifications of property and of labor as ambiguous forms of appearance, *Bonds of Citizenship* focuses on the laboring subject's multiple and historically varying forms of appearance, to explore the legal and cultural implications of that founding constitutional moment wherein the bondsman—the "person held to service or labor"—is inscribed as that name for the twinned labor subjections of slavery and indentured servitude. Pursuing Douglass's insight, this study reads the figure of the bondsman as a *trace* of both the slave and the indentured servant, which together serve as the absent presence of the Constitution.[19] That slavery was the absent presence of the Constitution was clear to Douglass and his contemporaries: the slave was not named in any of the so-called "slave clauses," and instead referenced only indirectly through the "equivocal" and "ambiguous" term "person held to service or labour." Yet as we have seen, Douglass pushed further on this point regarding the slave's ambiguous legal form of appearance, to apprehend that very form of appearance as a trace which codifies and masks another form of labor bondage: indentured servitude. This servitude is the other half of that labor bondage which is the absent presence of the "slave clauses"; and the intertwined history of slavery and servitude is marked in the Constitution by the figure of the bondsman as legal form of appearance.

The reading of Douglass's "man from another country" reveals how this form of appearance works in the Constitution to make invisible those other laboring subjects, indentured servants. In indentured servitude, individuals "voluntarily" contracted to serve for a term in exchange for compensation, such as transportation expenses and freedom dues. What type of labor exploitation did this practice constitute? As Barbara Fields's well-known argument indicates, the modern answer seems to be that it constitutes a form of slavery.[20] As Robert Steinfeld reminds us, however, this answer "depends upon a particular scheme of understandings that ignores the characteristics indentured servitude shares with free labor—contractual freedom, limited term, compensation—and that classifies it with slavery because of the legal compulsion both involve."[21]

At the time of the constitutional founding, indentured labor was a widespread form of labor bondage; and the recapture of escaped indentured servants was in fact one of the "originally intended" meanings of the fugitive labor rendition clause. William Wiecek notes that the interstate rendition of fugitive slaves among the American states "originated in intercolonial efforts to prohibit the absconding of white servants, and never lost its association with the problem of controlling elopement by those in limited-term servitude."[22] As Douglass and his contemporaries learned from reading James Madison's record of *The Debates in the Federal Convention of 1787* (first published in 1840), the original draft of this clause referred explicitly to both "fugitive slaves and servants," and provided for the return of both these types of laborers. Madison noted that this fugitive-from-labor clause was introduced initially as a supplement to the clause requiring the rendition of fugitive criminals to the "State having jurisdiction over the Crime": "Mr. Butler and Mr. Pinckney moved to 'require fugitive slaves and servants to be delivered up like criminals.'"[23] After several objections to this proposal—objections to its explicit inscription of slavery into the Constitution; and to its logical implication that nonslaveholding states would be required to pay for the labor practices of the slaveholding states—the proposition was withdrawn, "in order that some particular provision might be made apart from this article." What modern historians now call the "fugitive slave clause" was reintroduced the next day as a separate provision. Both "slave" and "servant" disappeared in the new formulation of the provision, replaced by the terms "person held to service or labour."[24] These twinned subjects of labor bondage are thus inscribed into the referential structure of the Constitution only indirectly, as the "person held to service or labor," their names erased from the letter of the law. Slave and servant are collapsed into the singular figure of the bondsman, "the person held to service or labor." The bondsman's legal form of appearance conceals the history of these other subjects of labor bondage implicated in the Constitution's fugitive rendition clause. As I elaborate in the next two sections of this introduction, a hermeneutic attuned to this absent presence and the ambiguities of law's forms can illuminate as well the other key term of that founding moment and of the present study, the citizen.

The Bondsman as Vanishing Mediator

Etienne Balibar has argued that the national revolutions of the late eighteenth century constituted a "break" in "the history of 'the problem of Man,' as 'citizen' and as subject,'" the crossing of an "irreversible threshold." This historical threshold was "crossed when secular and would-be democratic societies were constituted . . . namely during the 'revolutions' at the end of the eighteenth and the beginning of the nineteenth centuries in North America, France, Latin America, Greece, and elsewhere."[25] In contrast to the medieval figure of subjection to (religious and political) sovereign authority, with this second historical break man now "ceases to be a *subjectus*, a subject, and therefore his relationship to the Law (and the idea of law) is radically inverted: he is no longer the man called before the Law, or to whom an inner voice dictates the Law . . . he is rather the man who, at least virtually, 'makes the law,' i.e. constitutes it, or *declares* it to be valid."[26] This modern citizen-subject is now responsible or accountable because he is a legislator: "These men . . . were able to begin thinking of themselves as free subjects, and thus to identify liberty and subjectivity, because they had abolished the principle of their subjection . . . while conquering and constituting their political citizenship."[27] If the revolutions of 1776 and 1789 reconstituted citizenship such that modern "citizenship is not one among other attributes of subjectivity, on the contrary: it *is* subjectivity, *that form* of subjectivity that would no longer be identical with subjection for anyone," how do we understand the histories of slavery and servitude that inhered in these moments?[28] Supplementing Balibar's argument with the perspective of Douglass's "man from another country," we can see that during the historical moment of the constitutional founding, the bondsman mediates the two opposing poles of subjection and subjectivity codified in the letter of the law: that is, the complete subjection of chattel slavery on the one side and the "freedom" of self-constituted political subjectivity on the other.

As I argued in the previous section, the pairing of slavery and indentured servitude in the fugitive labor rendition clause also underscores their shared condition of legal compulsion. Such a provision for legal compulsion—this was a clause providing for the recapture and delivering up of *fugitive* labor, after all—would be mobilized later to consolidate the modern definition of "free labor" as that performed in "the absence of legal compulsion."[29] As the figure for criminal fugitive labor—criminal for having fled with the embodied labor purchased by another—whose recapture was a condition of the Constitution's ratification and thus of the founding of the nation, this bondsman (the "person held to service or labor") thus also serves as the vanishing mediator, between a pre-Revolutionary form of subjection to sovereignty and the imagined self-constituted subjectivity of U.S. citizenship.[30]

In Fredric Jameson's formulation, a vanishing mediator is "a catalytic agent that permits an exchange of [historical] energies between two otherwise mutually exclusive terms"; it is a dialectical figure whose form mediates the transition between two opposed concepts and thereafter disappears.[31] Jameson develops the concept of the vanishing mediator in his narrative analysis of Weber's famous account of Protestantism's role in the transition from the feudal mode of production to the capitalist mode of production; he proposes also that as a dialectical figure of historical transition, the vanishing mediator is likewise perceptible in Marx's analyses of political events (for example, his analyses of the revolutions of 1789 and

1848). Its origins in narrative analysis remind us of the dual function of the vanishing mediator, which is to "combine the twin requirements of narrative irreversibility, and of figuration into agents or characters."[32] In Weber's story of secularization, the movement called "Protestantism" is a historical character, a narrative agent that serves as a "mediation between the traditional medieval world from which it emerged and the modern secularized one that it in its turn prepared."[33] And it is a *vanishing* mediator in the sense that in "the final transition to the situation of modern capitalism ... what happens here is essentially that once Protestantism has accomplished the task of allowing a rationalization of innerworldly life to take place, it has no further reasons for being and disappears from the historical scene."[34]

As a narrative figure, the vanishing mediator need not be a historical movement, such as Protestantism; it can also be a singular character type, such as the figure of the prophet in Weber's account of secularization and charismatic power. I have argued thus far that Douglass's reading of the fugitive labor rendition clause, from the point of view of the "man from another country," recognizes the labor bondage of the slave and the servant as the absent presence of the Constitution. *Bonds of Citizenship* proposes that this reading thus also makes visible the ways in which the category of the bondsman—the figure for both enslaved and indentured labor—functions as a vanishing mediator, making possible that category of personhood equated with full legal freedom in the new republic, the citizen.

Douglass does not make this point, but surely his "man from another country" would. This reader would notice that the fugitive labor rendition clause is the supplementary clause to the only section of the original Constitution that refers to the "privileges and immunities of citizens" of the United States. The first clause of Article IV, Section 2 reads: "The Citizens of each State shall be entitled to all Privileges and Immunities of Citizens in the several States." Nowhere in the original Constitution is the term "citizen" defined.[35] National citizenship was clearly defined (over and against state citizenship) only after the Civil War, with the passage of the Fourteenth Amendment.[36] Yet of all the provisions of the Constitution, Article IV, Section 2 comes closest to delimiting, if not explicitly defining, the term "citizens."

I say delimiting because even in its narrowest interpretation, the clause recognizes the "citizen" as a figure always-already attached to certain "Privileges and Immunities," and likewise recognizes the citizens of each state as "entitled" to the privileges and immunities of citizens of all other states.[37] By entitling citizens of each state to privileges and immunities of citizens of all other states, this clause inscribes the citizen as a figure of unrestricted mobility, free to roam throughout the states of the new nation without legal disability. In explicit contrast to this new citizen's freedom of mobility, the second clause of Article IV, Section 2 states: "A Person charged in any State with Treason, Felony, or other Crime, who shall flee from justice, and be found in another State, shall on demand of the executive Authority of the State from which he fled, be delivered up, to be removed to the State having Jurisdiction of the Crime."[38] This fugitive criminal rendition clause is the necessary supplement to the extraterritoriality of the "privileges and immunities" clause. Just as a unified national space is imagined through the extraterritoriality of the state citizen's "privileges and immunities," the different legal spaces of the individual states are united through this supplementary provision for the capture and rendition of the fugitive criminal. The movement of this fugitive criminal maps the intersections between the local police powers of the states and the national reach of the federal Constitution.

The fugitive labor rendition clause was proposed as the political-economic *supplement* to this fugitive criminal rendition clause, which, as we have seen, served to delimit the freedom of the citizen. Indeed, the fugitive labor rendition clause likens escape from labor bondage to a flight "from Justice": in escaping from their economic bonds, fugitive slaves and servants fled the bonds of law and were, in the words of the authors of the clause, "to be delivered up like criminals."[39] Similarly, what is commonly known as the first federal "fugitive slave" act (of 1793), enacted to give force to the Constitution's fugitive labor rendition clause, was actually entitled "An act respecting fugitives from justice, and persons escaping from the service of their masters," and likewise linked to these different types of fugitives.[40] As I discuss at greater length in the first three chapters of this study, it is through these supplementary figures—the slave and the servant—that this founding law establishes one of the central categories through which "freedom" would be imagined—and racialized—throughout nineteenth-century American law and literature: "freedom" as free mobility.[41]

Nor would the "man from another country" ignore the bondsman's ambiguous forms of appearance in the Constitution's other "slave clauses," for there also the figure of the bondsman mediates the legal inscription of the passage from "subject" to "citizen." Article I, Section

2—the Constitution's all-important provision for apportionment of representation and taxation—scripts its infamous "three-fifths clause" thus: "Representatives and direct taxes shall be apportioned among the several states which may be included within this union, according to their respective numbers, which shall be determined by adding to the whole number of free persons, *including those bound to service for a term of years*, and excluding Indians not taxed, three-fifths of all other persons."[42] In chapter 1, I elaborate the significance of this negotiation of the "principle of representation" to late-eighteenth and nineteenth-century U.S. racial formations, and to the construction of blackness as "the badge of servitude." For now, I continue in the tracks of the bondsman as vanishing mediator. Historians are right to remark upon the absence of "black," "color," and "race" in the catalogue of this clause's accounting. The letter of the law, in its calculations for the purposes of representation and taxation, refers to only two types of "persons": "free persons" and "other persons."[43] While such arguments provide an important critical corrective, they forget another category of persons that adds significantly to our understanding of the relation between the unspoken terms of "race," "slavery," and "labor." Article I, Section 2 attempts a comprehensive survey of the persons then present in the states, even as it resists referring explicitly to racially marked freedom or unfreedom. Supplementing its description of "whole free persons," the clause adds: "including those bound to service for a term of years"—that is, indentured servants. In the context of the later mobilizations of the concepts of free and unfree labor, indentured servitude and its ambiguous position here between "free persons" and those "other persons" (slaves) become particularly important. While we might agree with David Brion Davis on a structural identity between indentured servant and slave, we should also recognize the difference between them, one important enough to be included as a supplement to the Constitution's calculus of representation. While indentured servants may be just like slaves in their material living conditions, their social standing, and the experience of corporal punishment, they are also legally different: for the purposes of political representation and direct taxation, indentured servants will be counted as whole persons; those "other persons" will not.[44] This third term adds productive problems to familiar critical narratives of slavery, and its various loose synonyms, such as bondage and involuntary servitude. One immediate question, for example, is: Why should they count as whole numbers? Yet this, too, is a misleading construction of the clause. It reads: "the whole number of free persons, *including those bound to service for a term of years.*"⁴⁵ The supplementary "including" describes free persons. Which is to say that according to the original Constitution, one could be bound, in a state of labor bondage, and also be "free." If in the fugitive labor rendition clause the bondsman's ambiguous legal form of appearance "codified and masked" the history of indentured servitude, here in the apportionment clause the bondsman foregrounds that history, in order to distinguish the nominally "free" personhood of the indentured servant from the unnamed slavery of those "other persons." The figure of the bondsman thus displaces that binary opposition between "free labor" and the unfreedom of black chattel slavery, one regularly assumed in readings of the Constitution and in histories of citizenship, racial formation, and class formation.

Finally, suppose the "man from another country" were to read the last of the "slavery clauses," the "migration and importation" clause? At first glance, this clause seems unequivocal in authorizing the continuation of the slave trade until (at least) 1808: "The migration or importation of such persons as any of the states now existing shall think proper to admit, shall not be prohibited by the Congress prior to the year one thousand eight hundred and eight, but a tax or duty may be imposed on such importation, not exceeding ten dollars for each person."⁴⁶ According to *The Federalist Papers* and other contemporary accounts, the clause was widely recognized as a "compromise" over the foreign slave trade.⁴⁷ Yet even those who recognized its slavery-sanctioning "original intent" remarked upon the ambiguity of its language and the unintended effects of such ambiguity. Arguing against ratification of the federal constitution, Luther Martin, delegate from Maryland, declared:

> The design of this clause is to prevent the general government from prohibiting the importation of slaves; but the same reasons which caused them to strike out the word "national" . . . influenced them here to guard against the word "*slaves.*" They anxiously sought to avoid the admission of expressions which might be odious in the ears of Americans, although they were willing to admit into their system those *things* which the *expressions* signified; and hence it is that the clause is so worded as really to authorize the general government to impose a duty of ten dollars on every foreigner who comes into a State to become a citizen, whether he comes *absolutely free*, or *qualifiedly so* as a servant; although this is contrary to the design of the framers, and the duty was only meant to extend to the importation of slaves.⁴⁸

Martin expressed the shared understanding that the immigrant (the man from another country) would be assimilated as a "citizen," and that the immigrant who came as an indentured servant was "qualifiedly" free, as opposed to the absolute unfreedom of the clause's "intended" subject, the unnamed slave. As we saw in Douglass's 1849 editorial response to Calhoun's "Southern Address," Douglass echoed Luther Martin's claim when he declared that "the framers of that cunning instrument were ashamed of the *name*, while they had not the honesty to renounce the *thing*, slavery."[49] The historical and literary-critical point to emphasize here is that this disjunction between the "expression" and the "signified," between "name" and "thing," is one that inhered in the original ambiguity of the Constitution's text.

Indeed, only a decade after the federal constitutional convention and long before the rise of broad antislavery agitation within the United States, the language of this apparently unequivocal "slave clause" came under scrutiny in the debates of the Alien and Sedition crisis. In the congressional debate over the Federalists' Alien Friends Act of 1798, Jeffersonian Republicans cited the 1808 provision of the "migration and importation clause" to argue that the Alien Friends Act was unconstitutional. While Federalists asserted that the "migration and importation clause" referred solely to the slave trade, Jeffersonian Republicans insisted that the clause also applied to the immigration of *free* persons. They argued that the word "person" was general, and included immigrants, and that in addition to "importation," which applied to the traffic in persons chattel—that is, slaves brought to the United States without their consent—the clause used the term "migration," which indicated a "free act of the will." This debate over the interpretation of that other key "slave clause" was resolved only when Abraham Baldwin (the only representative then in the House who had helped frame the Constitution) agreed that the clause applied to immigrants as well as to slaves. In doing so, Baldwin recalled the objections raised during the convention debates over the use of the word "slave" in the Constitution.[50]

As I have argued, the bondsman mediates the two opposing poles of personhood codified in the letter of the law: namely, the subjection of chattel slavery on the one side and the "freedom" of self-constituted political subjectivity on the other. The bondsman is thus a vanishing mediator in the strongest sense: as the "catalytic agent that permits an exchange of energies between two otherwise mutually exclusive terms," and thereafter disappears.

Literary History and Forms of Contingency

Douglass recognized the labor bondage of both the slave and the servant to be the absent presence of the Constitution, reading the figure of the bondsman as the *trace* of this erasure. By reinterpreting the so-called slave clauses as referring instead to the labor bondage of indentured servitude and apprenticeship, Douglass draws our attention to the figure of the bondsman, whose ambiguous form of appearance in the letter of the law registers the historical links between enslaved and "free" laborers. In doing so, Douglass points to labor exploitation as an underlying core of the slavery debates. Douglass recognized the fundamental historical role of both enslaved and bound-yet-free labor to the building of the republic; he also recognized the need for some proper accounting. In an insight that few modern scholars have taken up, however, he went further to argue that the erasure of the word, the refusal out of guilty shame "to name the thing," provided for the radical revision of the Constitution's meaning and purpose. For if ambiguities of reference arise from the slave's forms of appearance in the law, the words used to inscribe them in the Constitution could be given an altogether different "construction." As Douglass asserted: "The language in each of the provisions to which the [Calhoun] address refers . . . [bears] the very opposite of the construction given it by this wily band of slaveholders, and they have just reason to apprehend that such a construction may yet be placed upon that instrument as shall prove the downfall of slavery."[51] The point to emphasize here is that Douglass situated his own interpretation of those words written in the founding past within the diachronic movement of history itself, whose future, in what Douglass called "the ever-present now," was still undecided.[52]

One of my historical arguments thus far has been that Douglass's reading practice here illuminates the broader transformation in legal-literary hermeneutics caused by the political crises over slavery. Douglass's "man from another country" highlights as well one of the critical claims of this study, which is that in order to historicize more fully the cultural texts of the past, we must also attempt to recover their historical situations as moments of contingency, to recall a sense of that "ever-present now." This will require a rewriting of the historical context itself. It is to the question of how modern cultural historians can approach the texts of the past while recovering their historical situations of radical contingency to which we now turn.

Once again the bondsman, as legal form of appearance and as vanishing mediator between "subject" and "citizen," will aid us in this elaboration. As a narrative concept which finds its vocation in accounts of historical transition, the bondsman can likewise be deployed productively to specify the critical perspective on history and periodization employed throughout this study. In the passage from any precapitalist mode of production to what Marx designates "the specifically capitalist mode of production" (*Capital* 1: 1021), there remains the distinction between the *formal* subsumption of labor by capital and its *real* subsumption. The first key point of this distinction between the formal subsumption and the real subsumption of labor by capital is "that capital subsumes the labour process as it finds it, that is to say, it takes over an existing labour process, developed by different and more archaic modes of production" (*Capital* 1: 1021). In such moments of labor's formal subsumption by capital, the formal conditions for capitalist production arise or (depending upon the scale of development) are introduced by capital itself. The most central of these formal conditions is the transformation of the existing types of labor into wage labor. Marx refers to several examples of such formal subsumption of labor under capital:

> When a peasant who has always produced enough for his needs becomes a day labourer working for a farmer; when the hierarchic order of guild production vanishes making way for the straightforward distinction between the capitalist and the wage-labourers he employs; when the former slave-owner engages his former slaves as paid workers, etc., then we find that what is happening is that production processes of varying social provenance have been transformed into capitalist production. (*Capital* 1: 1020)

The formal subsumption of labor requires the transformation of these different types of bondsmen into "free" laborers. Marx emphasizes that this change in forms of labor will occur most spectacularly through the use of law (in "mystified" forms of appearance): wage laborer and capitalist will meet as formal equals on the market (as seller and buyer of labor), through the legal form of the wage contract; and the worker must enter this market precisely because the only legal "property" he owns is his labor, now a commodity for sale. Necessity subjects them to the laws of contract and wage labor because, with their formal subsumption by capital, these workers become "free in a double sense": "Free workers in the double sense that they neither form part of the means of production themselves, as would be the case with slaves, serfs, etc., nor do they own the means of production. . . . The free workers are therefore free from, unencumbered by, any means of production of their own" (*Capital* 1: 874). As I discuss in chapter 1, this formal subsumption of labor requires the assimilation and disciplining of these laboring subjects, their transformation into responsible and accountable free workers who recognize the obligations of contract and the bonds of debt.

However, while the labor process at this juncture is formally subsumed under capital, this "change does not in itself imply a fundamental modification in the real nature of the labour process" (*Capital* 1: 1021). Such subsumption of labor will remain "merely formal" (*Capital* 1: 1024) so long as it remains based on the production of absolute surplus-value (*Capital* 1: 1025). In contrast, with "the production of *relative-surplus* value the entire real form of production is altered, and a specifically capitalist form of production comes into being. . . . Based on this, and simultaneously with it, the corresponding relations of production between the various agents of production and above all between the capitalist and the wage-labourer, come into being for the first time" (*Capital* 1: 1024). Marx thus argues that the transition from any precapitalist production to the "specifically capitalist mode of production" actually involves two moments in the transformation of the relations of production, and of the workers ("the agents") in these relations. Whereas the formal subsumption of labor is characteristic of the period of manufacture, the real subsumption of labor is characteristic of large-scale industry, requiring that the capitalist be "the owner of the means of production on a *social* scale"; capital thus "assumes social dimensions, and so sheds its individual character" (*Capital* 1: 1035). This distinction between the formal subsumption of labor and the real subsumption of labor is crucial to a historicization of the transformations of citizenship, that modern "subjectivity" inscribed by the Constitution, and of the racialization of its slaves and bond servants. Such a distinction is one that maintains the Marxist claim for the "determination in the last instance" by the economic, yet registers as well the active role of "superstructural" changes in, for example, the legal form of appearance of labor during its formal subsumption. which in turn serves as the conditions of possibility for capital's subsequent real subsumption of labor.

Against the critical tendency of applying a static binary opposition between slavery and the "freedom" of wage labor to texts emerging in different historical situations—for example, to antislavery literature of the eighteenth century and antislavery literature of the mid-nineteenth century—we must emphasize the qualitative transformations constituted by that material shift from "mere" formal subsumption to the real subsumption of labor. These distinct historical situations will pose different expansions or contractions of any particular text's horizon of thematic and formal possibilities. For example, we must distinguish the significance of the formally "free" laborer, against which the slave was defined during the early national period (the period of manufacture, characterized by the formal subsumption of labor) from the later significance of "free labor" and "free-labor ideology" in mid-nineteenth-century America, under what Marx famously described as "capitalist production in full swing" (*Capital* 1: 717). As I argue in chapter 1, it will make all the difference to a historically precise interpretation of the slavery-freedom opposition as it appears in *The Interesting Narrative of the Life of Olaudah Equiano* (1789) that labor in this period is in the process of being formally subsumed, but not yet socialized as it would be under the large-scale industrial capitalism of the mid- and late nineteenth century, this latter socialization a "real subsumption of labor" wherein it is then necessary to speak of the "social productive forces of labour," and of a "collective labourer" (*Capital* 1: 1052–54).[53] Likewise, analyses of mid-nineteenth-century texts addressing the slavery-freedom opposition—be they legal-political debates over the Compromise of 1850 and the federal Fugitive Slave Act or literary texts such as *My Bondage and My Freedom* (the subject of chapter 4) and *Moby-Dick* (the subject of chapter 5)—would have to explore the various ways these texts register and apprehend the political and cultural mediations of the real subsumption of labor, and the transformation of slave and free laborers in the relations of production. This focus on the diachronic register of historical transformation is also marked by our "man from another country": In the midst of changes in the very conceptions of free personhood and citizenship initiated by the political struggles of the antebellum Union crisis, Douglass's reading recovered the significance of the bondsman to that original scene of writing, the constitutional founding of 1787–88. It is a historical materialist distinction maintained throughout this study.

Grounding the legal and cultural transformations of citizenship in this dialectic between slavery and free labor illuminated by Douglass, *Bonds of Citizenship* argues that in the age of Emancipation, the attributes of free personhood became identified with the rights and privileges of the citizen; and that individual "freedom" thus became identified with the nation-state, and understood as possible solely through national citizenship. The first part (chapters 1 and 2) situates early American citizenship and its literature, the early American novel, within the context of Atlantic slavery, Anglo-American legal culture, and the rise of nationalism. Chapter 1, "Bound by Law: Apprenticeship and the Culture of 'Free' Labor" examines the figures of apprenticeship and indentured servitude in a range of transatlantic texts of the late eighteenth century, in order to delineate the ambiguous legal and cultural spaces between slavery and "freedom." Throughout Hector St. John de Crèvecœur's *Letters from an American Farmer*, Benjamin Franklin's *Autobiography*, Ottobah Cugoano's *Thoughts and Sentiments on the Evil and Wicked Traffic of the Slavery and Commerce of the Human Species*, and Olaudah Equiano's *Interesting Narrative of the Life of Olaudah Equiano*, indentured servitude figures as an allegory of transformation, as a transitional state of passage by which the subject attains the freedom of self-mastery. Crèvecœur explicitly stages this transformational allegory as the coming-into-citizenship of "the American, this new man."[54] Franklin employs the allegory to depict his disruption of his own apprenticeship indentures as an exemplary moment of "asserting [his] freedom."[55] In the pioneering Black Atlantic texts of Cugoano and Equiano, apprenticeship and indentured servitude function as the formal structuring principles of textual self-representation. Further, they are proposed as practical models for gradual emancipation and the assimilation of the formerly enslaved into the late-eighteenth-century culture of merchant capitalism. As these texts reveal, in the late-eighteenth-century transatlantic world, the figure of indentured servitude had not yet been identified with "involuntary servitude" and instead could model the path to freedom. It is this cultural recognition of apprenticeship and indentured servitude as ambiguous, transitional states of labor bondage that the Constitution's erasures of race and slavery both depends upon and disavows.

In his early American novel *Arthur Mervyn; or, Memoirs of the Year 1793*, Charles Brockden Brown uses this same figure of apprenticeship as allegory of transformation to highlight the problems and potential dangers inhering in the representative subject of citizenship. In *Arthur Mervyn*, these dangers arise from the radical disjunction between an individual's civic persona and his invisible interior self, that imaginary space of moral sense and inner "character." This disjunction between visible persona and invisible character destabilized traditional republican conceptions of virtue and credibility. In chapter 2, "Civic Virtues: Narrative Form and the Trial of Character in Early America," I argue that the early

American novel mediates this change in social forms through innovations in literary form. Reading the shared epistemological forms and narrative structures of texts such as James Wilson's *Lectures on Law* and Brown's *Arthur Mervyn*, I show how legal theorists repeatedly rely upon the apparently distinct realm of aesthetic judgment to decide the truth of legal and historical facts. Situating both the novel and Anglo-American theories of evidence in relation to Enlightenment theories of natural language, I argue further that Brown's work is exemplary of the migration of procedures for ascertaining historical fact from the sphere of law to that of the novel. In *Arthur Mervyn*, the ideal republican citizen is a character whose testimony conforms to the law's rules of evidence, and the narrative testimony that ultimately prevails is that which the novel represents as a true account of the historical facts. Taking Brown's work as exemplary, this chapter thus situates the rise of the novel as a formal representation of the "imagined community" of the new nation in relation to what Christopher Tomlins describes as the concurrent "rise of the rule of law . . . to a position of supreme imaginative authority."[56]

This focus on apprenticeship and indentured servitude thus also advances the investigation of several key themes and concepts explored throughout the study. In these first chapters I explore, in particular, the interdependent relation between the rights and privileges of the formally free subject and the legal spaces of the nation—a relation elaborated through the construction of categories such as "jurisdiction" and "territory"; and the definition of "police powers" over freedom of mobility. I begin with this earlier literary-historical period in order to historicize both the continuities and the transformations in literary and legal discourses of race, labor, and citizenship, between the early republican period and the mid-nineteenth century. By beginning with this earlier period, my study shows how many of the concepts and themes central to nineteenth-century literature, law, and civic culture—such as freedom of mobility; or the opposition between private conscience and public law—have intellectual precursors and formal models in the literature of the late eighteenth century.

In the second part of my argument (chapters 3, 4, and 5), I study how citizenship was transformed by antebellum debates over slavery, free labor, and national union. While other studies have explored how slavery shaped the definition of freedom in antebellum America, few have examined how developments in the world of wage labor, such as changes in contract law, the movement for the ten-hour workday, or the rise of "free labor" ideology itself, influenced legal and cultural understandings of slavery, and conceptions of slave personhood. As I argue in these chapters, citizenship was the legal form through which slave law and wage-labor law articulated their representations of free personhood, and the attributes of subjectivity required for such personhood. Chapter 3, "Fugitive Bonds: Contract and the Culture of Constitutionalism," is organized around the reconfigurations of race, labor, and national citizenship during the Union crisis. Specifically, I examine the split within the antislavery movement between two radically opposed understandings of the constitutionality of slavery. I frame the chapter with a study of Frederick Douglass's speeches and editorials immediately prior to and immediately following the 1850 Compromise, in order to track the development of Douglass's shift from the Garrisonian position, which read the Constitution as a proslavery document, to the political- abolitionist position, which read the Constitution as fully opposed "in letter and spirit" to slavery. As we have seen, Douglass's writings on the Constitution elaborated the trope of "a man from another country," the figure for a legal hermeneutic whose perspective locates constitutional "intention" exclusively in the letter of the law. In this chapter, I historicize this trope as well as Douglass's shift more generally, and I ground the changes in the culture of constitutionalism in the debates over slavery and free labor. I do so through related analyses of Joseph Story's *Commentaries on the Constitution of the United States* (1833); the Supreme Court decision in *Prigg v. Pennsylvania* (1842); Wendell Phillips's *The Constitution: A Pro-Slavery Compact* (1844); and Lysander Spooner's *The Unconstitutionality of Slavery* (1845), all of which debated the Constitution's "original intent" regarding slavery. Further, I historicize the slavery debates themselves in relation to transformations in contract and labor law initiated with the antebellum market revolution.[57] In doing so, I make the case for a new understanding of the historical links between abolitionism, free-labor ideology, and the social construction of "race."

Building upon the revisionary historical arguments of the third chapter, chapter 4, "Hereditary Bondsman: Frederick Douglass and the Spirit of the Law," advances a new interpretation of Douglass's *My Bondage and My Freedom* (1855). If historians and literature scholars have underestimated the radical character of Douglass's change of political views in the 1850s, they have also underestimated the significance of Douglass's changed self-representation in *My Bondage and My Freedom*. The dominant critical and popular understandings of Douglass remain based on the 1845 *Narrative of the Life of Frederick Douglass*, published when

Douglass still adhered to the Garrisonian view of the Constitution as a "pro-slavery compact." As I argue, Douglass's transformed political views led to significant changes in the content and the form of his literary self-representation, from revisions of formative episodes in his life to changes in narrative structure and point of view. I focus in particular on the representations of slave women in *My Bondage and My Freedom* to describe Douglass's transformed understanding of the relation between gender and racial classifications; and on the depictions of Douglass's "apprenticeship life" to describe his transformed understanding of the political and economic links between slave labor, "free labor," and the formal freedom of American citizenship.

The slavery debates underscored a tension inherent in the very figure of modern citizenship, between the private self (of morality and ethics) and the public self (of market and law). As I discuss in chapter 3, for example, antislavery activists laid claim to the truths of the private self—"moral law," or "the higher law" of God—over and against the demands of positive law and civic duty. In the first two chapters, I describe this figure as the "split subject" of citizenship: the individual citizen understood as structured by this central division between private self and public *persona*. In chapter 5, "'If Man Will Strike': *Moby-Dick* and the Letter of the Law," I read Melville's novel as a symbolic mediation of the transformations in this "split subject" of citizenship caused by the antebellum market revolution. My readings historicize the novel in relation to the labor struggles of this period: "criminal conspiracy" labor cases, labor strikes, and the transformations of contract law. In contrast to influential readings of Ahab as a "dictator" or "totalitarian" figure, I read Ahab as a romantic figure of resistance to the market and the rule of law. In the historical perspective advanced in this chapter, the hunt for Moby-Dick is a battle against the expansion of the rule of law—an expansion which Melville depicts as the colonization of individual and collective freedoms by the nation-state.

1

Bound by Law

Apprenticeship and the Culture of "Free" Labor

The "case of the slaves," Publius declared in *The Federalist No. 54*, "is in truth a peculiar one."[1] Discussing the "three-fifths clause" of the Constitution's provision for apportionment of representation and taxation (art. 1, § 2, clause 3), Publius was not pleading the case of the slaves, but rather advocating the view of "our Southern brethren" the slaveholders, and appealing for "compromise" over the inclusion of three-fifths of their slaves in the Constitution's "numerical rule of representation" (*FP* 336). During the 1787 convention as well as the ratification debates for which *The Federalist Papers* were written, it was the three-fifths clause of the apportionment provision, more than any other "slave clause," that highlighted the ambiguity of the slave's form of appearance in the letter of the law, and exposed the contradictions of political representation in a slaveholding nation. Gouverneur Morris, the Pennsylvania delegate credited with writing the Constitution's celebrated preamble, highlighted this direct link between political representation and the rights of modern citizenship in his objections to the three-fifths clause: "Upon what principle is it that the slaves shall be computed in the representation? Are they men? Then make them citizens, and let them vote. Are they property? Why, then, is not other property included?"[2] Like Morris, many nonslaveholding state delegates objected to any inclusion of slaves in the apportionment clause, as against the very "principle of representation."[3] Slaveholding state delegates insisted, however, that their slaves be included in this "numerical rule of representation" on the grounds that the labor of these enslaved "other persons" contributed to the wealth of the nation. It was during these debates over the "true principle of representation" and this fundamental conception of modern citizenship that slavery emerged as the central point of division in the new nation.[4]

It was also in these debates that the Constitution first came to be described as a matter of "compact" between states with differing economic interests, requiring "compromise."[5] Because the case of the slaves was so peculiar, Publius continued: "Let the compromising expedient of the Constitution be mutually adopted which regards them as inhabitants, but as debased by servitude below the equal level of free inhabitants; which regards the *slave* as divested of two fifths of the *man*" (*FP* 339, emphasis in original). This characterization was a misleading rhetorical conceit, insofar as it implied that a slave was regarded in law as "divested" of manhood or humanity, rather than divested of legal rights and attributes. Historically, it has led to judicial and popular misunderstandings of the status of the slave in the original Constitution, and to critical misunderstandings of how slave personhood was recognized by state and society in the late eighteenth century. Yet there was partial truth in the characterization, insofar as slaves were regarded, by slaveholders and antislavery reformers alike, as "debased by servitude"; and they were included in the calculus of this constitutional provision for political representation only after extensive debate over the economic value of such servitude.[6]

The debates over the value of the slave's debasing "servitude" reveal the political-economic history concealed by the slave's form of appearance in the letter of the law, a form of appearance whose ambiguity would become central to the antislavery struggle, the Union crisis, and the definition of citizenship in a modern racial state. For the primary purposes of this chapter, the debates illuminate the historical understanding of freedom, slavery, and servitude as varying states of subjection to the law. As I observed in the introduction, the apportionment provision employed the bondsman as a figure to distinguish between the qualified freedom of those persons "bound to service for a term of years" and the absolute unfreedom of those "other persons" bound as slaves. Looking behind this form of appearance and recovering the social relations simultaneously codified and masked in this legal form supplements historical understandings of the "problem of slavery" and the "problem of freedom" in the Age of Revolution.[7] The peculiar case of the slaves' representation in the new Constitution was a political-economic problem, whose history reveals the intertwined roles of slave and "free" bond-laborers in the dialectical transformation of race as a mediation of class.

To appreciate the historical significance of the three-fifths clause to the Constitution's inscription of the rights of citizenship, it is important to note that the three-fifths ratio did not begin as a ratio for the apportionment of representation. The ratio came from the 1783 Congress, when James Madison—who would later wear the mask of Publius in *The Federalist No. 54* to explain its incorporation into the "compromising expedient" of the Constitution—proposed the ratio as a "compromise" in the context of negotiations over the calculation of property values, or "the index of wealth," for the purposes of taxation.[8] The application of the ratio to representation in the 1787 convention "was an entirely new concept."[9] While the bondsman's form of appearance in this clause would suggest that the provision was primarily about political representation, its repressed history reveals it to be equally about property, and the wealth-producing value of those laborers owned as property.

In fact, this debate over the ratio for the enumeration of enslaved "other persons" began with the American Revolution and the drafting of the Articles of Confederation, likewise as a debate over the "index of wealth" for taxation. The debates of the Second Continental Congress over assessing the financial contributions of states to the cost of the War of Independence introduced those terms of labor that would be central to the 1787 constitutional convention's debates over the three-fifths clause and "the true principle of representation" in the new republic: "the index of wealth," and the relative values of free and enslaved laborers. At the center of this ongoing debate, from 1776 through 1788, was the question of how slaves were to be regarded under national law as opposed to local state law: as property or as persons.[10]

In the 1776 Congress of Confederation, representatives of the non-slaveholding states argued for taxation based on all the people of a state, including its slaves: "John Adams (of Massachusetts) observed that the numbers of people were taken by this article as an index of the wealth of the State, and not as subjects of taxation. That as to this matter, it was of no consequence by what name you called your people, whether that of freeman or of slaves. That in some countries the laboring poor were called freemen, in others they were called slaves: but that the difference as to the state was imaginary only."[11] In Adams's argument, the difference between slaves and the laboring poor was merely nominal: considered in their material conditions—without property of their own and serving as the perpetual dependent hirelings of others—the laboring poor were the equal of slaves; and thus for the state's purposes, the laboring poor's difference from slaves, their nominal freedom, was "imaginary only." Adams elaborated upon the imaginary character of this distinction between slaves and the formally free laboring poor by proposing a hypothetical transformation: "Suppose, by any extraordinary operation of nature or of law, one half the laborers of a State could in the course of one night be transformed into slaves—would the State be made the poorer, or the less able to pay taxes?"[12] Adams's counterfactual reinforces the political-economic understanding that it was the slaves' "equal" status as laborers, as persons who "produce . . . profits," that mattered to the "wealth of the nation," and that the economic values of free and enslaved laborers were the same, insofar as the "surplus" produced by both types of laborers would be taxed to support the new nation-state: "Certainly five hundred freemen produce no more profits, no greater surplus for the payment of taxes, than five hundred slaves. . . . It is the number of laborers which produces the surplus for taxation; and numbers, therefore, indiscriminately, are the fair index of wealth."[13] Drawing together his arguments regarding the equality of conditions and the equal value of slave and free laborers, Adams concluded: "That it is the use of the word 'property' here, and its application to some of the people of the State, which produces the fallacy. . . . That a slave may, indeed, from the custom of speech, be more properly called the wealth of his master, than the free laborer might be called the wealth of his employer; but, as to the State, both were equally its wealth."[14] With this assessment of their equal status as producers of taxable surplus wealth for the state, Adams introduced those key words of the slavery debates, "property" and "persons," whose contested meanings as applied to the peculiar case of the slave are linked to that "imaginary" distinction between slave and free laborers.

Unsurprisingly, slaveholding state delegates opposed a numerical rule of taxation inclusive of those "people of the State" they owned as slaves, and disputed Adams's claims regarding the equal value of slave and free labor: "Mr. Harrison (of Virginia) proposed, as a compromise, that two slaves should be counted as one freeman. He affirmed that slaves did not do as much work as freemen, and doubted if two affected more than one."[15] Harrison's 1776 "compromise" ratio was premised upon a conception shared by many political elites of the period that slave labor was less productive than free labor, and so should not count as much as free labor in the calculus of taxable wealth. The antislavery Pennsylvanian James Wilson, who in the 1787 convention would introduce the three-fifths ratio into the Constitution's apportionment clause, objected in this 1776 debate to the slaveholders' labor-value calculus: "He acknowledged indeed that freeman worked the most; but they consume the most also. They do not produce a greater surplus for taxation."[16] What is of interest here is the point of agreement between the delegates of slaveholding and nonslaveholding states: both sides were of the view that "freeman worked the most." Both sides took for granted the point, elaborated most famously by Adam Smith in *An Inquiry into the Nature and Causes of the Wealth of Nations* (1776), that free labor was more productive than slave labor.[17] Yet the point of disagreement is equally significant to the debates over slavery in the early national period and later during the antebellum Union crisis, and to our historical understanding of modern citizenship. The value of labor, Wilson argued, ought to be considered in its relation to consumption as well as production: their relative values depended on the costs of reproducing these laborers.

This ratio for the enumeration of enslaved inhabitants as a state's "index of wealth"—as laborers and thus as the producers of a state's taxable surplus—was fine-tuned in the 1783 Congress, with an even greater number of positions on the relative values of slave and free labor: some delegates argued "that two blacks be rated as one freeman"; others argued "for rating them as four to three"; and still others "sincerely thought three to one would be a juster proportion."[18] In 1783, the debate again focused on the relative productivity of free and slave laborers—as calculated in the difference between the costs of reproducing the laborers and the value of those commodities produced by them. Nonslaveholding state delegates "were for rating the slaves high" in this ratio, arguing "that the expense of feeding and clothing them was as far below that incident to freemen as their industry and ingenuity were below those of freemen."[19] The slaveholding state delegates did not dispute the view of the nonslaveholding state delegates regarding the costs entailed in maintaining and reproducing slave laborers ("the expense of feeding and clothing them").[20] Slaveholders insisted, however, on the much lower relative productivity of slave labor and thus a lower "taxable surplus" with respect to costs of reproduction, insofar as "slaves were not put to labor as young as the children of laboring families." This relative productivity was lowered further, they asserted, because "having no interest in their labor, [slaves] did as little as possible; and omitted every exertion of thought requisite to facilitate and expedite it."[21] The slaveholders' conception of the lower productivity of slave labor recognized the direct coercion required by slavery—formulated as an absence of "interest in their labor"—even as they argued that in the broader view of labor reproduction, slaves worked less than "laboring families." This is the neglected prehistory of that legal form known as the "three-fifths compromise" of the 1787 constitutional convention.[22]

The three-fifths clause (of Article 1, Section 2) was of such importance in the debates of the 1787 convention because, as nonslaveholding state delegates recognized, if a state's representation in the federal legislature were based on the number of all of the state's inhabitants, including its slaves, the slaveholding states would have a representation vastly disproportionate to their free populations.[23] Delegates of both slaveholding and nonslaveholding states objected to the idea that the three-fifths ratio, derived as we have seen as a compromise "index of wealth" for taxation, should be applied to the apportionment of representation. Slaveholding state delegates opposed the ratio because they demanded that all their slaves be counted. South Carolina and Georgia "insisted that blacks be included in the rule of representation *equally* with whites, and for that purpose moved that the words 'three fifths' be struck out."[24] Their position was unsurprising since they would then have a greater number of representatives and legislative power. What is of special interest to our genealogy of the slave's absent presence in the Constitution is that once again the arguments turned upon the value-producing labor of slaves, as compared to free labor: "Mr. Butler insisted that the labor of a slave in South Carolina was as productive and valuable as that of a freeman in Massachusetts; that as wealth was the great means of defense and utility to the nation, they were equally valuable to it with freeman; and that consequently equal representation ought to be allowed for them in a government which was instituted principally for the protection of property."[25] As nonslaveholding state delegates recognized, this argument that slave labor was equally productive and valuable as free labor contradicted those arguments advanced by slaveholders earlier, in the context of taxation: "This ratio was fixed by Congress as a rule of taxation. Then, it was urged, by the delegates representing the States having slaves, that the blacks were still more inferior to freemen. At present, when the ratio of representation is to be established, we are assured that they are equal to freemen."[26]

If slaveholding state delegates opposed the three-fifths ratio because they supported "considering blacks as equal to whites in the apportionment of representation," nonslaveholding state delegates opposed the ratio because they did not want slaves counted at all.[27] As we have seen, many were categorically opposed to the very idea of "slave representation." In these objections, they returned to that point introduced by John Adams at the outset of the American Revolution regarding the contradictions in political representation produced by claiming "persons" as "property." William Patterson of New Jersey "could regard negro slaves in no light but as property. They are no free agents, have no personal liberty, no faculty of acquiring property, but on the contrary are themselves property, and like other property, entirely at the will of the master."[28] Focusing on those attributes of free personhood recognized by the laws of the state—personal liberty, free agency, and will—and pointing to the contradiction between these attributes of free personhood and the slave's legal condition as property, Patterson's arguments highlight the framers' shared conception of the direct link between legal "free agency" and "the acquiring of property," both of which require that the person not be subject entirely to the will of another. Elaborating these attributes of the self-willing "person" to be represented by the state, Patterson reminded the other delegates of "the true principle of representation," as "an expedient by which an assembly of certain individuals, chosen by the people, is substituted in place of the inconvenient meeting of the people themselves. If such a meeting of the people was actually to take place, would the slaves vote? They would not. Why then should they be represented?"[29] Invoking the classic republican scene of assembly wherein citizens gathered together to agree upon the democratic will, Patterson cites the slave's legal incapacities as marking the limits of the citizen. As property with no free agency or independent wills of their own, slaves would not in such a scene represent themselves; therefore they must not be represented.

The arguments of the nonslaveholding state delegates opposed to counting slaves equally with free persons in the apportionment clause centered upon this fundamental republican principle of representation: such inclusion of slaves defied the "true principle of presentation," effectively making a slaveholder the representative of his slaves. Gouverneur Morris argued further that it was "encouragement of the slave trade, as would be given by allowing them a representation for their negroes."[30] A corollary objection founded on this republican principle of representation was that the citizens of their states "would revolt at the idea of being put on a footing with slaves."[31] In these objections, we see once again the ways in which the figure of the slave functioned in the republican imaginary, as the opposite not only of the "free inhabitant" laborer but also of the citizen. This legal status of citizenship need not yet be obtained by the "free inhabitant," as was the case for thousands of immigrants, indentured servants, and apprentices. Those "bound to service for a term of years"—under the only form of labor bondage explicitly named in the Constitution—were understood to be "free persons." As free laborers, they were considered always-already becoming citizens, and thus a logical part of that population to be represented in the government of the new nation.

Proposing the three-fifths ratio in the 1787 convention (taking it from the compromise ratio introduced by Madison in the 1783 taxation debates), James Wilson agreed with those who argued that any apportionment of representation in the national legislature based on a population of slaves was illogical. Opposed to slavery and representing the state that had passed the first gradual emancipation act in 1780, Wilson "did not well see, on what principle the admission of blacks in the proportion of three-fifths could be explained. Are they admitted as citizens—then why are they not admitted on an equality with white citizens? Are they admitted as property—then why is no other property admitted into the computation? These were difficulties, however, which he thought must be overruled by the necessity of compromise."[32] The problem for those objecting to any inclusion of slaves in the numerical rule of representation was the other republican principle shared by all the framers: that "taxation and representation ought to go together."[33] This view was directly linked to the "true principle of representation" invoked by Patterson. At least since James Otis's famous speech declaring "taxation without representation is tyranny" (in other formulations, it was slavery), this "principle of representation" was one of the primary rallying cries of colonial opposition to the abuses of Parliament, and the American Revolution itself. Yet precisely because "eleven out of thirteen of the States had [already] agreed to consider slaves in the apportionment of taxation," they would also have to consider slaves in the rule of representation, if the slaveholding states were to enter into this "compact."[34]

Addressing this shared view of the necessary link between taxation of wealth and a corresponding representation in the national legislature, Wilson articulated most clearly both the substantive political logic and the literary "equivocation" by which the three-fifths ratio of "other persons" entered into the apportionment clause. Emphasizing, like Madison, "the necessity of compromise," Wilson "observed, that less umbrage would ... be taken against an admission of the slave into the rule of representation, if it should be so expressed as to make them indirectly only an ingredient in the rule, by saying that they should enter into the rule of taxation; and as representation was to be according to taxation, the end would be equally attained."[35] The law's desired object and intent—counting slaves for representation—could be reached indirectly if the clause was formulated as to count slaves solely for the purpose of taxation: slaves could enter the national body politic of legislative representation indirectly through the back door of wealth taxation. Wilson's argument thus highlights also the ways in which the "spirit" of a law, its "object and intent," could be separated from its "letter," that mode through which the law is "expressed." As we will see in the debates over the Union crisis, for those citing Madison's record of *Debates in the Federal Convention of 1787* as evidence of the "original intent" of this particular "slave clause," Wilson's turn to indirection as a way to address antislavery objections to the "admission of slaves into the rule of representation" confirmed their view of the Constitution as a document whose wording was deliberately "equivocal and ambiguous," not only in its avoidance of the term "slave" but also in its positive inscription of them as "other persons" in the apportionment clause. Wilson's suggestion for how to include slaves in the apportionment clause, proposed as a matter of "compromise" and avoiding "umbrage" through indirection, reveals the central political-economic truth of the slave's absent presence in the Constitution, and the bondsman's role as citizenship's vanishing mediator. As that "peculiar species of property" whose labor produced surplus value, the slave was "originally intended" to be included only for the purposes of taxation.[36] In a slaveholding nation adhering to the republican "principle of representation," however, there could be no taxation of the enslaved as wealth-producing property without the indirect, partial representation of them as "other persons."

If this history of the legal form of the three-fifths clause highlights the centrality of bond labor to the Constitution and to its inscription of political representation, as one of the fundamental rights of modern citizenship, it also underscores the framers' understanding of slavery as a peculiar form of labor bondage in a broader spectrum of labor exploitation. In 1776, John Adams asserted that "the difference" between poor freeman and slave "as to the state was imaginary only" when considering them as wealth-producing laborers.[37] In 1787, the Constitution's provision for the apportionment of representation and taxation regarded those who were "bound to service for a term of years" as "free persons." And as the framers debated the precise language of the apportionment provision's distinction between these bound-yet-free persons and enslaved "other persons," "the word 'servitude' was struck out, and 'service' unanimously inserted, the former being thought to express the condition of slaves, and the latter the obligations of free persons."[38] The broader Atlantic cultural history of this "imaginary" legal distinction between those free laborers "bound to service" and those slave laborers described by Publius as "debased by servitude below the equal level of free inhabitants" reveals the interdependence of slavery and servitude in the racialization of freedom and modern citizenship (*FP* 339). In the transatlantic eighteenth-century texts I examine together in this chapter, the bondsman figures as an allegory of transformation, a transitional state of passage by which the subject attains the freedom of independent self-mastery.

Visible and Invisible Characters in Letters from an American Farmer

For Hector St. John de Crèvecœur, the question, "What then is the American, this new man?" was answered by a "man from another country," the immigrant: "*Ubi panis ibi patria* is the motto of all emigrants."[39] *Letters from an American Farmer* is regularly invoked in nationalist histories of American literature; yet with this motto and throughout *Letters*, Crèvecœur focuses on the economic conditions of national affiliation, emphasizing the distinction between the "national" consciousness necessary to the imagined community of the nation on the one hand and the nationalist ideology of patriotism on the other.[40] Significant to this distinction is the narrative fact that Crèvecœur's emigrant is represented first as a figure of disaffiliation, and the failures of nationalist interpellation. Describing "the poor of Europe [who] have by some means met together" in America, Crèvecœur's Farmer James asks rhetorically:

> To what purpose should they ask one another what countrymen they are? Alas, two thirds of them had no country. Can a wretch, who wanders about, who works and starves, whose life is a continual scene of sore affliction or pinching penury; can that man call England or any other kingdom his country? A country that had no bread for him; whose fields procured him no harvest; who met with nothing but the frowns of the rich, the severity of the laws, with jails and punishments; who owned not a single foot of the extensive surface of this planet[?] (*Letters* 42)

Thus even as he introduces the question—"What then is the American?"—that would become central to later nationalist cultural projects, Crèvecœur's American farmer focuses on the immigrant, this "new man," as a figure that previously "had no country." He cannot identify with a "country that had no bread for him": *Ubi panis ibi patria*.

The recurring point of this famous Letter III is that individual subjects are tied to the nation not through affective bonds of "attachment" (*Letters* 43) but by the Lockean political-economic bonds of private property: "The American ought therefore to love this country much better than that wherein either he or his forefathers were born. Here the rewards of his industry follow, with equal steps, the progress of his labour. His labour is founded on the basis of nature, *self-interest*: can it want a stronger allurement?" (*Letters* 44).The series of contrasts between the lives of common men in Europe and the lives of common men in America all turn on the rewards of this self-interested labor: "From involuntary idleness, servile dependence, penury, and useless labour, he has passed to toils of a very different nature, rewarded by ample subsistence.—This is an American" (*Letters* 45). This economic basis of the immigrant's answer to the question of American identity continues throughout the later, famously pessimistic *Letters*, and indeed accounts for that very pessimism: the "Distresses of the Frontier Man" in Letter XII are initiated by the destruction of these economic bonds by the American War of Independence, which he calls "this unfortunate revolution" (*Letters* 191).

The central concern of Letter III is to explain the "metamorphosis" of the poor laboring immigrant from Europe, identified as a "man without a country," into the American, which Crèvecœur's Farmer James does by telling the "History of Andrew, the Hebridean" as "an epitome of the rest" (*Letters* 57). In tracing Andrew's "metamorphosis" (59), Crèvecœur's American farmer narrates an allegory of subject-formation, via the "invisible power" of political economy. The immigrant begins as a bond laborer, a servant indentured to a master, acquiring both technical training and moral cultivation through this "apprenticeship" (74). After fulfilling his contract and earning his freedom dues, he "become[s] a freeholder, possessed of a vote, of a place of residence, a citizen" (79): "From nothing, to start into being; from a servant, to the rank of master; from being a slave of some despotic prince, to become a free man, invested with lands.... It is in consequence of that change that he becomes an American" (59). By way of the Lockean *telos* of this transformational allegory, Crèvecœur's ultimate answer to the question, "What is an American?" is that the "American" is an immigrant, who through his labors and "the laws of naturalization" (59) becomes a citizen, "performing as a citizen all the duties required of him" (82). He is one of those to whom Luther Martin referred when objecting to the Constitution's "migration and importation clause": a "foreigner who comes into a State to become a citizen," coming not "absolutely free" but rather "qualifiedly so, as a servant."[41] His voluntary labor bondage serves as the ideal path to the freedom of American citizenship.

As representative "epitome of the rest," the history of Andrew the Hebridean introduces into American literature several narrative tropes which will recur throughout the debates over the cultural characteristics of this ultimate figure, the "citizen." The first is that already introduced in the structure of Andrew's metamorphosis: the political coming-into-being of the citizen is based on the socioeconomic model of the passage from dependent servitude to independent self-mastery. The other tropes emerge within this structure of transformation and, like this larger structure, depend on the primacy of labor. First, there is the trope of "incorporation" (the eighteenth-century term for assimilation), which we have seen staged by those laboring poor who previously "had no country" but then, following "the motto of all emigrants," become "American." This first trope names the narrative structure of that process of assimilation mediating between the individual subject and the civic community. Second, there is the related trope of "visible character," Crèvecœur's name for the social recognition of this assimilating subject, and the figure for the public persona of that subject of citizenship divided between "invisible character" and "visible character" (*Letters* 50).

Crèvecœur introduces these two tropes together when he compares the "incorporation" of Europeans into "Americans" to the "dissemination" of "religious indifference" (*Letters* 50):

> When any considerable number of a particular sect happen to dwell contiguous to each other, they immediately erect a temple, and there worship the Divinity according to their own peculiar ideas.... [They] are at liberty to make proselytes if they can ... and to follow the dictates of their conscience; for neither the government nor any other power interferes. If they are peaceable subjects, and are industrious, what is it to their neighbors how and in what manner they think fit to address their prayers to the Supreme Being? But if the sectaries are not settled close together, if they are mixed with other denominations, their zeal will cool for want of fuel, and will be extinguished in a little time. Then the Americans become, *as to religion what they are as to country*, allied to all. In them the name of Englishman, Frenchman, and European, is lost, and, in like manner, the strict modes of Christianity, as practiced in Europe, are lost also. (48, emphasis added)

36 *Bound by Law*

It is in this analogy, between the waning of religious sectarianism and the transformation of the "man without a country" into "an American," that Crèvecœur introduces the *split subject* of this "new man," the American citizen. Crèvecœur develops here the eighteenth-century view of religious belief as the primary index of the subject's individual personhood, distinct from the abstract legal-formal person of the citizen. The particularity of religious belief (a sect's "own peculiar ideas") is considered not only distinct from but entirely irrelevant to the civic life of the community: "If they are peaceable subjects, and are industrious," how they pray does not matter to their neighbors. Crèvecœur's analogy uses religion as the site of all things considered "private," as opposed to the public sites of the political ("peaceable subjects") and the economic ("industrious"). As we have seen, this opposition would be codified in the U.S. Constitution itself. And throughout *The Federalist Papers*, religion is explicitly compared to private interests and inner passions, and the proliferation of political factions is likened to the proliferation of religious sects.[42]

It is in the context of this division between private religion and public political-economic life that Crèvecœur introduces his figure for the split subject of citizenship, and the related trope of "visible character":

> Next to [the Catholic and the German Lutheran] lives a Seceder, the most enthusiastic of all sectaries; his zeal is hot and fiery; but, separated as he is from others of the same complexion, he has no congregation, where he might cabal and mingle religious pride with worldly obstinacy. He likewise raises good crops, his house is handsomely painted, his orchard is one of the fairest in the neighborhood. How does it concern the welfare of the country, or of the province at large, what this man's religious sentiments are, or really whether he has any at all? He is a good farmer, he is a sober, peaceable, good, citizen. . . . This is the visible character; the invisible one is only guessed at, and is nobody's business. . . . Thus all sects are mixed as well as all nations. Thus religious indifference is imperceptibly disseminated from one end of the continent to the other. (49–50)

Reiterating his claims regarding the community's "indifference" to the "peculiar ideas" of a particular sect, Crèvecœur makes explicit the role of religion as structural placeholder of the private, and underscores the split within the individual subject of citizenship, between the "invisible character" of the private person and the "visible character" of the public citizen. While the passage "from a servant, to the rank of a master" (*Letters* 58–59) structures the economic narrative of assimilation (or "incorporation"), its completion is marked not by any detectable transformation of the individual's inner character, but rather solely through the successes of "visible character," the outward signs of good citizenship. Whereas "incorporation" names the process of civic assimilation, whose ideal fulfillment is epitomized by Andrew the Hebridean, the dependent indentured servant become independent propertied citizen, "visible character" names a state of social being within this ideal process of assimilation, mediating the social recognition of its successful completion. The political-economic basis of this civic identity is underscored at the end of Letter III: the history of Andrew as epitome of the American closes with a ledger "account of the property he acquired with his own hands and those of his son," in "Pennsylvania currency.—Dollars" (*Letters* 82).

If in Crèvecœur's *Letters* the "visible character" of good citizenship takes the form of material prosperity (his crops, house, orchard), the success of such "incorporation" into citizenship is also marked by another type of "character." When Farmer James greets Andrew the Hebridean at the dock and asks him his plans, Andrew, still fresh off the boat bringing servants to America, replies:

> I do not know, Sir; I am but an ignorant man, a stranger besides:—I must rely on the advice of good Christians. . . . I have brought with me a character from our Barra minister, can it do me any good here? [To which Farmer James replies] Oh, yes; but your future success will depend entirely on your own conduct; if you are a sober man, as the certificate says, laborious and honest, there is no fear but that you will do well. (73)

One of the popular eighteenth-century uses of "character" was "to indicate reputation (including the formal giving of a character, a *character reference* as we would now say)."[43] In the eighteenth century, "character" was itself a document one could obtain, whose text would attest to the merits of an otherwise invisible because internalized possession. This character was "an outward sign," but one signifying the "inner character" of relatively fixed traits; and the bearer of the document was likewise considered an individual shaped by external forces.[44] It is in this latter sense that "character" converges with what Pierre Bourdieu has described as "social capital."[45] Because Andrew is a "stranger" not yet assimilated into the community of citizens in Pennsylvania, he does not possess that socially "visible character" of a reputation for industry and sobriety (like the "good name" left to Farmer James by his father), and so must rely instead on another outward sign of his inner self, the written document from a legitimating authority, his Barra minister. Here "character" is nothing less than embodied social capital, which Andrew can then build upon, through his own industry and performance of its claims, to accumulate economic capital.

Following the formal logic of the split subject of citizenship—the division between "visible character" and "invisible character"—the transformation of the social capital of this written character into direct economic capital is likewise marked by a series of texts as "outward sign[s]."[46] After reading Andrew's textual "character," Farmer James decides to assist in Andrew's "metamorphosis." After Andrew has "served a short apprenticeship at [Farmer James'] house," (*Letters* 74), Farmer James himself provides him with yet another character reference: "I went to Mr. A. V. in the county of——. . . I gave him a faithful detail of the progress Andrew had made in the rural arts; of his honesty, sobriety, and gratitude; and pressed him to sell him a hundred acres" (77), to which Mr. A. V. responds: "Well, honest Andrew, . . . in consideration of your good name, I will let you have a hundred acres of good arable land" (78). Significant to our understanding of the development of the representations of "character" in American literature is that the "character" written by Crèvecœur's Farmer James in the pages of Letter III is a supplementary text which displaces that initial "character" written by Andrew's Barra minister. Andrew's minister, a legitimating authority from his old world, had provided Andrew with his initial character, yet it is the respected citizen of his new world, Farmer James, who functions as the legitimating authority necessary to Andrew's accumulation of greater economic capital. From these two visible (because textual) characters, Andrew then obtains yet another document, a "lease" securing his property. As Mr. A. V. informs Andrew, still ignorant of such legal terms, "If ever you are dissatisfied with the land, a jury of your own neighborhood shall value all your improvements, and you shall be paid agreeably to their verdict" (78–79).

Crèvecœur closes this narration of the translation of "character" into lease, of "good name" into freehold property, with a discussion of the ways in which the terms for the attributes of free, independent personhood converge with the language of the economic. After Andrew tells them he "know[s] nothing of what [they] mean about lease, improvement, will, jury, &c," Farmer James reflects: "[Those] were hard words, which he had never heard in his life. . . . No wonder, therefore, that he was embarrassed for how could the man, who had hardly a *will of his own* since he was born, imagine he could have one after his death?" (79). The scene marking Andrew's crossing of that threshold from dependent bond-servitude to independent self-mastery turns upon this movement, from "will" in the sense of a necessary attribute of free personhood, to "will" as that legal document through which he can pass on his property, and the social capital of his good name, through the laws of inheritance.

Benjamin Franklin, who suggested to those inquiring about emigration to America that they read Crèvecœur's *Letters from an American Farmer,* likewise employed this division between "invisible" and "visible" character in the depictions of his representative self.

Benjamin Franklin and the Character of the Fugitive Apprentice

Early in his *Autobiography,* Benjamin Franklin relates that he "lik'd [the printer's profession] much better than that of [his] Father, but still had a Hankering for the sea. To prevent the apprehended Effect of such an Inclination, my Father was impatient to have me bound to my Brother. I stood out some time, but at last was persuaded and signed the Indentures, when I was yet but 12 years old."[47] Critics have remarked upon both the oedipal structure and the self-consciously "representative" character of Franklin's literary self-fashioning throughout part 1 of the *Autobiography*.[48] In their focus on these psychological and psychoanalytic themes, they ignore the economic reality to which Franklin refers, and the character-determining, formative role Franklin himself assigns to this period.[49] Franklin repeatedly emphasizes the significance of this apprenticeship under his brother, and characterizes the ploy he uses to free himself from his indentures as "one of the first Errata" of his life. In fact, it is the first of Franklin's famous "errata" to be named as such in the *Autobiography*. And it is during this apprenticeship under his brother that the young Franklin "now had access to better Books" (Franklin 14), an initial store of cultural capital he links directly to his accumulation of social and economic capital later in life. Further, in introducing this moment of signing his indentures, Franklin is keen to point out that his life could have taken a different path, depending on the vocation to which he was bound: he might have become a clergyman, as his father had originally intended; or a tallow chandler and soap boiler (his father's trade), a joiner, bricklayer, turner, or brazier; or he could have gone to Sea, as his brother Josiah "had done to his [father's] great Vexation" (Franklin 12). Thus to appreciate the complexity of Franklin's famous self-fashioning, we should attend to the ways in which Franklin narrates how he was formed in this apprenticeship period, for it is in his narration of the dynamic relation between social formation and the individual subject that Franklin becomes "representative" of the new American.

One of the books Franklin read during this period was "Locke on Human Understanding" (Franklin 17), whose conceptions of agency and freedom would be enacted in Franklin's narrative of his escape from the bonds of his apprenticeship. What is most significant to our understanding of this formative period in Franklin's apprenticeship is his narration of the conflict between the economic bonds of labor and the affective bonds of the family: "Tho' a Brother, he considered himself as my Master, and me as his Apprentice; and accordingly expected the same Services from me as he would from another; while I thought he demean'd me too much in some he required of me, who from a Brother expected more Indulgence" (20). Franklin highlights the conflicting expectations of the contracting parties: his brother, viewing him solely as an apprentice, expected "the same Services" from Franklin as he would any other bound servant; in contrast, Franklin considers the familial relation and so "expected more Indulgence." Significantly, Franklin never refers to his brother as his master; rather, it is the brother who "considered himself as my Master": for his brother, the familial bond had been displaced by the economic, once the indentures were signed. Thus while there may very well be an oedipal drama subtending Franklin's departure from his family, the political unconscious of this departure begins first and foremost as the apprentice's flight from the laws of the master-servant relation.

Franklin underscores the significance of this political-economic relation in the transition to the narration of his escape from these indentures:

> Our Disputes were often brought before our Father, and I fancy I was either generally in the right, or else a better Pleader, because the Judgment was generally in my favour: But my Brother was passionate and had often beaten me, which I took extremely amiss; and thinking my Apprenticeship very tedious, I was continually wishing for some Opportunity of shortening it, which at length offered in a manner unexpected. *Note.* I fancy his harsh and tyrannical Treatment of me, might be a means of impressing me with that Aversion to arbitrary Power that has stuck to me thro' my whole Life. (20–21)

Franklin locates the origins of his lifelong "Aversion to arbitrary Power" in his own subjection as an apprentice to the "tyrannical treatment" by his brother, and thus proposes a direct allegorical reading of their master-apprentice contract as a socially and politically representative power relation.

Appearing in a text published after the success of the American Revolution, whose leaders famously cited Locke's justification of the Whig Revolution (in his *Second Treatise of Government*) in their own justifications of colonial resistance to abuses of Parliament, Franklin's allegory is suggestive in many ways. First, James Franklin's character-function in this allegory of power is made explicit: disregarding the familial bond, the brother identifying as master is characterized as "passionate," and the treatment of his apprentice "tyrannical." In the conceptual grammar of Locke's *Essay Concerning Human Understanding* (which, as Franklin points out immediately prior to narrating this episode, he had read at this time), "passionate" is opposed to the calm of just reason and true liberty of thought: "But if any extreme disturbance ... possesses our whole mind, as when the pain of ... an impetuous uneasiness, as of love, anger, or any other violent passion, running away with us, allows us not the liberty of thought, and we are not masters enough of our own minds to consider thoroughly and fairly; God ... will judge as a kind and merciful Father. But ... the moderation of and restraint of our passions, so that our understanding may be free to examine, and reason unbiased give its judgment ... it is in this we should employ our chief care and endeavors."[50] While James Franklin cannot master his passions and thus behaves as a tyrannical master over his own brother, the apprentice Benjamin Franklin, having read "Locke on Human Understanding" (Franklin 17), is the figure of reason (and his father, not unlike God, the "kind and merciful Father," thus often showed him favor). As Locke elaborated in this chapter "On the Idea of Power," the mind has the "power to suspend the execution and satisfaction of any of its desires," that is, the power to contain unreasonable "passions."[51] Locke argued that this "power to suspend the prosecution of this or that desire" was "the source of all liberty.... This is so far from being a restraint or diminution of freedom, that it is the very improvement and benefit of it; it is not an abridgment, it is the end and use of our liberty; and the further we are removed from such a determination, the nearer we are to misery and slavery."[52] Locke incorporated this conceptualization of power and "freedom" (along with its contrasting metaphorical "slavery") into his *Second Treatise of Government* (1690) based on the same analogy Franklin invokes in his apprentice's allegory of "Arbitrary power": just as "a man ... cannot subject himself to the arbitrary power of another ... but only so much as the law of nature gave him for the preservation of himself ... this is all he doth, or can give up to the common-wealth, and by it to the legislative power."[53] Thus while the legislative power is "the supreme power in every common-wealth ... [i]t is not, nor can possibly be *arbitrary power* over the lives and fortunes of the people."[54] It is on this fundamental philosophical principle regarding the nature of man, that "no man or society of men [have] a power to deliver up their preservation ... to the absolute will and arbitrary dominion of another," that Locke would rest his political defense of the "supreme power of the people" to free themselves from the social contract: "when ever any one shall go about to bring them into such a slavish condition, they will always have a right ... to rid themselves of those who invade this fundamental, sacred, and unalterable law of self-preservation, for which they entered into society."[55] Locke's philosophical defense of the natural right of resistance to "arbitrary power" circulated widely, and Franklin's allusion to it in these lines introducing the representation of his escape from his indentures thus frames the significance of that act, and inflects its subsequent "representative" meaning, even before Franklin narrates it. Franklin, who describes (immediately prior to the narration of this episode) how to "inform and to persuade" through humility and subtle indirection, compares his own subjection under his master's "tyrannical treatment" to the colonies' subjection to the "arbitrary power" of Britain, and suggests an analogy between his apprenticeship indentures and the contract of civil government. Thus even before naming it his life's "first errata," Franklin has excused himself of breaking his indentures, assigning blame to the master for abusing his contractual powers.

Throughout the *Autobiography*, Franklin focuses on the split between the public self and the private self. This is especially so in part 1, which narrates his formative years as an apprentice and then journeyman printer—that period during which, as Benjamin Vaughn asserted in his letter to Franklin (included by Franklin in the *Autobiography*), "the private and public character is determined" (Franklin 74). What is equally significant to our understanding of the influence of Franklin as a literary model for that "new race of man, the American" is the device through which Franklin escapes the indentures binding him to his master, for the device turns upon the division between public character and private character, what Crèvecœur described as the difference between "visible character" and "invisible character." And the "manner unexpected" by which Franklin's "Opportunity of shortening" his apprenticeship occurred is likewise significant for what it reveals about this split subject: "One of the Pieces in our News-Paper, on some political Point which I have now forgotten, gave Offense to the Assembly. [James Franklin] was taken up, censur'd and imprison'd for a month.... During my Brother's Confinement... I had the Management of the Paper, and I made bold to give our Rulers some Rubs in it.... My Brother's Discharge was accompany'd with an Order of the House, (a very odd one) *that James Franklin should no longer print the Paper called the New England Courant*" (Franklin 21). The "visible character" of "Benjamin Franklin" first appeared in the public sphere of print in the circumstances of the state's attempts to suppress political speech. It is also significant that it was thus publicly known that Franklin, the apprentice, was managing the paper during his master's confinement, and giving "Rubs to our Rulers in it," which led others to "consider [him] in an unfavourable Light, as a young Genious that had a Turn for Libelling & Satyr" (21). Franklin represents himself as a young apprentice already fully capable of taking on the duties of the master printer, and already overstepping the limits of his station. In order "to evade" the House's "very odd" injunction

> it was finally concluded... to let it be printed for the future under the Name of *Benjamin Franklin*. And to avoid the Censure of the Assembly that might still fall on him, as still printing it by his Apprentice, the Contrivance was, that my old Indenture should be returned to me with a full Discharge on the Back of it, to be shown on Occasion; but to secure to him the Benefit of my service I was to sign new indentures for the Remainder of the Term, [which] were to be kept private. (Franklin 21)

The "contrivance" thus relies on a twofold split between "private" and "public" character. First, as I have noted, with the newspaper now printed officially under the "Name of Benjamin Franklin," the textual character of Benjamin Franklin as a master printer (what would become his most iconic role) made its public debut. Further, for the "very flimsy scheme" to work, this new public character required that Franklin be "discharged" from his apprenticeship indentures: the contract, which only bound him because it was a publicly recognized document, would be dissolved, while his "new Indentures for the Remainder of the Term ... were to be kept private" (Franklin 21). As a secret, "private" contract in direct contradiction to the public character Benjamin Franklin had since assumed, these new indentures did not really bind him.

It is this very split, between Franklin's public character as one discharged from the bonds of his indenture on the one hand, and his private character as an apprentice still bound by secret contract on the other, that Franklin would manipulate when, as he describes, "a fresh Difference arising between my Brother and me, I took upon me to assert my Freedom, presuming he could not venture to produce the new Indentures" (Franklin 21). Franklin manipulated the already existing split between public and private character, while thus revealing the greater significance of the former to the social order of early America. Ultimately Franklin says that "it was not fair in me to take this Advantage, and this I therefore reckon one of the first Errata of my Life" (22). Yet we should note that what Franklin calls an errata was his manipulation of that split between public and private enacted in their contrivance to evade the House's order; Franklin does not say it was an errata to have "assert[ed] my freedom" (23). Franklin here is "representative" not of patience, but rather of the individual capable of mastering the split between public and private, visible and invisible "character," in order to leap past that period of apprenticeship inscribed in the laws of master and servant.[56]

Nor should we underestimate this aspect of the "character" Franklin represents in his *Autobiography*: twice in the next pages narrating the journey of his escape he refers to himself as the "figure" of the fugitive indentured servant: "I cut so miserable a figure too, that I found by Questions ask'd me I was suspected to be some runaway Servant, and in danger of being taken up on that suspicion" (Franklin 24). And later, after having arrived in Philadelphia, "several sly Questions were ask'd me, as it seemed to be suspected from my youth & Appearance, that I might be some runaway" (27). It is this representative version of Franklin, as the young apprentice who appropriated the discourse of his master (it was his master's "contrivance" after all) and manipulated the terms of his subjection in order to assert his freedom, that made the *Autobiography* popular among "the youth"—young apprentices and journeymen—throughout the post-Revolutionary republic of the 1790s and the first half of the nineteenth century. It was a period of the early republic which saw the rapidly decreasing structural mobility promised by the eighteenth-century political-economic model of apprenticeship, and the breakdown of its cultural ideology: the individual's gradual and orderly movement from bound, "qualifiedly free" subject to a position of independent self-mastery.[57]

Mixed Character and *The Interesting Narrative of Olaudah Equiano*

In an influential interpretation of the significance of Olaudah Equiano's representation of his manumission certificate to the larger cultural work of *The Interesting Narrative*, Houston Baker has argued that the "document ... signals the ironic transformation of property by property into humanity."[58] Baker resituated Equiano's *Interesting Narrative* in the "social ground" of eighteenth-century mercantilism with the critical insight that the *Narrative* "vividly delineates the true character of Afro-America's historical origins in a slave economics and implicitly acknowledges that such economics *must be mastered* before liberation can be achieved."[59] This understanding needs to be supplemented with a more expansive view of the political-economic "social ground," one which comprehends the broader spectrum of labor subjection and bondage through which antislavery writers like Equiano imagined freedom, and those attributes of social personhood required for its realization.[60] The claim that the document "signals the ironic transformation of property by property into humanity" is based on a historically inaccurate opposition between property and humanity. While there were eighteenth-century proslavery texts, such as James Tobin's *Cursory Remarks upon the Rev. Mr. Ramsay's Essay*, that questioned or denied the humanity of Africans, most of the eighteenth-century literature defending slavery accepted the philosophical and religious recognitions of their humanity, if only to claim it to be an uncivilized and a naturally inferior one. And in the context of a historical analysis of Equiano's manumission certificate as not only a "linguistic occurrence" but a legal document, we should note that eighteenth-century British and American laws governing slave property did not deny the humanity of slaves. In British colonial and American slavery law, property and humanity were not absolutely opposed terms, and the slave was recognized throughout the transatlantic world as both property and person. In the United States, the recognition of slave humanity was extended to the legal recognition of the slave "as a moral person." Writing behind the mask of Publius in *The Federalist No. 54* (1788), James Madison cited this dual recognition to explain the Constitution's three-fifths clause and its ratio for the counting of slaves as persons ("three-fifths of all other persons"). Madison argued that though legally the slave was chattel property, "the slave is no less evidently regarded by law as a member of society, not as a part of the irrational creation; as a moral person, not as a mere article of property." The proposed federal Constitution, Madison continued, thus "views them in the mixed character of persons and of property. This is in fact their true character. It is the character bestowed on them by the laws under which they live."[61]

The recognition of the slave's humanity as coextensive with the slave's legal condition as property was inherited from English common law. Blackstone's *Commentaries*, for example, while recognizing slaves as property in the West Indian and North American colonies, took for granted the law's recognition of them as men and by natural right free: "[the] spirit of liberty is so deeply rooted in our soil, that a slave or negro, the moment he lands in England, falls under the protection of the laws, and with regard to all natural rights becomes *eo instanti* a freeman."[62] Lord Mansfield's famous 1772 ruling in *Somerset v. Stewart* (brought to litigation by Equiano's friend Granville Sharp) proceeded from the accepted view that all humanity, including Africans, are by natural right free, and that the slave's condition as property was the artificial creation of local (municipal) positive law.[63]

Moreover, Equiano himself reminds us of the legal and cultural recognitions of this "mixed character" of the slave as person and property through the two other documents embedded within the *Interesting Narrative*, his certificates of "good character." As with Andrew the Hebridean's passage from servitude to self-mastery in Crèvecœur's *Letters*, the major steps in Equiano's passage from slavery to freedom—through the cultivation narrative of apprenticeship—are marked by these textual "outward signs" of "visible character." After having bought his manumission from his master, Robert King, and continuing to work for him for a year, Equiano decides to "return" to England: "I then requested he be kind enough to give me a certificate of my behaviour while in his service, which he very readily complied with, and gave me the following: Montserrat, 26th of July, 1767. The bearer hereof, Gustavas Vassa, was my slave for upwards of three years, during which he has always behaved himself well, and discharged his duty with honesty and assiduity. Robert King. To all whom this may concern."[64] Equiano has been formally free for over a year when he obtains this certificate of his behavior (his manumission certificate is dated 11 July 1766); yet the certificate, for Equiano's use as a free laborer (seeking employment as a sailor or hired servant), is given its social-textual authority through the signature of his former owner; and those attributes of "good character" to which the document attests ("he behaved himself well, and discharged his duty with honesty and assiduity") are based on his performance of these traits while

Equiano was Robert King's slave. Indeed, Equiano's "certificate of character" speaks the same language as the Quaker reformer David Barclay's broadside "Advice to Servants," whose central message was that "a good character" should be the highest goal of servants, "for it is their bread."[65] As we have seen, this good "visible character" was also one of the primary lessons in Crèvecœur's history of Andrew the Hebridean, whose motto was that of all poor immigrants: *ubi panis ibi patria* (*Letters* 43).

These continuities between the good character traits of the slave and those of the formally free servant are then reaffirmed when Equiano later obtains another certificate, this time from another "old and good master," Dr. Irving. This "certificate of [his] behaviour" reads: "The bearer, Gustavus Vassa, has served me several years with strict honesty, sobriety, and fidelity. I can, therefore, with justice recommend him for these qualifications; and indeed in every respect I consider him as an excellent servant. I do hereby certify that he always behaved well, and that he is perfectly trust-worthy" (Equiano 210). The formal difference in servile status indicated in these two certificates of character is worth noting: in the first certificate, the attributes of "good character" were demonstrated through Equiano's services to his master as a slave, whereas in the second, they were demonstrated through his role as a servant. However, as documents signed by authorities identified with the full freedom of a master (over slaves and servants), these certificates of character serve the same social function. And as their contents reveal, the attributes of "good character" for the slave and for the "free" servant were the same; these were the traits of the ideal laboring subject, enslaved or free: the tractable person accepting his subjection to the mastery of another, willingly bound "to serve well and faithfully."[66]

Equiano's two certificates of "good character" together reveal a more complex conception of slave personhood than is represented in Equiano's oft-cited manumission certificate. The writing of such "characters" for slaves signaled the social recognition of their possession of those attributes of the "moral person" considered necessary to the "free" laborer. While slavery is still exemplary here of the most extreme form of labor bondage and unfree personhood, it is also represented as existing along a spectrum of labor subjection, not in static binary opposition to "freedom" or "humanity." Even as in the late eighteenth century to be a slave of "good character" was to be "honest," "well-behaved," and above all *faithful* to a master while bound in involuntary servitude, such an understanding proceeds from the cultural and legal recognition of the slave as both a member of humanity and a "moral person." Thus while we can agree with the importance of the manumission certificate as exemplary of Equiano's "mastery" of slave economics, we should not ignore the significance of these other embedded texts marking the narrative of Equiano's passage from slavery to formal freedom. These social documents reinforce the political-economic fact that the attributes of "good character" for the slave were the same as those for the servant (in the words of these certificates: "honesty, sobriety, fidelity"), and that the primary difference between them was the legal freedom inscribed in the more spectacularly "peculiar" manumission certificate (Equiano 137).

In the narration of his passage from bondage to freedom, Equiano dwells on scenes that typify those traits listed in the two certificates of character he receives: honesty and fidelity. For example, Equiano repeatedly points out that while his mind was "replete with inventions and thoughts of being freed," especially when faced with the horrors of slavery in the West Indies, he wished to obtain his freedom "by honest and honourable means, for I always remembered the old adage, and I trust that it has ever been my ruling principle, 'that Honesty is the best policy'" (119).

In order to model the practicability of both slave emancipation and black civic assimilation, Equiano presents himself throughout the *Interesting Narrative* as "ruled" not by exterior restraints or fear of his master—as he declares, "I used plainly to tell him [the Captain] ... that I would die before I would be imposed upon as other negroes were" (120)—but rather by the interior governance of the moral principle of "honesty," that trait later listed as Equiano's first distinctive trait in the certificate of "good character" given to him by his former owner, Robert King. This "good character" trait distinguishes Equiano from that most representative of unruly slaves, the fugitive: "Had I wished to run away, I did not want opportunities, which frequently presented themselves" (Equiano 123). Equiano's contrast with the figure of the fugitive appealed to antislavery reformers and political elites alike. Throughout the transatlantic slavery debates, all sides referred to the maroon communities of escaped slaves that regularly "terrorized" the planter population with raids, and whose very existence provided a dangerous example to a restive slave population.

We should note further the political-economic significance of describing such a contrast with runaway slaves as "honesty," which is to say we should remember that in the emergent bourgeois ideology of the late eighteenth century, "moral sense" necessarily carried political-economic significations. In the model of black assimilability Equiano stages in the

Interesting Narrative, the "honest and honourable means" of obtaining freedom is equated with its "purchase" (126), such that slaveholders would be compensated for any losses sustained, by manumission or emancipation, of what Equiano calls the "first cost" (103) of their slaves. To make this last point is not to argue that Equiano sincerely believed that masters should be compensated for their freed slaves. Rather, it is to focus on slave autobiography's relation to the discourse of the master, and thus to attend to how such traits defining "good character" are represented by Equiano as profitable to the slave who would be free. For instance, in his narration of the episode wherein he passes on the opportunity to escape, Equiano repeats that principle by which he was governed ("honesty is the best policy"), and adds: "Indeed my captain was much afraid of my leaving him and the vessel at that time, as I had so fair an opportunity: but ... this fidelity of mine turned out much to my advantage hereafter" (123). Significant here is that Equiano uses the second of those terms listed as a trait of good character, "fidelity," and once again characterizes it in the terms not of the slave's religious or moral self but rather in its material "advantage" to him.

As described by Equiano, the value of this "fidelity" arose from how it gained him credibility with his master. After the ship's mate accuses Equiano of planning to run away, his master, Robert King, tells Equiano that he must therefore sell him. In response to this accusation and to the threat of being sold, Equiano refers to the several prior opportunities he had to escape, and repeats to his master the declaration he had made earlier to the reader of *The Interesting Narrative*, of his belief that "if ever I were freed, whilst I was used well, it should be by honest means" (Equiano 124). Equiano is not categorically opposed to escape as the means of becoming free for he qualifies this belief in the "honest means" of becoming free with the condition of good treatment ("whilst I was used well"). Likewise, in the beginning of this chapter he tells the reader he had agreed to serve as a sailor because he thought he might "possibly make [his] escape if [he] should be used ill" (115). And immediately after declaring to his master that he had never *intended* to escape, Equiano tells the reader, "at that instant my mind was big with inventions, and full of schemes to escape" (125). In this dialogue between the slave accused of infidelity and the master as judge of the slave's credibility, Equiano distinguishes between what the slave says in the face of the master and what the slave is thinking. What this disjunction highlights is the performative aspect of Equiano's "good character" of fidelity to his master. The slave does not have to actually believe in the idea of "being freed... by honest means," yet the value of his fidelity—of not attempting escape despite many opportunities—comes from the credible performance of this trait for the master, as well as for readers debating the practicability of abolition of the slave trade, slave emancipation, and the assimilation of the formerly enslaved into the culture of free (because voluntary) labor subjection.

Equiano elaborates this point further through the corroborating testimony of the captain:

> I then appealed to the captain, whether ever he saw any sign of my making the least attempt to run away.... [The] captain confirmed every syllable I said, and even more; for he said he had tried different times to see if I would make any attempt of this kind, both at St. Eustatia and in America, and he never found that I made the smallest; ... and he did really believe, if ever I meant to run away, that, as I could never have had a better opportunity, I would have done it the night the mate and all the people left our vessel at Guadaloupe. (Equiano 125)

The captain corroborates the truth of Equiano's claims of fidelity not by reference to anything Equiano has said (e.g., the assertion of his belief that whether he would be free depended on God's will), but rather through reference to Equiano's performance of such fidelity by remaining with the ship in the absence of an overseer and passing over his many opportunities to escape.

The episode closes with the translation of this fidelity to the master, as a trait of "good character," into its economic value to the slave seeking freedom:

> [My] master immediately [said] that I was a sensible fellow, and he never did intend to use me as a common slave; and that, but for the entreaties of the captain, and his character of me, he would not have let me go from the stores about as I had done; that also, in so doing, he thought by carrying one little thing or other to different places to sell I might make money. That he also intended to encourage me in this, by crediting me with half a puncheon of rum and half a hogshead of sugar at a time; so that, from being careful, I might have money enough, in some time, to purchase my freedom: and, when that was the case, I might depend upon it he would let me have it for forty pounds sterling money, which was only the price he gave for me. (Equiano 126)

If Equiano's manumission certificate documents how "chattel has transformed itself into freeman through the exchange of forty pounds sterling," Equiano's narration of this transformation highlights that the price Equiano later pays to purchase his freedom is a price originally suggested here by his master, and is represented as the reward for the slave's honesty and fidelity.[67]

The dialogue was an especially popular form in antislavery literature. In addition to reminding us that Equiano's *Narrative* belongs to a wider literary tradition (not an exclusively Anglo-African, African American, or Black Atlantic one), the dialogic form of this key episode emphasizes that conceptions of freedom, and of its contrasting degrees of unfreedom, were produced through the dialectic of master and bondsman, a dialectic whose very imaginative possibility depended upon both the implicit and explicit recognitions of slave humanity, and of the "mixed character" of the slave as both chattel property and moral person. Equiano employs the narrative symmetry of the dialogue form to emphasize the economic value—to the slave and to the master—of slave fidelity as a "good character" trait. This narrative symmetry is marked by the master's promise, at the dialogue's close, to let Equiano purchase his freedom "for forty pounds sterling money, which was only the price he gave for me" (Equiano 126). This dialogue between master and slave had opened, we recall, with Robert King learning of Equiano's possible infidelity—"he heard that I meant to run away" (124)—and consequently telling him, "And therefore ... I must sell you again; you cost me a great deal of money, no less than forty pounds sterling; and it will not do to lose so much. You are a valuable fellow ... and I can get any day for you one hundred guineas, from many gentlemen in this island" (124). Whereas in this opening exchange of the dialogue, Equiano's master, fearing the loss of the forty pounds he had paid for Equiano, threatens to sell him to a West Indian slaveholder, in the dialogue's conclusion, the master, after having been reassured of Equiano's fidelity, promises to sell to Equiano his manumission for this same price of forty pounds. The trial of Equiano's "good character" is framed by these dialogic exchanges between master and slave, and the success of Equiano's performance of fidelity is marked by the change in the master's address to his slave from *threat* to *promise*, from believing forty pounds too great a sum to lose ("it will not do to lose so much") if the slave were to escape from his bondage, to considering it an equitable price ("only the price he gave for me"), if the slave could earn it while continuing to serve his master faithfully.

While Equiano mentions his "thoughts of being freed" (119) prior to this moment, he highlights in this dialogue that it is his owner Robert King who initiates the material possibility of this transformation from chattel property to free man—in Equiano's words, to become "my own master" (137)—by "credit[ing] me with a tierce of sugar and another of rum" (126). The visible character trait of fidelity thus becomes of direct financial value to Equiano, marked by this translation of the credibility of Equiano's claims of fidelity into merchant "credit"—that is, by the conversion of the *social capital* of good "character" into *economic capital*.[68]

The dialogue form also illuminates the ways in which the master's promise introduces those very terms later inscribed into Equiano's manumission certificate and his certificates of good character, thus underscoring the widespread recognition, in the interdependent discourses of the master and the slave, of the continuities between the "moral person" of the slave and the free servant. These continuities are represented here through the combined narratives of assimilation and accumulation contained in the master's address to his slave at the dialogue's conclusion. Based on both "the captain's character of [Equiano]" and Equiano's own successful performance of the good character trait of fidelity, the master recognizes his slave as a "sensible fellow" and decides to "encourage" his industry. The master ties his promise of manumission to the inculcation of the market's values: "from being careful, I might have money enough, in some time, to purchase my freedom" (Equiano 126). Through the voice of the master, Equiano represents freedom here as something "earned," both in its direct economic sense—the individual accumulation of capital—and in its assimilative, moral sense: the slave must *learn* to trade well and to "be careful" with his time and money if he is to obtain freedom.

"Being careful" is especially significant in the context of this promise of a *future* opportunity to purchase his freedom, for it emphasizes that attribute of moral personhood considered a distinguishing feature of the free laboring subject: foresight. Even as the slave is enjoined to accept his present bondage, he is "encouraged" to practice his industry and the self-discipline of being careful with his money—to behave like a "sensible" free laborer—with a view toward a possible future, the end of his enslavement "in some time."[69] Countering the proslavery view of black slaves as living solely in and for the present, Equiano depicts the master's recognition of his slave as a moral person with the foresight necessary to comprehend the significance of the master's promise.

Assimilation and Universal Emancipation

Equiano's representation of the master's promise of manumission as a reward for the slave's fidelity draws directly from the proposals for practicable emancipation made by fellow abolitionists such as Anthony Benezet, Granville Sharp, Benjamin Rush, and Ottobah Cugoano. In his influential *Historical Account of Guinea* (1771), Benezet discussed the "expediency of a general freedom being granted to the Negroes" through the gradualist model of assimilation.[70] Benezet opposed sending to Africa those slaves already imported to the colonies, or those "born in our families," on the grounds that such a deportation "would be to expose them, in a strange land, to greater difficulties than many of them labour under at present."[71] He acknowledged, however, the possible difficulties attending immediate emancipation, due to what was described as the degraded moral characters of these slaves, which Benezet argued were the artificial "effects," the social product, of an unnatural enslavement: "To let them suddenly free here, would perhaps be attended with no less difficulty; for, undisciplined as they are in religion and virtue, they might give a loose to their evil habits, which the fear of a master would have restrained. These are objections, which weigh with many well disposed people, and it must be granted, there are difficulties in the way."[72] Speaking directly to the economic concerns of the political elite, Benezet "offered for consideration" this proposal:

> That all further importation of slaves be absolutely prohibited; and as those born among us, *after serving so long as may appear to be equitable*, let them by law be declared free. Let every one, thus set free, be enrolled in the county courts, and *be obliged* to be a resident, during a certain number of years, within the said county, under the care of the *overseers of the poor*. Thus being, in some sort, still *under the direction of governors*, and the notice of those who were formerly acquainted with them, they would be *obliged to act the more circumspectly*, and make *proper use of their liberty*, and their children would have an opportunity of obtaining such *instructions*, as are necessary to the common occasions of life; and thus both parents and children might *gradually become useful* members of the community. And further, where the nature of the country would permit . . . suppose a small tract of land were assigned to every Negroe family, and they *obliged* to live upon and improve it, (when not hired out to work

for the white people) this would *encourage them* to exert their abilities, and *become industrious subjects.*[73]

Benezet's proposal both assumes and projects a narrative of moral cultivation, and its concomitant "inculcation" of "economic virtues."[74] The transformation from slave subject to free (because voluntary) laborer is imagined through the reciprocal inducements of "obligation" and "encouragement." Even when formally free, the formerly enslaved would be "under the direction of governors," and thus continue to feel "obliged to act the more circumspectly, and make proper use of their liberty." The discipline of the lash—the "restraint" provided by "the fear of a master"—would be replaced by the slave's moral self-discipline, marked here by that recurring term, "obliged."

The result of such an assimilation of slave subjects into the world of "free" labor, Benezet concludes, is that "both planters and tradesman would be plentifully supplied with cheerful and willing-minded labourers, much vacant land would be cultivated, the produce of the country be justly increased, the taxes for the support of government lessened to the individuals, by the increase of taxables, and the Negroes, instead of being an object of terror, as they certainly must be where their numbers are great, would become interested in their safety and welfare."[75] I should emphasize as well that in order to imagine this transition to formal freedom, Benezet draws from the extant models of labor discipline applied to the British and colonial American "white" working class, as indicated here by his references to the "the overseers of the poor" and "the direction of governors" as the disciplinary mode through which the formerly enslaved would "become industrious subjects."

Ottobah Cugoano concludes his *Thoughts and Sentiments on the Evil and Wicked Traffic of the Slavery and Commerce of the Human Species* (1787) with proposals for the abolition of slavery that follow the same gradualist model of apprenticeship and assimilation invoked by Benezet:

> I would propose that a total abolition of slavery should be ... proclaimed; and that a universal emancipation of slaves should begin from the date thereof, and be carried out in the following manner: ... [T]hat it should require all slaveholders to mitigate the labor of their slaves to that of *lawful servitude*. ... And that it should be made known to the slaves that those who had been above seven years in the islands or elsewhere, if they had obtained any *competent degree of knowledge* of the Christian religion, and

the laws of civilization, and had *behaved themselves honestly and decently*, that they should immediately become free; and that their owners should give them reasonable wages and maintenance for their labor.[76]

While Cugoano appealed to religious feeling and moral sentiment throughout the preceding pages, his positive proposals for the practical implementation of "universal emancipation" transposes the religious assimilation of conversion onto the economic assimilation of the "lawful servitude" of apprenticeship and indenture. The time period of seven years proposed by Cugoano may have come from the Bible—the jubilee, when bond servants were set free, arrived every seven years—yet more likely came from the standard term limits of the contracts for apprentices and indentured servants: as early as 1562, the Statute of Artificers imposed a minimum of seven years of service for all persons entering an industrial calling and specified that the apprenticeship was not to expire before the worker reached the age of twenty-four.[77]

Cugoano's transposition of conversion onto servitude underscores the double nature of the structure of assimilation, as, on the one side, an "incorporation" of the individual subject by the community, which enjoins, on the other side, a transformation of the individual subject, such that this subject would be deemed worthy of such incorporation. The seven years thus figure as a period of apprenticeship, in the sense of what Cugoano pointedly calls a "lawful servitude" governed by training and instruction: "For in the course of that time, they would have sufficiently paid their owners by their labor, both for their first purpose, and for the expenses attending their education. By being thus instructed in the course of seven years, they would become tractable and obedient, useful laborers, dutiful servants and good subjects."[78] Thus, while the proposed "universal emancipation of slaves" would be immediate, their labor subjection would continue as a "lawful servitude" until they paid their former masters "for their first purpose and for the expenses attending their education," just as apprentices paid theirs; and until the formerly enslaved were themselves transformed into "good subjects," and acquired the moral "character" of free laborers: "tractable and obedient, useful and dutiful."

In addition to the extant models of labor discipline for "free" laborers, abolitionists looked to the slavery laws of other colonial states to describe the practical transition from slavery to freedom. To argue the practicability of gradual emancipation in the British West Indies, for example, Granville Sharp invoked the Spanish colonial system of slave self-purchase, *coartación*, as a model "worthy our imitation, in case we should not be so happy as to obtain an entire abolition of slavery":

> As soon as a slave is landed, his name, price, &c., are register'd in a public office, and the master is obliged to allow him one working day in every week to himself, besides Sundays, so that if the slave chuses to work for his master on that day, he receives the wages of a freeman for it, and whatever he gains by his labor on that day, is so secured to him by law, that the master cannot deprive him of it. This is certainly a considerable step towards the abolishing [of] absolute slavery. As soon as the slave is able to purchase another working day, the master is obliged to sell it to him at a proportional price, viz. 1–fifth part of his original cost: and so likewise the remaining 4 days at the same rate, as soon as the slave is able to *redeem them*, after which he is absolutely free. This is such an *encouragement to industry*, that even the most indolent are tempted to exert themselves. Men who have thus *worked out their freedom* are inured to the labour of the country, and are certainly the most useful subjects that a colony can acquire. Regulations might be formed upon the same plan to *encourage the industry* of slaves that are already imported into the colonies, which would *teach them how to maintain themselves and be as useful*, as well as less expensive to the planter. They would by such means *become members* of society, and have an interest in the welfare of the community, which would greatly add to the security of the colony; whereas, at present, many of the planters are in continual danger of being cut off by their slaves—A fate which they but too justly deserve![79]

The *coartación* system differed from British abolitionist proposals for "immediate emancipation" of slaves (to be followed by a period of their "apprenticeship" as bound servants), insofar as under *coartación*, laborers remained enslaved until they had purchased all the days of the work week. In Sharp's view, however, their gradualist models of slave assimilation into the culture of free labor, through technical training and moral reform, were the same: slaves who steadily "worked out their freedom" would become "inured to the labour of the country"; taught "how to maintain themselves and be . . . useful," they would "become members of society." Similarly, both labor models, apprenticeship and *coartación*, were premised upon the replacement of physical coercion with the positive inducement of wages and formal freedom.[80]

The practicability of both slave trade abolition and slave emancipation was one of the most urgently debated questions of antislavery politics in this period. No matter how often antislavery activists such as Sharp, Benezet, Cugoano, and Equiano cited religion and natural justice or referred to the threat of slave insurrection, they had to address as well the economic concerns of political elites—what Equiano, recognizing the demand to speak the language of political economy, repeatedly refers to as "interest." As historians of emancipation in the age of revolution have demonstrated, political elites were concerned with maintaining social order and economic stability—specifically, labor production levels—if abolition of the slave trade or slave emancipation were ever enacted.[81]

The Interesting Narrative presents in narrative form this discourse of "universal emancipation" through gradualist assimilation, whose possibility was conceptualized through the bound, yet "qualifiedly free," laborers of apprenticeship and indentured servitude, and stages the practicability of both abolition of the slave trade and immediate slave emancipation. In the dialogic scene of the master's promise to his slave, Equiano gives narrative form to the proposals made by abolitionists like Benezet, Cugoano, and Sharp for the assimilation of the formerly enslaved into the "free" culture of market society. Equiano's representation of the master's promise to his slave combines manumission with instruction, and identifies the moral and economic "cultivation" of the slave with the slaveholder's self-interest. As Cugoano suggested, in the now "lawful servitude" of this apprenticeship period, the slaves "would have sufficiently paid their owners by their labor, for their first purpose"—that is, repaid what Equiano refers to as the slave's "first cost" (Equiano 103).

Literary critics arguing Equiano's "containment" within "liberal ideology" have focused on Equiano's claim for the high labor productivity of slaves: "I have sometimes heard it asserted that a negro cannot earn his master the first cost, but nothing can be further from the truth.... I have known many slaves whose masters would not take a thousand pounds current for them" (Equiano 103). One has cited it to argue Equiano's complicity with slavery: "And where human worth is measured in wealth, Equiano's attempts to make money on deck while slaves languish below become intelligible."[82] Another cites it to lament the reduction of "African humanity to what African slaves can produce in the capitalist market. This engenders a terrible irony: the value of humanity becomes indistinct from capital, or property, in this case figured as the exemplary slave worth more than a thousand pounds."[83] In order to characterize Equiano as complicit with that "world where human worth is measured in wealth," these commentators isolate this passage from its context within the *Interesting Narrative* as well as from its broader literary historical context. Nowhere in this passage does Equiano discuss "African labor," "humanity," or "human worth"; rather, his focus here is exclusively on the productivity of enslaved laborers. As Equiano notes, he does so in order to rebut the claims made by slavery's defenders that Africans were unproductive laborers, and that because they were unsuitable for "free" labor, they must be enslaved. Likewise, Equiano explicitly addresses that broader debate (discussed at the beginning of this chapter) over the relative values of slave and free labor, values estimated by considering labor productivity in relation to the costs of reproducing these laborers. These critical readings of Equiano's statement arise from the historical assumption that economic terms such as "first cost" and labor value were in this period absolutely opposed to conceptions of "humanity." They ignore the wider discursive field Equiano is addressing here (despite Equiano's direct reference to it in the passage), namely the much-debated practicability of abolition of the slave trade, gradual emancipation, and the assimilation of the formerly enslaved into the world of "free" labor. In literary-critical terms, what these readings ignore is the dialogic narrative form of Equiano's *Interesting Narrative*; instead reading the text as merely expressive of the views of an isolated individual. They ignore, in other words, the broader class dialogue within which Equiano's claims are made, a class *langue* registered here by the always present figure of the slaveholder, to whom Equiano speaks implicitly and explicitly throughout the pages of his *Interesting Narrative*. Equiano's narration does not assign the decision to manumit him solely to the relative "good character" of the Quaker slaveholder Robert King, but rather makes his master a representative of the emergent view that considerations of "humanity," based on religious duty or moral sentiment, could be reconciled with the "true interests" of individuals and "the welfare of the community."[84]

Bonds of Promise

Finally, the conditions contained in the master's address to his slave link the informal promise to its legal form, the *contract*. While the slave was not recognized in law as a free agent and was thus disabled from contract, Robert King's promise to let Equiano purchase his freedom depends upon the recognition of him as a moral person, capable of contract: as a "sensible fellow" possessing those attributes—what Crèvecœur called "invisible character"—required for an agent of contract, such as will, foresight, and responsibility. In the scene of his self-purchase, Equiano makes explicit the promise's implicit recognition of the slave as a moral person capable of contract:

> I went in and made obeisance to my master, and with my money in my hand, and many fears in my heart, I prayed him to be as good as his offer to me, when he pleased to promise me my freedom as soon as I could purchase it. This speech seemed to confound him.... "What!" said he, "give you your freedom?... Have you got forty pounds sterling?... How did you get it[?]"... I told him, "Very honestly." The captain then said he knew I got the money very honestly, and with much industry, and that I was particularly careful. (Equiano 135)

Once again employing the dialogue form in his representation of the master-slave relation, Equiano pointedly reemploys those keywords of the master's original promise in this description of his successful performance of its conditions: earning "the money very honestly, and with much industry," and being "particularly careful." Equiano organizes the narration of this scene of the slave's self-purchase around the conceptual status of the promise itself. The scene begins with Equiano's request for his manumission articulated indirectly, as a plea that the master "be as good as his offer": Equiano's entreaty is that the master keep his promise to his slave—renamed by Equiano an "offer," the significance of which Equiano reveals as the dialogue unfolds. Surprised at how quickly Equiano has earned the forty pounds, King at first resists, by saying that "he would not have made me the promise he did if he had thought I should have got money so soon" (Equiano 135). Even as a slaveholder is not legally bound by promises to his slave, in this representative dialogue Equiano's master expresses his reluctance to "give" Equiano his freedom not by refusing the request outright, but rather by regretting having made the promise itself. Significant as well is the master's expression of regret: "if he had thought I should have got money so soon"—that is, if King had foreseen how quickly Equiano could meet the conditions of the "offer," he would not have made the "promise." Whereas the time of a promise's fulfillment depends on the one who makes the promise, the time of a contract's fulfillment depends on the meeting of its conditions. It is precisely this fixed temporality entailed in the conditions of the master's promise to his slave that reveals its direct link to the contract. For while King may not have foreseen Equiano's rapid accumulation of this "first cost," King had made the promise in order to "encourage" (Equiano 126) such industry and foresight in his slave, as those defining character traits required of a free laboring subject.

Equiano's "worthy captain" helps persuade King to keep his promise of manumission to Equiano by likewise using the terms of contract—or, more precisely, the language of the *debt bond*:

> "Come, come" said my worthy captain, ..."I think you must let him have his freedom;—you have laid your money out very well; you have received *good interest* for it all this time, and here now is the *principal* at last. I know Gustavus has earned you more than a hundred a-year, and he will still save you money, as he will not leave you." (Equiano 135)

The captain here echoes Equiano's earlier claims regarding the productivity of black laborers: "I have sometimes heard it asserted that a negro cannot earn his master the first cost; but nothing can be further from the truth" (Equiano 103). Yet the metaphor of the debt bond also shifts these terms, identifying the "first cost" of the slave with the "principal" of a loan, and the money earned for the master by his slave with the "interest" on that principal. Even as he translates its terms into the contemporary idiom of merchant capitalism, Equiano incorporates into his narration here the metaphor of debt-bondage, and its corollary trope for freeing the servant from these bonds: "redemption."

These related figures of debt-bond and redemption circulated widely throughout antislavery discourse. They were first used as a way to distinguish biblical servitude from modern slavery, but then employed both as rhetorical tropes and as practical models through which antislavery activists could imagine the transition from slavery to freedom. For example, in Cugoano's rebuttal of the proslavery claim that slavery was sanctioned by the "historical" accounts of such bondage in the Bible, Cugoano described the latter as a "lawful servitude" of temporary debt-bondage, which thus distinguished it from the permanent (and hereditary) chattel principles of modern slavery:

> Now, in respect to that kind of servitude which was admitted into the law of Moses, that was not contrary to the natural liberties of men, but a state of equity and justice, according as the nature and circumstances of the time required. There was no more harm in entering into a *covenant*

> with another man as a *bond servant*, than there is for two men to enter into *partnership* the one with the other. ... There was no harm in buying a man who was in a state of captivity and bondage by others, and keeping him in *servitude* until such time as *his purchase was redeemed* by his *labor and service*. And there could be no harm in paying a man's *debts*, and keeping him in servitude until such time as an equitable agreement of composition was *paid by him*.⁸⁵

Precisely because Cugoano can describe biblical debt-bondage as a "lawful servitude"—comparing it in the next lines to "a vassalage state ... equivalent to a poor man in England paying rent"—and thus distinguish it from the modern enslavement of Africans, Cugoano can also employ the biblical "redemption" of the bond servant's debts—whether these were "just debts ... or were brought from such as held them in an *unlawful captivity*"—as both metaphor and model for modern slave emancipation, through the bond servitudes of apprenticeship and indenture.⁸⁶

Equiano incorporates these popular antislavery metaphors for the "redemption" of the slave's "debts" through "labor and service" into his own narrative of self-purchase, presenting the slaveholder as a moneylender, the slave as his debtor, and the chains of the slave replaced by these "lawful" bonds. While legally the chattel property of his master, the slave is represented through this metaphor as a social agent possessing all the attributes necessary for legal contract. The contract implied in the promise, the legal form implicit in the symbolic form, is then made explicit through the dialogue's concluding act of economic exchange: "My master then said, *he would not be worse than his promise*; and, taking the money, told me to go to the Secretary at the Register Office, and get my manumission drawn up" (Equiano 135). Significantly, the dialogue concludes with King, before accepting the purchase money, echoing Equiano's opening request that the master "be as good as his offer," that he deal with his slave as a "sensible fellow" and abide by their implied contract. In Equiano's representation of his manumission as the slave's redemption from debt-bondage, the word is bond.

Indeed, the "peculiar" (Equiano 137) language of the manumission certificate itself confirms Equiano's view of the master's promise to his slave as an implied contract. In the words of the manumission certificate, the master does not merely declare he has "manumitted, emancipated, enfranchised, and set free" his slave; rather, he declares he does so "*for, and in consideration of* the sum of seventy pounds current money of the said island" (137). "Consideration" is precisely what distinguishes a binding contract from a mere promise: in contract law, consideration is "the thing given or done by the promisee in exchange for the promise.... In law, no promise is enforceable without consideration."[87] The purchase of the manumission certificate thus represents the completion of Equiano's passage to freedom through "faithful" bond-servitude—in his words, "I who had been a slave in the morning, trembling at the will of another, now became *my own master,* and completely free" (137). It was the reward for Equiano's successful apprenticeship in the "way of the world."[88]

2

Civic Virtues

Narrative Form and the Trial of Character in Early America

In his influential description of the novel's formal realism, Ian Watt proposed an analogy with the epistemological procedures of philosophical realism. He went on to suggest that such representational strategies and

> procedures are by no means confined to philosophy; they tend, in fact, to be followed whenever the relation to reality of any report of an event is being investigated. The novel's mode of imitating reality may therefore be equally well summarised in terms of the procedures of another group of specialists in epistemology, the jury in a court of law. Their expectations, and those of the novel reader coincide in many ways: both want to know "all the particulars" of a given case—the time and place of the occurrence; both must be satisfied as to the identities of the parties concerned, and will refuse to accept evidence about anyone called Sir Toby Belch or Mr. Badman—still less about a Chloe who has no surname and is "common as the air"; and they also expect the witnesses to tell the story "in his own words."[1]

In Watt's analogy between the novel's mimetic mode and that of the law, the procedures of the jury trial serve as the analogous narrative model. The novel's readers are like members of the jury, and the novel's "mode of imitating reality," or the "descriptive realism" that characterizes the novel as a genre, must meet certain standards of proof and evidence. Several questions arise from this insight, which will need to be addressed if we are to understand its implications for the formal development of the novel. First: why are the novel's readers analogous to the jury? If it is the novel's mimetic mode that is like the procedures of the jury in a court of law, would not the analogy be, more precisely, between the jury and the novel itself? Watt seems to return to this proposition of the analogy when he concludes: "The jury, in fact, takes the 'circumstantial view of life,' which T. H. Green found to be the characteristic outlook of the novel."[2] The propositional form of the analogy makes an important distinction in critical perspective on the novel. One form of the analogy—the novel's readers are like a jury—makes a claim regarding the novel's strategies of "imitating reality," or its mode of *representing* the truth. A second form of the analogy—the novel itself is like a jury—makes a claim regarding the novel's own strategies and procedures for *ascertaining* the truth. The first form perceives the novel primarily as a matter of representation; the second form, as a matter of epistemology.

We should note also that Watt's influential characterization of the novel's formal realism relies upon a characterization of the law as a realm of "realism." Watt's characterization of the legal sphere is not fully accurate. During the rise of the novel, legal fictions abounded which defied both the epistemological and representational demands of "realism." If necessary facts did not exist for the court to apply a known rule, or the absence of facts compelled the court to treat a claim under a set of rules that inconvenienced the parties involved, "the common law allowed facts to be contrived to fit the rule; known to all as 'fictions,' they were legal and thereby accepted by the court. A legal fiction was a 'feigned Construction of the Law ... when in a similitudinary and colourable Way the Law construeth a Thing otherwise than it is in Truth.'"[3] To avoid the constraints of existing ancient forms of legal action for example, "the common law welcomed before its bar fictitious figures John Doe and Richard Roe and accepted pledges from the fictitious John Den and Richard Fen. By the time Blackstone wrote, it also allowed 'Fairclaim' to commence an action against 'Shamtitle.'"[4] Throughout the seventeenth and eighteenth centuries, evidence was heard by and about persons who, while not named "Sir Toby Belch or Mr. Badman," were recognized to be "false," fictive," and as much "artifices" and "pretenses" as Richardson's *Pamela* or Fielding's *Shamela*.

Viewing the "truth" or "reality" of the facts as less important than their functionality in a particular judicial narrative, English and early American courts admitted fictitious facts if they served in "expediting Justice."[5] Because they expedited justice, entirely "fictitious proceedings" were described by Blackstone as "a kind of *pia fraus*," or "honorable deceit."[6] While the novel as a genre may be defined, as Watt argues, "by the premise, or primary convention, that the novel is a full and authentic report of human experience," the history of legal fictions suggests that human experience itself—the referent of the novel's authentic report—is full of situations wherein "details of the story" need not be "presented through a more largely referential use of language."[7] In light of the law's widespread acceptance and circulation of obvious fictions and accepted untruths, an examination of the novel should attend to legal fictions as much as literary facts, and investigate the "realism" of the law as much as the *verisimilitude* of the novel. Indeed, it could be said that the novel is "like" the trial not because both depend on true facts, but rather because both depend on fictions, in order to produce their narratives of truth.

What the history of legal fictions reveals, and what I will be elaborating in relation to the novel in early America, is that the law demands a singular narrative of truth. In the long transformation of Anglo-American law, the jury trial displaced archaic and "irrational" modes of ascertaining the truth of the "facts" of the past, as were used in the feudal system of ordeal.[8] As Michael McKeon describes, in the feudal system, "the *vera*, the 'facts,' of a history are relevant but subordinate to its *veritas*, or 'truth,' and in cases of apparent conflict the pure abstraction is superior to the concrete attribute."[9] While the law developed more "rational" procedures for judging the factuality of the past, however, it retained the conceptualization of a singular narrative as the standard of historical "truth" as such. As the "legal fiction" highlights, Anglo-American law courts continued to subordinate discrete "facts," or *vera*, to the production of a singular narrative *veritas*. Indeed, the broader narrative truth takes such precedence over the discrete facts that the latter can be invented to ensure the completion—and inscription—of an historical *veritas*. I will elaborate the importance of this narrative distinction throughout my readings of the culture of evidence in early America.

Watt's analogy is as complicated as it is suggestive. One objection that might be raised is that belief in the novel is different from belief in the law. The law requires that a jury reach certainty "beyond a reasonable doubt," whose logic expects (and requires by oath that) the jurors sincerely believe in the historical truth of the narrative upon which they base their verdict.[10] This is not the case with the novel. Readers are expected to believe in the possibility, and even the *probability*, of the truth of the novel's narrative, but they are not expected to believe the novel to be actually true: "the probable mediates between the falsehood of the fictional work and the truth of the reality it imitates."[11] To be an imitation of nature, a novel must be probable, but no more than probable. "As the Narration ought to be probable, so it ought to be only probable, and not actually true . . . for otherwise it would not be an imitation of Nature, but Nature itself."[12] While a novel must meet certain standards of *verisimilitude* shared by the law, it does not need to meet the same standards of *proof* as the law.

This paradox of probability which inheres in the novel's form—the countervalent tension of "truth" through fiction—is the point of departure for the investigations of truth conducted by the early American republic's first major novelist, Charles Brockden Brown. Brown's novels signal the transformation of legal and literary forms occasioned by the representational and epistemological debates of the early republic. This chapter argues for the importance of legal forms in the rise of the novel in America. In my reading of *Arthur Mervyn* (1799–1800), I argue that Brown translates, into the genre of the novel, the law's procedures for both ascertaining and representing the historical "truth" of facts. Even as I argue this line of influence in some of the formal developments of the novel, however, I also demonstrate the ways in which the law itself continually relies on literary forms in particular, and cultural artifacts in general, in the development of its own evidentiary procedures and fact-finding methods. Exploring this early moment in the rise of both the law and the novel in the United States, I trace their distinct yet interconnected developments, and their convergence in the cultural production of an aesthetic of evidence.

Fictitious Histories

In the preface to *Arthur Mervyn; or, Memoirs of the Year 1793*, Charles Brockden Brown cited the yellow fever epidemic in Philadelphia and the civic crisis it caused as the historical and philosophical subject of his novel, noting that "the evils of pestilence by which this city has lately been afflicted will probably form an aera in its history," and predicting that "the change in manners and population which they will produce, will be, in the highest degree, memorable."[13] As the introduction to his own novel's account of the plague year, Brown's claim about the likelihood of the recent past becoming an "aera" of a future "history" carries both an assessment of the historical significance of the epidemic's effects—some future historians may write these events into a history—and a self-conscious literary aspiration. Brown's account is that future "history" to which he refers: the evils of pestilence will form an "aera" in the city's history through his novel.[14]

Brown claims a place for the novel among other civic projects of Enlightenment belles lettres. In addition to historical writing, Brown cites "the schemes of reformation and improvement" to which "the periodic visitations of this calamity" will "give birth":

> They have already supplied new and copious materials for reflection to the physician and the political economist. They have not been less fertile to the moral observer, to whom they have furnished new displays of the influence of human passions and motives.
>
> Amidst the medical and political discussions... relative to this topic, the author of these remarks has ventured to weave into an humble narrative, such incidents as appeared to him most instructive and remarkable among those which came within the sphere of his own observation. (3)

The physician, the political economist, and the moral observer—these are the three ideal-typical republican citizens, whose thoughts and reflections can instruct others. Posing novel writing in the republican public sphere as a matter of civic virtue, Brown adds: "It is every one's duty to profit by all opportunities of inculcating on mankind the lessons of justice and humanity" (3). Speaking of his own role as moral observer, Brown proposes to construct a literary narrative as his contribution to the republican project of enlightenment and civic improvement.

What type of history of this period can the novel tell? The answer, Brown continues in the preface, seems to be that novels can tell history better than historical writing can. In Brown's theory, at the level of descriptive realism the novel can perform the service of the historical account: it can "deliver to posterity a brief but faithful sketch of the condition of this metropolis during that calamitous period" and the catalogue of descriptive details, or "facts" that historical accounts provide. Writing a narrative woven out of incidents "which came within the sphere of his own observation," the author as "moral observer" can relay with faithful accuracy the true facts of the historical event. Even as he locates the novel as an equal among other republican civic sciences, Brown claims for the early American novel a greater depth of descriptive realism, and an ability to depict moral truths of the past, a broader truth beyond the mere factual history, unavailable to those other civic sciences. Brown credits the moral observer with the ability to "snatch from oblivion" the "influences of hope and fear, the trials of fortitude and constancy." Such qualitative motivations for human actions are lessons made most evident through the novel. The moral observer "depicts, in lively colours, the evils of disease and poverty," and thus "performs an eminent service to the sufferers"; portraying "examples of disinterestedness and intrepidity," he "confers on virtue the notoriety and homage that are due to it, and rouses in the spectators, the spirit of salutary emulation" (3).

In 1799, the same year he began serial publication of *Arthur Mervyn*, Brown published in his *Monthly Magazine and American Review* "Walstein's School of History," his critical reflections on the relationship between history and novel writing. In this fictional review of the works of an imaginary German historian named Walstein, Brown elaborates a theory of "fictitious history" as that mode through which narrative fiction can better represent the historical truths of the past. As in the preface to *Arthur Mervyn*, in this review Brown first draws an analogy between the "physician attentive to the constitution and diseases of man in all ages and nations" and the "moral reasoner [who] may discover principles equally universal in their application" (146). Discussing Walstein's history of Cicero and the late Roman republic, Brown elaborates the special advantages of fictitious history:

> To assume the person of Cicero, as the narrator of his own transactions, was certainly an hazardous undertaking. Frequent errors and lapses, violations of probability, and incongruities in the style and conduct of this imaginary history with the genuine productions of Cicero, might be reasonably expected, but these are not found.... The whole system of Roman domestic manners, of civil and military government is contained in this work. The facts are either collected from the best antiquarians, or artfully deducted from what is known, or invented with a boldness more easy to admire than to imitate. Pure fiction is never employed but when truth was unattainable.[15]

Remarking upon the fictional narrative device of writing from the assumed persona of a historical actor, Brown cites the "felicity of the imposture," its faithfulness to the "authentic monuments," and its avoidance of "violations of probability" as a proof of its historical truth. As with the moral observer's narrative in *Arthur Mervyn*, Walstein's fictitious history catalogues for posterity the collected facts of the past with a depth of descriptive realism that evokes the totality of past experience, the "whole system" of Roman life. Yet the difference between Walstein's version of the Cataline conspiracy and the "factual" historical account of Sallust is due not only to "a more accurate acquaintance with the facts"; it is a difference "of that kind which result from a deeper insight into human nature ... more correctness of arrangement [of these facts], and a deeper concern in the progress and issue of the story." The "true" totality of the past is thus only successfully depicted because historical "facts" are subordinated to the broader *narrative* aspects of that truth: arrangement, progress, and theme (or "issue"). In Walstein's history, the "invented" or "false" fact is "so conformable to Roman modes and sentiments"—so probable, or verisimilar—"that one is almost prompted to accept it as the gift of inspiration."[16] Brown underscores here the centrality of narrative to the epistemological concerns of historical understanding.[17]

In his preface to *Arthur Mervyn* and in this theory of "fictitious history," Brown emphasizes two interdependent points. The first is fictitious history's representation of the social totality: Brown asserts that in Walstein's fictitious history of the Cataline conspiracy, "the whole system of Roman domestic manners, of civil and military government, is contained." The second point is the representation of how the individual subject is situated within this social totality. For Walstein's portrait of Cicero, and for Brown's "humble narrative" of *Arthur Mervyn*, the task of fictitious history is to "display a virtuous being in opposite conditions," to model virtue through its response to civic crisis.

In Mathew Carey's popular pamphlet *A Short Account of the Malignant Fever Which Prevailed in Philadelphia in the Year 1793*, the historical account from which Brown drew many of the descriptive details of his novel, Carey notes that communities neighboring Philadelphia refused to accept refugees from Philadelphia, stage and ferry lines were blocked, ports tightly controlled, and private citizens strongly warned not to admit Philadelphians to their homes: "Our citizens were proscribed in several cities and towns—hunted up like felons in some—debarred admittance and turned back in others, whether found or infected."[18] Rumors and exaggerated accounts of the epidemic circulated in newspapers throughout the mid-Atlantic. New York newspapers reported that as many as fifteen thousand had died. Theft and looting was widespread; it was widely reported that husbands and wives abandoned one another, and their children, out of fear of contracting the disease. The yellow fever epidemic was thus considered both a public health crisis, and, in the words of accounts from the time, a crisis of "civic virtue."

The novel's frame narrator, Dr. Stevens, is represented throughout the novel as the most exemplary of disinterested, virtuous republican citizens, choosing to stay to care for the sick out of a sense of civic duty. The frame narrator is thus immediately identified with the civic virtue of that self-reflexive moral observer described in "Walstein's School of History" and *Arthur Mervyn*'s preface. When Dr. Stevens assists a dying stranger he finds in the street (who we later learn is Arthur Mervyn), Stevens does so mindful of the "virulence and activity of this contagion, the dangerous condition of [his] patient, and the dubiousness of his character" (8). Dr. Stevens soon restores Mervyn to health. After this framing narrative, the novel's central plot begins when Dr. Stevens's longtime friend Mr. Wortley accuses Mervyn of being the accomplice of a wanted criminal, Thomas Welbeck. The primary motivating device of *Arthur Mervyn*'s narrative is thus an accusation which casts further doubt and suspicion upon Mervyn. In addition to arrest and imprisonment, Mervyn faces the loss, as Dr. Stevens warns him, of his "character" (13). In the context of the novel's representation of the early republic's symbolic economy of virtue, wherein the social capital of good reputation, or "character," is vital to republican life and civic identity, this threat is the most serious. For like the social characters examined in the previous chapter, Arthur Mervyn is "free in a double sense": no longer tied to family or estate, owning neither property nor means of production, he is a free-floating laborer, wandering the new republic.[19] When found by Dr. Stevens, Mervyn is a stranger to Philadelphia. Respected citizens, "venerable for [their] discernment and integrity," charge this stranger with abetting criminal fraud, possibly murder. For all its complicated subplots and narrative incidents, the novel is organized around this trial of what characters such as Dr. Stevens and his friend Wortley call, as various synonyms, Mervyn's "character," "credibility," and "virtue."

It is this narrative frame, and the series of embedded narratives that appear within it, that becomes the central structural concern of the novel. Embedded narrative is one type of embedded text. In Mieke Bal's precise formulation, "the narrative text constitutes a whole, into which, from the [primary] narrator's text, other [subordinate] texts are embedded."[20] "The content of an embedded text may be anything: assertions about things in general, discussion between actors, descriptions, confidences, etc."[21] While the "majority of embedded texts are non-narrative" (that is, no story is related in them), embedded narratives are those types of embedded texts "in which at the second or third level a complete story is told."[22]

It is through the confrontation of the novel's several embedded narratives (as narrated by individual characters such as Mervyn, Wortley, Welbeck, Mrs. Wentworth, Mrs. Althorpe, and other republican citizens) that the novel tries the "truth" of Mervyn's story, and thus the credibility of his "character."

This trial of virtue, enacted through the novel's embedded narrative structure, is the mode through which the individual is assimilated into that civic totality represented in the world of the novel.[23] The two thematic representational aims of that "fictitious history" theorized by Brown—the representation of the social totality of the republic; and the representation of an individual model of civic virtue—are in *Arthur Mervyn* mediated through the symbolic form of embedded narrative. Even as embedded narrative provides the novel's formal structure for the trial of Mervyn's "character," his civic virtue, it also enables the novel's representation of that social totality into which Mervyn is ultimately assimilated. In other words, embedded narrative mediates the reciprocal determinations between the novel's *bildung* and the novel's chronotopes.

In his classic study "Forms of Time and of Chronotope in the Novel," Mikhail Bakhtin introduces the concept of the chronotope to theorize the temporal-spatial parameters that limn the worldview of a fictional genre and its internal rules of operation. This formal concept is especially useful in our understanding of the republican novel's relationship to post-Revolutionary nationalism in the early republican period, when considered in relation to Benedict Anderson's theory of the imagined spatial-temporal "simultaneity" necessary to the rise of nationalisms in the late eighteenth and early nineteenth centuries. In *Imagined Communities*, Anderson argues that social and political-economic developments of the eighteenth century led to a transformation in the apprehension of time, a new imagining of temporality. Drawing on Walter Benjamin's idea of "homogenous, empty time," Anderson argues that this apprehension of 'simultaneity' is "marked ... by temporal coincidence, and measured by clock and calendar." "Why this transformation should be so important for [the birth of] the imagined community of the nation," Anderson goes on to suggest, "can best be seen if we consider the basic structure of two forms of imagining which first flowered in Europe in the eighteenth century: the novel and the newspaper. For these forms provided the technical means for 'representing' the *kind* of imagined community that is the nation."[24] To further specify the claims of this reading, my argument is that the embedded narrative structure of *Arthur Mervyn*, by bringing together individual *bildung* and national *chronotope*, thus links the central themes of the early republican novel—the stability of the post-Revolutionary republic's experiment in democracy; and the fate of civic virtue in crisis—to the novel's formal representation of the temporal-spatial "simultaneity" of the nation itself.

Only in Mervyn's extended embedded narrative does the novel depict the yellow fever epidemic, that contagion which threatens the dissolution of social bonds. Narrating to Dr. Stevens his encounter with the epidemic, Mervyn says he first learned of it as

> a rumour, which had gradually swelled to formidable dimensions, and which, at length, reached us in our quiet retreats. The city, we were told, was involved in confusion and panick, for a pestilential disease had begun its destructive progress. Magistrates and citizens were flying to the country. The numbers of the sick multiplied beyond all example. . . . Terror had exterminated all the sentiments of nature. Wives were deserted by their husbands, and children by their parents. Some had shut themselves in their houses, and debarred themselves from all communication with the rest of mankind. . . . Men were seized by this disease in the streets; passengers fled from them; entrance into their own dwellings were denied to them; they perished in the public ways. . . . Such was the tale, distorted and diversified a thousand ways, by the credulity and exaggeration of the tellers. (128–29)

Mervyn first encounters the yellow fever epidemic as a rumor; as an extended narrative composed of various individual stories, exaggerated by their individual tellers. Before its depiction of the epidemic itself, the novel here presents the "transverse, cross-time 'simultaneity' of the nation" through the circulation of the rumors of the contagion's spread. Even as the chronotope of the "city" is distinct from the quiet retreat of "the country," the citizens of these spaces are conceived as inhabiting the same "nation"; and their spatial-temporal simultaneity is made visible in the representational field of the novel through the otherwise invisible circulation of the epidemic. The yellow fever epidemic is represented first as narrative, and the space of the republic itself is thus mapped by the circulation of this narrative. Of equal significance to the novel's "imagining" of this simultaneity is that Brown should use disease, and the civic crisis it occasions—that is, a civic crisis heightened by the atomization of narrative within the nation—to represent the space of the "public ways." The imagined republican community can only be imagined in its state of real or rumored crisis, in its state of symbolic dissolution: as its magistrates and citizens flee; as its now atomized individuals "shut themselves in their houses, and debarred themselves from all communication with the rest of mankind."

If this rumor of the yellow fever epidemic makes visible the imagined community in its dissolution, we should notice as well that its narrative structure mirrors the larger embedded narrative structure of the novel. The yellow fever epidemic first appears to Mervyn as a rumor composed of various disparate narratives, which had "swelled to formidable dimensions," accumulating into a singular "tale, distorted and diversified a thousand ways, by the credulity and exaggeration of the tellers." This particular embedded narrative of the yellow fever epidemic further mirrors the novel's larger structural form when Mervyn's initial skepticism yields to the accumulation of evidence: the growing number of witnesses and the overlapping consistency of their individual testimonies: "I expected that every new day would detect the absurdity and fallacy of such representations. Every new day, however, added to the number of witnesses, and the consistency of the tale, till, at length, it was not possible to withhold my faith" (129). Once again linking its representation of temporality and this unfolding narrative of the epidemic, the novel here emphasizes that it is the growing number of witnesses, the growing number of testimonies corroborating the same story, and thus the cumulative narrative consistency that leads to credible representation and so requires belief.

What is of further interest to our understanding of the early republican novel's unique contribution to the thinking of the nation in the post-Revolutionary period is the way in which the novel's individual embedded narratives work together to represent the implied history of the yellow fever epidemic's outbreak and circulation. Throughout *Arthur Mervyn*, Brown makes explicit reference to yellow fever as a disease associated with merchant ships arriving from the transatlantic and Caribbean trade routes. Early in the narration of one of the novel's many embedded narrative subplots, for example, the criminal (forger and imposter) Thomas Welbeck, revealing to Arthur Mervyn how he came into his fortune, tells of his encounter with a dying stranger in the streets of Philadelphia.

> His malady was such as is known in the tropical islands, by the name of the Yellow or Malignant Fever.... His father's name was [also] Vincentio Lodi. From a merchant at Leghorn, he had changed himself into a planter in the Island of Guadaloupe. His Son had been sent, at an early age, for

the benefits of education to Europe. The young Vincentio was, at length, informed of his father, that, being weary of his present mode of existence, he had determined to sell his property, and to transport himself to the United States. The son was directed to hasten home, that he might embark, with his father, on this voyage.... The summons was cheerfully obeyed. The youth on his arrival at the Island found preparation making for the funeral of his father. It appeared that the elder Lodi had flattered one of his slaves with the prospect of freedom, but had, nevertheless, included his slave in the sale that he made of his estate. Actuated by revenge, the slave assassinated Lodi in the open street, and resigned himself, without a struggle, to the punishment which the law had provided for such a deed. (92–93)

In this early scene, the novel links its representation of the crisis of the yellow fever epidemic in Philadelphia to a wider transatlantic chronotope. The Russian formalists' distinction between *sjuzhet* and *fabula* is pertinent here: the *sjuzhet* is the plot of the narrative as it is narrated, while the *fabula* is that implied "actual" chronology of events within the world of the novel. While we are introduced to the presence of the yellow fever epidemic in the very first pages of the novel (when Dr. Stevens encounters the dying Mervyn) in the implied chronology of the novel's *fabula*, yellow fever actually first enters the world of the republic in this scene of Welbeck's encounter with the dying Lodi. This embedded narrative, whose revealing *fabula* underscores again that "transverse, cross-time 'simultaneity'" of the nation in the strong sense of that term, thus represents as well the structural link between the central plot of *Arthur Mervyn* and the apparently distant historical events occurring in the slave plantations of the West Indies. Vincentio Lodi, whose character functions as the bearer of Welbeck's sudden reversal of fortune (indeed, he dies immediately after handing it to Welbeck), had sailed from the Island of Guadalupe to Baltimore after the sale of his father's plantation and slaves, and from there traveled by coach to Philadelphia. This is the very route that yellow fever was rumored, in writings from the period and within the world of the novel, to have traveled. Mathew Carey reported in his *Short Account* that many newspapers throughout the mid-Atlantic suspected that yellow fever was brought by ships from the West Indies.

Describing the "expanding chronotopes" of the late-eighteenth-century British novel, Katie Trumpener has argued in *Bardic Nationalism* that "from the 1790s to the 1820s, the British novel remains preoccupied with the integrity and interpenetration of cultural spaces: successive novelistic genres establish a dialectical relationship between nationalist ways of thinking about place and the consciousness of empire, a dialectic crucial not only to romantic nationalist, regionalist, and local-color writing but also to early colonial literature."[25] As the Lodi episode highlights, a similar literary historical development occurs in the post-Revolutionary novel in America. Yet Brown's early republican novel goes further, in that it explicitly links what Trumpener calls a "rhetoric of the interdependence of domestic and colonial interests" to the material conditions of the transatlantic slave trade, connecting Europe, Africa, the Caribbean, and the new United States.[26] Brown makes the links between the circulation of literature and the economic circuits of the transatlantic even more explicit at the close of this embedded narrative. Before dying of yellow fever, Lodi entrusts Welbeck with the fortune obtained from the sale of his father's plantation and slaves, and with "a manuscript, written by the elder Lodi in Italian" (93). Even as Welbeck uses Lodi's wealth to pose as a wealthy merchant, he also plans to translate the manuscript into English and publish it as his own literary invention. The relation between Welbeck and Mervyn begins in the novel when Welbeck hires Mervyn as his scrivener, to assist him in this literary project (100). Brown's novel thus repeatedly links the production and circulation of the literary commodity itself to circuits of the growing and much-debated slave trade in the new republic. If embedded narrative is that symbolic form through which the novel represents the simultaneity of the nation's time-space, it is also through these individual embedded narratives that the novel situates the chronotope of the new republic within the broader historical chronotope of the slave routes and markets of the transatlantic.

Discourses of Legitimacy in Early America

In the critical debate over whether print or orality was more central to the culture of the early American republic, both sides have claimed the novels of Charles Brockden Brown as exemplary. Proceeding from the thesis that "republican print discourse" constitutes the central form of legitimation in the early republic, Michael Warner argues that *Arthur Mervyn* enacts a "fantasy of publicity" through which the novel's representations attain a validity "that carries the full authority of law."[27] In this perspective, "disclosing information, making things public, is understood as ensuring a civic source of validity. For that reason, the strategy of disclosure in this novel can be taken to be a fantasy-equivalent of the act of publication, even when no thematic connection with writing occurs."[28] This reading interprets Arthur Mervyn's disclosure of his tale thematically, as a "publication" that automatically grants his story legitimacy. From this thematic interpretation of Mervyn's narrative (wherein publication displaces speaking as the equivalent for "disclosure"), Warner equates such "publication" with the material medium of print itself: Mervyn's friend Dr. Stevens, and later Mervyn himself, writes and "publishes" the story, as does the novel's author, Charles Brockden Brown. Through such a strategy of disclosure, "Brown implicitly identifies his writing with the validity of the public sphere"—thus the novel's "fantasy of publicity."[29]

Warner's equation of publicity with legitimacy ignores the many epistemological problems that arise in the very act of disclosure. In *Arthur Mervyn*, publicity does not guarantee legitimacy for the simple reason that one's public disclosures are not necessarily believed. Indeed, most characters in *Arthur Mervyn* are suspicious, rather than credulous, and the truth of narratives is more often in doubt than it is given credit. For example, while Brown presents Dr. Stevens, Mervyn's friend and primary audience, as the one character in the novel most inclined to believe Mervyn's story, he also repeatedly depicts Dr. Stevens's moments of doubt:

> Surely the youth was honest. His tale could not be the fruit of invention; and yet, what are the bounds of fraud? Nature has set no limits to the combinations of fancy. A smooth exterior, a show of virtue, and a specious tale, are, a thousand times, exhibited in human intercourse by craft and subtlety. Motives are endlessly varied, while actions continue the same; and an acute penetration may not find it hard to select and arrange motives, suited to exempt from censure any action that an human being can commit. (229)

Through Dr. Stevens's repeated narrative interventions, the novel presents the philosophical skepticism to which any and all acts of disclosure can be subject. All narratives involve the "selection" and "arrangement" of "motives," and because "Nature has set no limits to the combinations of fancy," it is very possible that Mervyn's narrative, however compelling, is a fraud. Dr. Stevens is far less skeptical of Mervyn's tale than are other characters in the novel (Wortley, Mrs. Wentworth, and Mrs. Althorpe, to name a few, continually suspect the truth of Mervyn's disclosures). In its recurring emphasis on the skepticism of a character as ready and willing to believe as Dr. Stevens, the novel suggests that "publicity" alone is no guarantee of legitimacy in the early American republic.

Similarly, the novel does not equate such disclosures with the legitimacy of print material, or print culture. Dr. Stevens emphasizes that it is neither the content nor the act of disclosure, but rather its medium that matters most: "Had I heard Mervyn's story from another, or read it in a book, I might, perhaps, have found it possible to suspect the truth; but, as long as the impression, made by his tones, gestures and looks, remained in my memory, this suspicion was impossible" (229). Contrary to the thesis that print culture served as the *sine qua non* of legitimacy in the early American public sphere, the printed word is here viewed as one of a range of forms of evidence through which one might have access to truth. In Stevens's formulation, reading a narrative in a book is just like hearing it from another—as a type of evidence much farther removed from the immediacy of hearing eyewitness accounts, the printed word allows for greater suspicions of its truth. In this classification of various forms of evidence, Stevens also emphasizes the merits of direct testimony, over and against the secondhand evidence of print ("Had I heard Mervyn's story from another, or read it in a book . . .").

Framing evidence as a question of prior mediations, Brown highlights Dr. Stevens's confidence in the accessibility of truth through direct testimony. Dr. Stevens's doubts are allayed by his own "direct inspection" of Arthur's oral narration of the story. Because Stevens can witness Mervyn's very act of disclosure, he says, "his tones, gestures and looks, remained in my memory," and "suspicion was impossible."

> Wickedness may sometimes be ambiguous, its mask may puzzle the observer; our judgment may be made to falter and fluctuate, but the face of Mervyn is the index of an honest mind. Calm or vehement, doubting or confident, it is full of benevolence and candor. He that listens to his words may question their truth, but he that looks upon his countenance when speaking, cannot withhold his faith. (229)

Dr. Stevens claims that Mervyn's narration, more than the narrative he tells, persuades the listener of the truth of his story. Passages like this one might be used to support Christopher Looby's thesis that the culture of orality, and "acts of voice," were equally significant to the project of republican legitimation in early America.[30] Yet Dr. Stevens's expression of faith in the reliability of testimonial narrative is a complicated one. It assumes a direct causal relationship between oral narration and narrative truth: the manner in which words are spoken, Mervyn's "tones, gestures, and looks," all confirm the truth of those words. However, Dr. Stevens's description also severs those spoken words from the body that speaks them, and in so doing focuses more upon the physical appearance of the speaker than upon either his voice or his words. As Dr. Stevens says, even he that "listens to his words may question their truth" (229). The truth of the spoken word can still be suspect, and ultimately it is not Mervyn's voice that persuades Stevens of the truth of his words, but rather his "countenance when speaking": the "face of Meryvn is an index" of his honest mind.

The oral-culture thesis posits a "difference between the abstract, alienated, rational polis of print culture and the more passionately attached, quasi-somatically experienced nation for which many Americans longed." In his analysis of Brown's *Wieland* (1798), Looby argues that "the rational-legal foundation of the United States could seem dangerously inadequate by virtue of its neglect of the visceral needs of citizens for more psychically compelling modes of attachment to their nation."[31] While this argument provides a useful counterpoint to the view of the early republic as a public sphere of print, it shares with the print-culture thesis the premise that "law" and "print" are thematically identical discourses. Identifying print and law with an "abstract" and "rational" polis conflates the culture of print with legal discourse itself. Linking law and print is certainly important, insofar as legal development has been tied historically to the rise of literacy and the print medium.[32] Within the legal sphere of the early republic, however, there existed no clear opposition between "oral" and "print" culture as such. Evidence was presented at trial as much by way of the written as by the oral. While testimony could appear in the form of print, much testimony was delivered orally, and the jury's judgment of oral testimony involved evaluations of a witness's physical traits (including, in Dr. Stevens's words, his "countenance"), demeanor, and the very manner in which the testimony was given. The credibility of testimony often depended upon the performance of the witness. Indeed, it would be perhaps more accurate to suggest that Dr. Stevens's reference to "the impression, made by his tones, gestures and looks" highlights the importance of natural language and the culture of rhetorical performance in early America.[33]

The discourses of print and orality were both significant to the questions of narrative truth and cultural legitimacy in the early American republic. Yet what *Arthur Mervyn* returns to repeatedly, and what serves as a conceptual framework for both these discourses, is the question of evidentiary procedure, and of direct testimony as one central, if necessarily limited, means of obtaining knowledge. Viewed as a question of evidence, Mervyn's disclosures, and *Arthur Mervyn* as a whole, illuminate the possibilities and problems of both print and orality in the new republic. Self-expression in the early American republic is thus not merely a matter of the public sphere of print, nor only an effect of the special metonymy of voice—it is a question of evidence, of the truth of matters of fact, and of the attributes required of the individual subject for recognition, by both state and society, of his testimony.

Res Publica, Res Facta

"Walstein was conscious," Brown wrote of his imaginary historian, "of the uncertainty of history. Actions and motives cannot be truly described. We can only make approaches to the truth. The more attentively we observe mankind, and study ourselves, the greater will this uncertainty appear, and the farther shall we find ourselves from the truth." False and invented facts can serve the ends of historical "truth"—or *veritas*—precisely because history, as John Locke argued, does not lend itself to "the certainty of true *knowledge*."[34] In Locke's *Essay Concerning Human Understanding* of 1690, which was the best-known discussion of probability in the eighteenth century, very little knowledge is considered *certain*: "in the greatest part of our concernment [God] has afforded us only the twilight, as I may so say, of *probability*."[35] The specter of skepticism appears often in "Walstein's School," as it does throughout Brown's novels. If most knowledge is always uncertain, this "uncertainty, however, has some bounds. Some circumstances of events, and some events, are more capable of evidence than others. The same may be said of motives. Our guesses as to the motives of some actions are more *probable* than the guesses that relate to other actions."[36] The skeptical strain of Brown's work is thus tempered by the concept of probability, to which Brown grants great weight. Using the language of evidence, Brown argues that probability provides the grounds for the delimitations of uncertainty.

James Wilson, first professor of law at the College of Philadelphia, associate justice of the U.S. Supreme Court, and primary author of the Pennsylvania and U.S Constitutions, similarly drew upon this Lockean "scale of probability" in his *Lectures on Law*. Throughout the *Lectures*,

Wilson draws upon the experimental moral philosophy that predominated in Anglo-American thought throughout the eighteenth century.[37] Drawing from Thomas Reid, the central figure of the Scottish philosophy of Common Sense, Wilson divides "the evidence, which arises from reasoning... into two species—demonstrative and moral."[38] The difference between these two species of evidence was fundamental to Anglo-American law's understanding of truth and certainty. "Demonstrative evidence has for its subject abstract and necessary truths, or the unchangeable relations of ideas. Moral evidence has for its subject the real but contingent truths and connexions, which take place among things actually existing. Abstract truths have no respect to time or place; they are universally and eternally the same."[39] Demonstrative evidence would be found in mathematics, for example, where logically necessary truth claims could be deduced from abstract universals. The contingent truths of moral evidence, which constitute the *res facta* tried by the jury and are thus liable to the "fluctuation or uncertainty arising from the characters or conduct of men," can never attain the absolute certainty of demonstrative evidence.[40]

Wilson's elaboration of the difference between demonstrative and moral evidence assumes the Lockean "scale of probability," wherein the knowledge acquired by moral evidence is always considered *probable* knowledge. "In demonstrative evidence, there are no degrees.... Every necessary truth leaves no possibility of its being false. In moral evidence, we rise," instead, "by an insensible gradation, from possibility to *probability*, and from probability to the highest degree of moral certainty."[41] While thus asserting the necessarily asymptotic nature of the "certainty" produced with moral evidence, Wilson does not reject altogether the possibility of "certain" knowledge. This "certainty" was what philosophers called *moral certainty*. This knowledge, in other words, was a matter of belief, or "assent." Sufficient evidence of a fact led one to assent to its truth. Probable knowledge, such as the contingent truths decided by a jury, can be ascertained to "the highest degree of moral certainty."[42]

Throughout his *Lectures on Law*, Wilson remarks as well upon the connections between the epistemological procedures of the jury trial and the concept of "truth" as a matter of fact.[43] Well before "fact" was used to designate objective description of the natural world (e.g., "facts of nature"), the term was used to signify an act or an event whose truth was unproven. There existed, in other words, such things as "false facts." Maintaining a distinction between *res facta*, the matter of fact of which the jury was judge, and *res ley*, the matter of law decided by the court, law courts developed normative procedures for proving the truth of the facts. As legal historians have noted, this legal distinction between "matter of fact" and "matter of law" was well known by the sixteenth century.[44] "Fact" in the legal context "implied a human deed or action which had occurred in the past and which had to be substantiated or proved to the satisfaction of the jurors, who were 'judges of the fact.' The 'fact' or 'matter of fact' was not considered 'true' or suitable to be believed until satisfactory evidence had been presented."[45] Thus, in the trial of the "truth," jurors first ascertained the truth of the *vera* of the matter, before judging its *veritas*.[46]

In the early republic, this conception of "fact"—and the epistemological task assigned the jury in "trying the truth of the fact"—was considered fundamental to the civic aims of Anglo-American law. While early American jurisprudence certainly attempted to depart from English common law for various theoretical and practical reasons, the common-law distinction between "matters of fact" and "matters of law" was maintained throughout the republican period in America.[47]

Citing the imbrication of the concept of the *res facta* with the ultimate truth-claims of the law, Wilson argues that the "discretionary power" assigned the jury was of such importance to justice in the new republic because the "truth of facts is tried by evidence." And as Wilson emphasizes, the evidence of facts is uncertain: "The evidence of the sciences is very different from the evidence of facts. In the sciences, evidence depends on causes which are fixed and immovable, liable to no fluctuation or uncertainty arising from the characters or conduct of men. In the sciences, truths, if self-evident, are instantly known.... In facts, it is otherwise. They consist not of principles which are self-evident."[48] Locating the *matter of fact* in the uncertain, contingent world of human characters and conduct, Wilson argues that that most rational means of delimiting such uncertainty, and of thereby approaching the truth of the facts, is to bring it before a jury. "*Ad quæstionem facti respondent juratores.*"[49] (To questions of fact respond the jurors.) While claiming for law a place among the other "sciences" of man, Wilson emphasizes the special qualities of legal epistemology, whose modes of proof and procedures for ascertaining "certainty" deal in the evidence of facts.

In the law's taxonomy of evidence, the evidence of facts must be classified as a species of moral evidence. "Truths alone ... which depend on abstract principles, are susceptible of demonstrative evidence: truths, that depend on matters of facts, however complete may be the evidence by which they are established, can never become demonstrative." Thus "we may see the impropriety of Lord Chief Baron Gilbert's remark, when he says, that 'all demonstration is founded upon the view of man's proper senses.' From hence we may see likewise the inaccuracy of Sir William Blackstone's description of evidence, when he mentions it as demonstrating the very fact in issue."[50] In this critique of the dominant common-law understanding of the evidence given at jury trial, Wilson departs from what he characterizes as the common law's failure to appreciate the several degrees of uncertainty involved in the "contingent truths" of everyday life. All knowledge based upon observation is subject to uncertainty: "The objects of our senses," he argues, "are objects of moral, but not of demonstrative evidence."[51] Wilson undercuts here the claim that man's senses can be the source of absolute certainty, a claim, in Wilson's view, which works within a model of demonstrative knowledge that assumes an immediacy between the objects of the senses and the "facts" whose very truth is being tried.[52]

Wilson's discussion of the "scientific distinction" between these "species" of evidence highlights the ultimate truth of the law: that the jury trial, in the process of ascertaining the truth of facts, constructs a narrative of truth. Toward the close of this discussion of reasoning as a source of evidence, Wilson adds: "In moral evidence, there not only may be, but there generally is, contrariety of proofs.... [T]here is... real evidence on both sides. On both sides, contrary presumptions, contrary testimonies, contrary experiences must be balanced. The *probability*, on the whole, is, consequently, in the proportion, in which the evidence on one side preponderates over the evidence on the other side."[53] Invoking the familiar image of the scale of Justice, Wilson thus closes his discussion of the law's moral evidence with a negotiation between the qualitative and the quantitative aspects of judgment: presumptions and experiences can be "balanced," and their relative probabilities measured against the other. More than a figure for the "scientific" possibilities of the law, the image of the scale here highlights the "contrary," agonistic nature of moral evidence itself.

Praising the legal procedures of the jury trial as the most just mode of judging between reality's "contrariety of proofs," Wilson remarks further upon the "beautiful and exquisite propriety of a form, which is used every day in criminal trials," whereby the clerk of the court informs the jury that the accused "has put himself upon his country" for trial—"'which country,' adds he, 'you are.'" A jury may be called "the country of the person accused, and the trial by jury, indeed, be denominated the trial *per patrium.*"[54] Wilson's metonymic characterization of the jury as representative of the nation underscores the material and symbolic connections between citizenship and legal judgments in the early American republic.[55] "When I speak of juries," Wilson declares, "I mean a convenient number of citizens, selected and impartial, who, on particular occasions, or in particular causes, are vested with discretionary powers to try the truth of facts, on which depend the property, the liberty, the reputation, and the lives of their fellow citizens."[56] Here the fundamental rights and privileges of citizenship depend upon the ascertainment of the truths of the matters of fact. "An abstract of the people is selected for the occasional exercise of [this discretionary power]. The moment that the occasion is over, the abstracted selection disappears among the general body of the citizens."[57] Wilson thus describes the civic project of the entire *res publica* itself as reliant upon the just trial of the *res facta*. Wilson's taxonomy of evidence and legal procedure provides us also with the conceptual definitions of those legal forms which Brown translated into the structuring literary forms of the early American novel.

For practitioners and theorists of law in the early American republic, the law's pursuit of "justice" was a pursuit of the truth of the matters of fact. Because the matters of fact depended upon moral evidence, the jury trial was ultimately a confrontation of contrary narratives. Thus "it is impossible," Wilson continues, "to establish general rules, by which a complete proof may be distinguished from a proof that is incomplete, and presumptions slightly *probable* may be distinguished from conjectures altogether *uncertain*.... The farther consequence unavoidably is, that power of deciding on the evidence of facts must be a discretionary power" vested in that metonymic abstract of the nation, the jury, whose verdict represented both the symbolic and material "voice" of the people.[58]

In the days of the feudal trials by *ordeal*, the courts were understood to be querying God in their testing of the truth of the facts; the ultimate outcome of the ordeal was considered the *vox dei*, the voice of God. In the early American republic, the courts relied upon a jury to try the truth of the facts, and the verdict of the jury was the *vox populi*, the voice of the people. As Wilson's *Lectures* emphasize, this verdict was a singular narrative of truth, produced by the adjudication of competing narratives: "Evidence is the foundation of conviction: conviction is the foundation of persuasion: to convey persuasion is the end of pleading."[59] While bound by rules of legal form, the logic of persuasion that defines the jury trial underscores the essentially "cultural" character of the law's forms for ascertaining truth. Such a framework of persuasion also raised some troubling questions. If it is the case, as Wilson declares at the close of his lectures on evidence, that "much depends on the pleadings of the counsel" and "his pleadings depend much on a masterly... management of the principles of evidence," it is likewise possible, as Dr. Stevens suggests in *Arthur Mervyn*, that "motives are endlessly varied, while actions continue the same; and an acute penetration may not find it hard to select and arrange motives, suited to exempt from censure any action that an human being can commit" (229). In such a framework of persuasion, how does one contain the possibility that the *vox populi* might be swayed by "a smooth exterior, a show of virtue, and a specious tale," which "are, a thousand times, exhibited in human intercourse by craft and subtlety"? (229).

Testimony and the Legal Subject

If Wilson's *Lectures* serve as an index, Anglo-American law underwent significant conceptual and formal shifts as it was developed by jurists and practitioners of the early American republic. While not breaking with common law, Wilson insists that the common law must find its authority in experience, and its legitimacy in the principles of common sense: "The proceedings of the common law are founded on long and sound experience; but long and sound experience will not be found to stand in opposition to the original and genuine sentiments of the human mind."[60] As with other elements in the development of what I call the epistemological forms of the law, witness testimony underwent significant transformations as the law's empire entered the era of the new republic.

Witness testimony long held a fundamental place in the law's taxonomy of evidence. In the long transformation of legal forms, "irrational" proofs (as used in the feudal ordeals) were replaced by witness testimony, "character" witness credibility, corroboration of evidence, and other such delimitations on belief and certainty. As Barbara Shapiro remarks, "Witnesses played a central role in the rationalization of evidence, perhaps the single most important change in later medieval law."[61] In his *Essay Concerning Human Understanding* (1690), Locke describes testimony as the main source of historical knowledge in "matters of fact."[62] By the time of Sir Geoffrey Gilbert's *Law of Evidence* (1754), it was common to claim that the only way "to understand the true Theory of Evidence, we must consider two Things. First, the several Sorts of testimony. Secondly, the Force of Testimony to prove the Matter which is alleg'd."[63] Often citing Locke's *Essay*, jurists and legal treatise writers from Gilbert on described testimony as the primary form of legal evidence.[64]

James Wilson cites Gilbert in his description of the persuasive force of testimonial evidence:

> "This is very plain," says my Lord Chief Baron Gilbert, "that when we cannot see or hear any thing ourselves and yet are obliged to make a judgment of it, we must see and hear from report of others; which is one step farther from demonstration, which is founded upon the view of our own senses: and yet there is that faith and credit to be given to the honesty and integrity of credible and disinterested witnesses, attesting any fact under solemnities and obligation of religion, and the dangers and penalties of perjury, that the mind equally acquiesces therein as in knowledge by demonstration; for it cannot have any more reason to be doubted that if we ourselves had heard or seen it. And this is the original of all trials, and all manner of evidence." [Gilbert, Ev. 4][65]

In Gilbert's description, Wilson argues, "the *restraints*, which are wisely calculated, by human regulations, to *check*, are mistaken for the *causes* intended to produce this belief" in testimony. "Every gentleman," Wilson declares, "in the least conversant about law proceedings, knows very well, that the qualifications and solemnities enumerated by the learned Judge [Gilbert] are requisite to the *competency*, not to the *credibility*, of the witness—to the admission, not to the operation, of his testimony."[66] Against Gilbert's common-law valuation of witness testimony, which assumes, as with the "testimony of the senses," a certain immediacy of relation between testimony and true knowledge ("as in knowledge by demonstration"), Wilson argues that the "true language of the law" wisely restrains jurors from crediting, rather than instructing them to grant credit to witness testimony. Such restraint is necessary because "belief in testimony springs not from the precepts of the law, but from the propensity of our nature. This propensity we indulge in every moment of our lives, and in every part of our business, without attending, in the least, to the circumspect precautions prescribed by the law."[67] Just as he had critiqued the common-law understanding of demonstrative knowledge and its faith in the "testimony of our senses," Wilson elaborates a common sense philosophy of the law's necessary restraints on the credibility of testimony as evidence.[68] Like Thomas Reid, Wilson sees the "original sentiments of the human mind" to be naturally predisposed toward credulity, not skepticism.[69] Wilson writes that "the propensity to believe testimony is a natural propensity. It is unnecessary to encourage it; sometimes it is impracticable to restrain it. The law will not order that which is unnecessary: it will not attempt that which is impracticable. In no case, therefore, does it order a witness to be believed; *for jurors are triers of the credibility of witnesses,* as well as of the truth of facts."[70]

This last distinction is especially important to an understanding of the long process of rationalization in the epistemological forms of the law. As judges of the *res facta*, jurors likewise must judge the credibility of those witnesses giving testimony to the truth of the facts. Indeed, just as jurors may tend to credit a single testimonial given into evidence, the "positive testimony of a thousand witnesses is not conclusive as to the verdict. The jury retain an indisputable, unquestionable right to acquit the person accused, if, in their private opinions, they disbelieve the accusers."[71] This expressly subjective operation necessitates that distinction between witness competence and witness credibility, which Gilbert's much-cited common-law definition had left unclear.

Wilson's point is that there exists no necessary connection between the criteria used by the court to judge the competence of a witness, and the criteria used by the jury in its trial of the credibility of that witness. This does not mean, however, that the jury and court do not share similar criteria for evaluating the credibility of witnesses. In *The Country Justice*, the most influential legal handbook of the seventeenth century, used by generations of English and American legal practitioners, Michael Dalton cites "two old verses that derived from Romano-canon tradition" to describe criteria used to evaluate witness testimony;

> *Conditio, sexus, discretio, fama,*
> *Et fortuna, fides: in testibus esta requires.*[72]

Here the competence of testimony was based upon what were called the *indicia*, drawn from the social personhood of the witness: circumstances such as sex; discretion, or ability to distinguish truth; reputation; economic and social status; and religious beliefs (especially one's reputation for piety and adherence to oaths).[73] For the law recognizes only certain types of testimony. The ability to present legal testimony was itself an important index of one's subject status within the nation: as native citizen, as naturalized citizen, as denizen, or as resident alien. One's class, sex, and social position were also significant details of personhood that affected the credibility granted testimony, if allowed.

These social markers were especially significant to the jury's direct observation of oral testimony. In his praise of the public character of the jury trial, Sir Mathew Hale described oral testimony as superior to written testimony precisely because it allowed for direct observation of the witness: "Echoing the Romano-canon law maxims that were ultimately derived from classical rhetorical sources, Hale suggests that 'The very Quality, Carriage, Age, Condition, Education and Place of Commorance of a Witness' is best appreciated when the jurors can see and hear the witnesses and thus give 'the more or less Credit to their Testimony.'"[74] Like Brown's characters would do throughout *Arthur Mervyn*, Hale emphasized that "the very Manner of a Witness's delivering his Testimony will give a probable Indication whether he speaks truly or falsely."[75] Hale supplements this valorization of the direct observation of witness testimony with the point Wilson would make in his *Lectures*, "that jurors were not bound to give verdicts according to the testimony and were free to credit one witness over several who disagreed."[76]

Following Hale, Wilson links those criteria derived from legally recognized indices of social personhood to the degrees of probability by which the truth of moral evidence was measured. Citing what legal theorists and philosophers since Locke called the "degrees of assent," Wilson adds that "belief arises from many different sources, and admits of all possible degrees, from absolute certainty down to doubt and suspicion."[77] The jury is the most "proper" judge in matters of evidence, Wilson concludes, precisely because "evidence is much more easily felt than described":

> "It is much easier, says the Marquis of Beccaria, "to feel the moral certainty of proofs, than to define it exactly. For this reason I think it an excellent law, which establishes assistants to the principal Judge, and those chosen by lot: For that ignorance which judges by its feelings is little subject to errour." (Bec.c.14.p.39)[78]

It is through feeling the moral proof of evidence that a juror (or any man of common sense) is persuaded of the truth of a "fact." Wilson likewise highlights that point so central to the debate between Dr. Stevens and Wortley in Brown's *Arthur Mervyn*: in addition to those indices of his social personhood that could be observed directly by the juror, the "manner in

88 *Civic Virtues*

which he delivers his testimony" may likewise augment that feeling of moral certainty which constitutes the persuasive force of his testimony.

Natural Signs, Natural Testimony

> When he espy'd me, he came running to me, laying himself down again upon the Ground, with all the possible Signs of an humble thankful Disposition, making a great many antick Gestures to show it: At last he lays His Head flat upon the Ground, close to my Foot, and sets my other Foot upon his Head, as he had done before; and after this; made all the Signs to me of Subjections, Servitude, and Submission imaginable, to let me know, how he would serve me as long as he liv'd. I understood him in many Things. . . . [I]n a little Time I began to speak to him, and teach him to speak to me; and first I made him know his Name should be Friday, which was the Day I sav'd his Life; I call'd him so for the Memory of the Time; I likewise taught him to say, Yes and No, and to know the meaning of them.
> —*Robinson Crusoe*

In Wilson's taxonomy of evidence, a discussion of the evidence of "natural" and "artificial" signs immediately precedes his extensive description of the evidence of testimony.[79] Wilson argues that the evidence of testimony, the key mediating concept between *vera* and *veritas*—between discrete "facts" and the law's ultimate narrative of "truth"—can only be understood in relation to the evidence of natural and artificial signs. Elaborating that type of evidence "which arises from natural signs," Wilson alludes to the novel scene of encounter between Robinson Crusoe and the "savage" who would become "his man Friday." "These first interviews," Wilson explains, "are interesting, because we immediately perceive them to be natural. Two dumb persons, in their intercourse together, carry the use of these natural signs to a wonderful degree of variety and minuteness." Defoe's novel offers "very picturesque and interesting representations" of the evidence arising from natural signs, which is of such great and extensive importance, to society generally, and to the law in particular.[80]

Wilson characterized witness testimony as fundamental not only to man's knowledge of the law, but to "our knowledge of history, of criticism . . . for all that acquaintance with nature and the works of nature, which is not founded on our own personal observations and experience, but on the attested experience and observations of others; and for the greatest part of that information concerning men and things, which is necessary ... to the ease, comfort, and improvement, and happiness of human life."[81] Like Brown's *Arthur Mervyn*, Wilson distinguishes between the knowledge acquired by "personal observations and experience" and the knowledge received from others. In law, testimony mediates between the former and the latter.

Yet just as in the novel, the question of testimonial credibility becomes central to the law's attempts to ascertain the truth of the matter of fact. If jurors are not merely triers of the truth of the fact, but triers of the *credibility* of the testimony to facts; and if they often try such credibility through *feeling* the moral proof of evidence, how does the law order this latter trial, which is so important to the court's binding narrative conclusions? The answer to this question lies in the law's invocation of natural language. To better understand the jury's trial of the credibility of witness testimony, we thus need to remark upon the convergence, in Anglo-American theories of evidence, between those indices of social personhood I have described and the theory of natural language, developed by one of James Wilson's most profound influences, Thomas Reid.[82]

Wilson's elaboration of the connections between natural language and testimony draws directly from Reid's *Inquiry into the Human Mind, on the Principles of Common Sense* (1764). In his *Inquiry*, Reid argues that language consists of two kinds of signs: "First, such as have no meaning but what is affixed to them by compact or agreement among those who use them—these are artificial signs; Secondly, such as, previous to all compact or agreement, have a meaning which every man understands by the principles of his nature. Language, so far as it consists of artificial signs, may be called *artificial*; so far as it consists of natural signs, I call it *natural*."[83] In his discussion entitled "Of the Analogy between Perception and the Credit We Give Human Testimony" (chap. 6, sec. 24), Reid adds that "the signs in the natural language of the human countenance and behaviour, as well as the signs in our original perceptions have the same signification in all climates and in all nations; and the skill of interpreting them is not acquired, but innate."[84] It is through such analogies that Reid (and, later, Wilson) *naturalizes* the subjects of law: "The signs in original perception are sensations.... The signs in natural language are features of the face, gestures of the body, and modulations of the voice." For both original perception and natural language, "Nature hath established a real connection between the signs and the things signified; and Nature hath also taught us the interpretation of signs—so that previous to experience, the sign suggest the thing signified, and create the belief of it."[85] Through this analogy of original perception and testimony, the universal man (of Scottish Common Sense philosophy) becomes identified with the modern legal subject.[86]

Following Reid, Wilson argues that through natural signs "we gain information and knowledge of the minds, and of the thoughts, and qualities, and affections of the minds of men": "We have no immediate perception of what passes in the minds of one another. Nature has not thought it proper to gratify the wish of the philosopher, by placing a window in every bosom, that all interiour transactions may become visible to every spectator. But, although the thoughts, dispositions, and talents of men are not perceivable by direct and immediate inspection; there are certain external signs, by which those thoughts, and dispositions, and talents are naturally and certainly disclosed and communicated."[87] Like *Arthur Mervyn*, Wilson valorizes knowledge obtained by direct observation and firsthand experience and witnessing. There exists a perceptual divide, however, between man's interior consciousness—the space of emotions, motivations, wills, and desires—and the external world. Natural signs bridge this divide. Like testimony, natural signs are mediations: here, they serve to externalize, and thus display, that interiority which "spectators" cannot perceive by "direct and immediate inspection."

Natural signs operate as more "certain" mediations than testimony: as part of the natural language of mankind, an understanding of which is innate to the species, natural signs are always understood. These signs "naturally denote our thoughts." The theory of natural language assumes this universalist *a priori*; thus it is that those "two dumb persons," Crusoe and Friday, from completely different "cultures," can understand the signs made by the other. Like common sense itself, the language of natural signs is shared by all men.

Reid reduces "the elements . . . or the signs that are naturally expressive of our thoughts" to "these three kinds: modulations of the voice, gestures, and features. By means of these, two savages who have no common artificial language, can converse together; can communicate their thoughts in some tolerable manner; can ask and refuse, affirm and deny, threaten and supplicate; can traffic, enter into covenants and plight their faith. This might be confirmed by historical facts of undoubted credit, if it were necessary."[88] According to Reid, the historical record would readily provide the "facts" to confirm the theory. In his lectures on evidence, Wilson recites this same series of "natural" human acts enabled by natural language. Instead of looking to historical facts, however, Wilson confirms the theory by reference to literary facts: the novel exchange between Robinson Crusoe and Friday. By means of these same natural signs, Wilson says, "two persons who never saw one another before, and who possess no knowledge of one common *artificial* language, can, in some tolerable degree, communicate their thoughts and even their present dispositions to one another: they can ask and give information: they can affirm and deny: they can mutually supplicate and engage fidelity and protection."[89]

Following Reid, Wilson divides natural signs into "the different motions of the hand, the different modulations or tones of the voice, the different gestures and attitudes of the body, and the different looks and features of the countenance, especially what is termed, with singular force and propriety, the expression of the eye."[90] The reader will recall that *Arthur Mervyn*'s juror-character, Dr. Stevens, invokes the same catalogue of natural signs when explaining his reasons for granting credit to Mervyn's testimony.[91] Of particular significance is the visual emphasis of Wilson's descriptions of natural language. While voice (including its tones and modulations) is among the natural signs, all of Wilson's examples of natural language are visual, and all highlight the physical, bodily gestures revealing inner thought. What is most striking here is the extent to which the law's criteria for the evaluation of testimony rely upon the interpretation of bodily gestures and facial expressions. Witness testimony played a central role, we recall, in the rationalization of legal procedures for ascertaining the truth of "facts." As both mediating concept and evidentiary form, testimony reveals that the law, in its attempt to ascertain the "truth" of the facts, must pass first through the body.

The importance of natural signs to the interpretation of testimony highlights the aesthetic turn of legal epistemology. Wilson refers to mankind as so many "spectators." This language of spectatorship is one index of the law's reliance on aesthetic judgments in its ascertainment of the objective "facts." Wilson underscores this point through his examples of the evidence arising from natural signs. In addition to citing the (relatively new genre of) the novel, Wilson continues:

> The variety, the certainty, and the extent of that evidence, which arises from natural signs, may be conceived from what we discover in the pantomime entertainments on the theatre; in some of which, the whole series of

a dramatick tale, and all the passions and emotions to which it gives birth, are represented, with astonishing address, by natural signs. By natural signs, likewise, the painters and statuaries infuse into their pictures and statues the most intelligible, and, sometimes, the most powerful expression of thought, of affections, and even of character.[92]

The logic of Wilson's examples is one of voiceless signification. Beginning with the already speechless theater of pantomime, with its emphasis on physical acting and bodily expression (like the savage Friday's "antick Gestures"), Wilson concludes with the mute natural signs of pictures and statues. Paradoxically, it is in the aesthetic sphere that civilized man "discovers" the extent and variety of natural signs. Natural signs are employed by the artist to "infuse" into silent aesthetic objects—paintings and statues—psychic interiorities ("thoughts," affections," even "character"), which these objects then "express" to a spectator. Describing such a tension between artifice and nature in contemporary oratory, Jay Fliegelman has characterized it as the paradox of "natural theatricality (simultaneously imitating and realizing nature)."[93] Yet the aesthetic uses of natural signs constitute the fullest expression of the philosophical heart of Reid's theory of natural language: that signs of the living body's exterior surfaces naturally (and often involuntarily) communicate inner affect and meaning.

The figural aesthetic of Wilson's invocation of natural language, with its accompanying emphasis on visuality and spectatorship in the interpretation of testimony, is significant also to the consideration of testimony's mediating role, between the direct observation of the facts and the trial of those facts. Again, in the law's formulation, testimony is the "attested experience and observations of others." Eyewitnesses are thus conceived as those who have seen for, in the place of, the jury and the court. Yet in the translation from "direct observation" to attested words, from witnessing to telling, the "subject" of testimony becomes both the narrated facts and the witness narrating them. The question arises: in trying the "truth" of testimony, which is granted greater evaluative weight—the scene narrated by the witness, or the scene of witness narration? The theory of natural language applies to the testifying witness as well: natural signs externalize and thus make accessible to the spectator-juror the "true" thoughts, emotions, and intents of the witness. As Wilson's reflections on natural language suggest, the observation of natural signs during the scene of narration—what in my analysis of *Arthur Mervyn* I call the scene of testimony—is often the deciding criteria for jurors in granting credit to testimony. In the trial of the credibility of testimony in particular, and in legal culture more generally, this figural aesthetic of natural language becomes a key form of evidence.

In the new republic, virtue is rewarded with credit. Within the world of *Arthur Mervyn*, the trial of the truth of Mervyn's narrative turns upon the trial of his credibility—itself a trial of his "character." Mervyn's character-function is to provide the locus for the debates in the novel's republican world over the concept of "character," as bearer of cultural capital and social value within a symbolic economy of credit and civic virtue.[94] As the aesthetic reflections of both Wilson and Brown reveal, the trial of credibility—or the trial of character—is very often conducted through the interpretation of natural signs: "We acquire information, not only of the thoughts and present dispositions and affections, but also of the qualities, moral and intellectual, of the minds of others, by the means of natural signs.... In the same manner, and by the same means, we receive evidence concerning his benevolence, his fortitude, and all his other talents and virtues."[95] Extending the theory of natural language, Wilson argues that natural signs can reveal not only the fleeting thoughts and dispositions of a man but also his deepest inner character traits. What Wilson says of paintings and statues representing the human body is even truer of a living man: his countenance and other natural signs constitute the "most powerful expression of thought, of affections, and even of character." The reader may recall here as well Dr. Stevens's reflections on the credibility of Mervyn's testimony: "He that listens to his words may question their truth, but he that looks upon his countenance when speaking, cannot withhold his faith." *Arthur Mervyn* elaborates the logical conclusion of the notion that the credibility of testimony can be judged by the direct observation of the manner in which a witness testifies. Severed from his voice and his words, "the face" of Arthur Mervyn truly "is the index"—because it is the *natural sign*—"of an honest mind."

Embedded Narrative and the Trial of Character

Many literary critics have remarked upon the legal themes of Brown's novels, and of *Arthur Mervyn* in particular.[96] Few have examined the formal distinctiveness of this ingenious novel, or the novel forms through which it performs its cultural work. In what follows, I trace the cultural link between the epistemological forms of law we have just explored and the narrative form of *Arthur Mervyn*. Brown's work exemplifies the migration, from the sphere of law to that of the early American novel, of evidentiary procedures for ascertaining historical fact.[97] The law does not merely ascertain the truth of discrete facts (*vera*), but rather produces a narrative of truth. The history of legal fictions attests to the law's insistence on a singular narrative truth, which the disparate "true" facts, the discrete *vera* of everyday life, must be employed to support. As we saw in the history of legal fictions, this demand for narrative closure will even accept invented and wholly fictitious "facts." This singular narrative, the law's *veritas*, is produced through the jury trial. At the close of his discussion of reasoning as a source of evidence, Wilson elaborates the philosophy of evidence subtending the narrative logic of the evidence of facts: "In moral evidence, there not only may be, but there generally is, contrariety of proofs. . . . [T]here is . . . real evidence on both sides. On both sides, contrary presumptions, contrary testimonies, contrary experiences must be balanced. The probability, on the whole, is, consequently, in the proportion, in which the evidence on one side preponderates over the evidence on the other side."[98] As with the jury trial, *Arthur Mervyn* is a "contrariety of proofs" that begins in uncertainty. *Arthur Mervyn* employs an embedded narrative structure to position the disparate testimonies of various characters as competing narratives: the novel's structure is a "contrariety of proofs" whose confrontation is the novel's homology for the law's procedures for producing its truth. Through the translation of legal forms into its embedded narrative structure, the novel articulates the figure of "the citizen" as witness—as one whose testimony conforms to the law's rules of evidence. The epistemological uncertainty at the center of Brown's novel demands that the central characters provide explanatory accounts of themselves, of their status as credible deponents of the facts. Such an epistemological demand produces not only a particular type of "character," the narrating witness, but also the structural form of embedded narrative itself. Through the structure of embedded narrative, Brown's novel represents the truth of a narrative as a "matter of fact" in the epistemological sense derived from the evidentiary culture of law.

As James Wilson argued in his *Lectures*, and as the debate between Dr. Stevens and Wortley over the truth of Mervyn's tale reminds us, the jury must try not only the truth of the facts, but also the credibility of testimony. The first-person (or testimonial) account requires that some credit be given the narrator's story. *Arthur Mervyn* actually consists of two overlapping trials. The first, initiated by Wortley's accusations against Mervyn, tries Mervyn's actions and his implication in Welbeck's crimes. The first part of the novel is Mervyn's testimony in his defense. The novel's second part comprises the trial of the truth of Mervyn's story itself (i.e., the truth of the novel's first part). Trying the truth of Mervyn's testimony, this second trial necessarily examines Mervyn's "character," and his credibility. As is quickly revealed by Dr. Stevens's investigations into Mervyn's family history, belief in the truth of Mervyn's account of his relationship to the known villain Welbeck depends upon belief in the truth of Mervyn's personal history.

It is appropriate to the central uncertainty of *Arthur Mervyn* that the main point of disagreement for literary critics has been the character of its eponymous hero. One's view of the novel as a whole depends upon one's view of Mervyn, and, most importantly, the credibility of his narration.[99] Cathy Davidson and Michael Warner have suggested that critics who do not credit Arthur's character, and thus disbelieve his testimony, assume an ironic distance between the author and his novel's protagonist.[100] We might add that those who read Arthur's self-representation as sincere and credit his tale assume an identification of Brown with Mervyn.[101] The literary-critical history reproduces a debate staged by the novel itself: the organizing center of the novel is the dispute between Dr. Stevens and his friend Wortley over the "dubiousness" of Arthur Mervyn's "character," and the credibility of his testimony (8).

Another approach to this critical debate is with a question of literary form: Why stage Mervyn's testimony at all? Why present Mervyn's oral narration as one told to Dr. Stevens, a character who then writes a very long text that reads as if Arthur were speaking to the reader directly? As we have noted, Mervyn's oral testimony is framed by the written narration of Dr. Stevens (15).[102] Indeed, Mervyn's entire oral narration of his life in the novel's first part is mediated through the written narration of Dr. Stevens, as are most events of the novel's second part. It is this narrative frame, and the series of embedded narratives that appear within it, that become the central structural concern of the novel. Through the confrontation of the novel's several embedded narratives—as narrated by individual characters such as Mervyn, Wortley, Welbeck, Mrs. Wentworth, Mrs. Althorpe, and other republican citizens—the novel tries the "truth" of Mervyn's story, the credibility of his "character." It is through this very structural confrontation of differing embedded narratives that *Arthur Mervyn* represents the citizens of the early republic as so many legal subjects: as witnesses and jurors, and as suspect characters.

By staging testimony, I mean the novel's recurrent employment of scenes in which characters are called upon to recount their knowledge of past facts. In these scenes of testimony, Brown goes to great lengths to present not only the character's account (through an embedded narrative told in the first person) but to describe, through another frame narrator, the "very manner" in which the witness narrates the account: from the "tones, gestures and looks" of this witness's oral performance to various subtle changes in his "countenance"—"calm or vehement, doubting or confident"—as he recounts his tale. These scenes draw upon the figural aesthetic of testimonial evidence I discussed with respect to "the face of Mervyn" as the "index of an honest mind."

Yet the novel, like the court of law, recognizes only certain types of testimony. The reader will recall the "two old verses" cited in Dalton's *Country Justice* to describe criteria used to evaluate witness testimony:

> *Conditio, sexus, discretio, fama,*
> *Et fortuna, fides: in testibus esta requires.*[103]

While Dalton cites this maxim in connection with examination by the justice of the peace, the "criteria to be considered by the justices in preliminary examination of witnesses were almost identical to those which came to be used *to test the credibility of witnesses* who appeared before juries in criminal cases. Both dealt with witnesses, albeit in a different procedural context. Indeed, they involved the same persons."[104] Barbara Shapiro notes that Dalton's "successors [in the legal handbook tradition] sometimes used the same verses and similar materials in a section labeled 'witnesses.'" As early as Richard Chamberlain's *Complete Justice* (1681), legal handbook and treatise writers applied this verse-maxim and similar descriptive materials to the evaluation of witness testimony. Shapiro suggests that this should be considered "an example of how evidentiary criteria designed for one purpose or procedure could *migrate* to another. If Dalton's criteria for examination were in large part borrowed from the Romano-canon *indicia*, they might be borrowed again as criteria for assessment of witness credibility."[105] Such *indicia* were drawn from the social personhood of the witness: circumstances such as sex; discretion, or ability to distinguish truth; reputation; economic and social status; and religious beliefs (especially one's reputation for piety and adherence to oaths).[106]

In his description of the qualities of a witness that add to the persuasive "force" of testimonial evidence, Wilson elaborated upon these indices, incorporating criteria outlined by Locke, Reid, and Hale: "The reputation of the witness, the manner in which he delivers his testimony, the nature of the fact concerning which his testimony is given, the peculiar situation in which he stands with regard to that fact, the occasion on which he is called to produce his testimony, his entire disinterestedness as to the matter in question—each of these taken singly may much augment the force of his evidence—all of these taken jointly may render that force irresistible."[107] Wilson begins with the ever-recurring criterion of "reputation." This attribute recurs throughout the legal and philosophical literature on testimony. As an index of credibility, it speaks to the witness's reputation for honesty and truth-telling; as such, it was directly linked to conceptions of "virtue" and "character." The recurrence of this term in the genealogy of epistemological forms highlights the persistence of a language of republicanism in the "Americanization of virtue."[108]

Legal and cultural historians have yet to note the striking similarity between these social indices of witness credibility used within the law and the descriptions of literary "character" that made literary representations *credible*—or in the language of contemporary aesthetic theory, "probable." Just as such evaluative criteria were capable of migration *within* the legal sphere, they were capable of migration to the aesthetic and literary spheres, and to the (relatively) new genre of the novel. One index of this migration is that aesthetic theorists would cite these same criteria in discussions of the "probable" qualities of aesthetic representations—with "probable" in the aesthetic context meaning "plausible," "credible," "natural," and "verisimilar" all at once.[109] In his *Essays: On Poetry and Music* (1776), for example, James Beattie (a student of Thomas Reid) cites the legal definition of "condition" in his description of the "naturalness" of literary-aesthetic representations of "character." In his aesthetic theory, Beattie extends Reid's theory of natural language to include "all those features of discourse that may be understood as the causal products of character."[110] May we not infer, Beattie argues, that literary "language is then according to nature, when it is suitable to the supposed *condition* of the speaker?'—meaning by the word *condition*, not only the outward circumstances of *fortune, rank, employment, sex, age, and nation*, but also the internal temperature of the *understanding* and the *passions*, as well as the peculiar nature of the *thoughts* that may happen to occupy the mind."[111] While extending Reid's model of a naturally expressive language to the artificial signs of literary speech generally, and to the *decorums* of character portrayal in particular, Beattie cites, as *a priori* conditions of its literary uses, the series of social markers applied by the law to the evaluation of witness credibility.

In the republican world of *Arthur Mervyn*, scenes of testimony include detailed descriptions of characters as more or less "reputable," credible witnesses. Such descriptive details, which always accompany the introduction of a character's account, correspond to those social markers of personhood used in the law to evaluate testimonial credibility. Throughout *Arthur Mervyn*, Brown's frame narrator, Dr. Stevens, remarks upon the same "outward circumstances" or "conditions" of the novel's various witnesses. Likewise, all the novel's characters cite such social markers as indices of testimonial credibility. Thus Stevens introduces Mrs. Althorpe—whose account of Mervyn's family history runs entirely contrary to Mervyn's testimony—as "a sensible and candid woman" from a well-respected family. When asked by Stevens "what proof" she had of "the immoral conduct" of Mervyn, Mrs. Althorpe responds: "I have no proof but the unanimous report of Mervyn's neighbors. Respectable and honest men have affirmed, in my hearing, that they have been present when the boy treated his [step-]mother in the way that I have described" (232). As for the fact of Mervyn "being seen in the city the next day after his elopement, dressed in a most costly and fashionable manner," she continues, "I can doubt that as little as the rest, for he that saw [Mervyn] was my father, and you who know my father, know what credit is due to his eyes and his word" (232). When judging the credibility of Mervyn's testimony alone, Stevens had focused on the figural aesthetics of Mervyn's testimonial performance, as the most persuasive *sign* of his credibility. In its representation of peripheral witness-characters such as Mrs. Althorpe, Mrs. Wentworth, Wortley, and Williams, the novels highlights instead social markers such as reputation and status as the greater indices of testimonial credibility.

Dr. Stevens is that disinterested, virtuous character who had remained in the city to tend to those afflicted with the yellow fever. As Stevens says, "my office required me to go daily into the midst" of "the receptacles of infection." When Stevens encounters the dying stranger (whom we later learn is Mervyn), "to take this person into my house, and bestow upon him the requisite attendance was the scheme that first occurred to" him (6). Stevens first consults his wife; her response, one expected by Stevens, is equally revealing of their roles as virtuous, dutiful citizens: "I have no fear about me for my part, in a case where the injunctions of duty are so obvious" (6). Repeatedly describing his actions as motivated by selfless duty and disinterest, Brown presents Dr. Stevens, the "composer" of the present "narrative," as a model of republican virtue. This is not to oppose the critical identification of Brown and Mervyn with an alternative identification, of Brown and Dr. Stevens. Rather it is to suggest that the novel, having established Stevens as the ideal-typical republican citizen and privileged moral observer, will use Stevens as the most appropriate judge of the facts.

The novel's many scenes of testimony also emphasize the epistemological concept, developed within the law, of the corroboration of facts. In James Wilson's formulation,

> in a number of concurrent testimonies, there is a degree of probability superadded to that, which may be termed the aggregate of all the probabilities of the separate testimonies. This superadded probability arises from the concurrence itself. When, concerning a great number and variety of circumstances, there is an entire agreement in the testimony of many witnesses, without the possibility of a previous collusion between them, the evidence may, in its effect, be equal to that of strict demonstration. That such concurrence should be the result of chance, is as one to infinite; or, to vary the expression, is a moral impossibility.[112]

Again describing the moral certainty of legal judgment as probable knowledge, Wilson elaborates a logic of narrative coincidence as epistemological grounds for proof: coincidence without collusion constitutes "evidence [which] may, in its effect, be equal to that of strict demonstration." Through the novel's embedded narrative structure, Brown juxtaposes independent accounts, highlighting those facts narrated by them that coincide, thus granting greater probability to the truth of these discrete facts. Stevens's extensive intervention into the trial of Arthur's credibility continues, for example, with his own corroboration of the facts of Arthur's strange narrative. While remarking upon the uncommon nature of Mervyn's facts, Dr. Stevens assures the reader that the Clemenza Lodi of Mervyn's narrative, "the lady whom Welbeck had betrayed and deserted, was not unknown to me. I was but too well acquainted with her fate" (221). Dr. Stevens adds that he was told of her fate by someone well known to himself:

> I have mentioned that the source of my intelligence was a kinsman.... No tidings was received of him, till a messenger arrived intreating my assistance. I was conducted to the house of Mrs. Villars, in which I found

no one but my kinsman.... Before he died, he informed me fully of the character of his betrayers. The late arrival, name and personal condition of Clemenza Lodi were related. Welbeck was not named, but was described in terms, which, combined with the narrative of Mervyn, enabled me to recognize the paramour of Lucy Villars in the man whose crimes had been the principal theme of our discourse. (222)

Dr. Stevens's acquaintance with these facts comes from someone close to him, who did have not any acquaintance with Mervyn, and thus no possibility of collusion with Mervyn. By describing at length the circumstances of how he came to know of these facts in Mervyn's narrative, and emphasizing that he came to this knowledge independently of Mervyn's testimony, Dr. Stevens persuades the reader of their truth.

The corroboration of facts is given greater narrative weight as the novel's plot grows more complicated. The debate between Dr. Stevens and Wortley, for example, revolves around not only Mervyn's face but also the tense relation between the truth of discrete facts and the truth of their narration.

> It cannot be denied, continued [Wortley], that [Mervyn] lived with Welbeck at the time of his elopement; that they disappeared together; that they entered a boat, at Pine-street wharf, at midnight; that this boat was discovered by the owner in the possession of a fisherman at Red-bank, who affirmed that he had found it stranded near his door, the day succeeding that on which they disappeared. Of all this, I can supply you [Dr. Stevens] with incontestible proof. If, after this proof, you can give credit to his story, I shall think you made of very perverse and credulous materials. (226)

Cataloguing the series of facts that collectively point toward Mervyn's criminal conspiracy with Welbeck, Wortley then deduces, from the incontestable evidence of these individual facts, the proof of Mervyn's duplicity. Wortley insists that the truth of these facts is sufficient evidence against the truth of any testimony narrated by Mervyn. Dr. Stevens counters, however: "The proof you mention, said I, will only enhance his credibility. All the facts which you have stated, have been admitted by him. They constitute an essential portion of his narrative" (226). Dr. Stevens argues for the relation between the truth of discrete facts (*vera*) and the truth of a total narrative (*veritas*): because these individual facts, which

Wortley testifies are true, corroborate facts already admitted independently in Mervyn's testimony, they "only enhance his credibility" and the truth of Mervyn's narrative. While Dr. Stevens was convinced of the truth of Mervyn's testimony largely by the narration and the "face of Arthur Mervyn," the existence of these other facts corroborate Mervyn's tale, granting greater credit to his narrative testimony. Testimony is an overdetermined epistemological form: its evidence persuades through both narrative and narration.

What is also significant to the novel's elaboration of the law's epistemological forms is the way in which discrete facts are employed in the narrative construction of truth. Whereas Dr. Stevens focuses on the interpretive aesthetics of testimony, Wortley focuses on facts as object-givens. While the evidence of facts is moral, and not demonstrative, evidence, Wortley's argument employs them as an aggregate objectivity, "equal to that of strict demonstration." Wortley's exclusive focus on the narrative facts of a testimony, rather than the manner of narration, is underscored when he declares to Dr. Stevens: "You say [Mervyn] means to return; but of that I doubt. You will never see his face more" (226).

While Mervyn is away, Wortley returns with new evidence against him. As in his previous debate with Dr. Stevens, Wortley employs the language of "objective" facts to assert the truth of his account: "Facts have come to light of which you are wholly unaware, and which, when known to you, will conquer even your incredulity as to the guilt of Mervyn" (249). Now charging Dr. Stevens with ignorance of "all the facts," Wortley thus uses the argument Stevens had earlier made against Wortley's allegations of Mervyn's duplicity. This logic of narrative totality, in which the truth of one's perspective depends upon its comprehension of all the true facts, is thus shared by both sides of the case. "Facts?," Dr. Stevens responds. "Let me know them, I beseech you. If Mervyn has deceived me, there is an end to my confidence in human nature. All limits to dissimulation, and all distinctions between vice and virtue will be effaced. No man's word, no force of collateral evidence shall weigh with me an hair" (249). Dr. Stevens's plea for the true facts in the case of Arthur Mervyn raises the stakes of his debate with Wortley, to question the epistemological status of all human testimony: if Mervyn's testimony was a lie, there will be no basis for Stevens's confidence in any testimony. As we have seen, direct eyewitness testimony has been represented, in the scale of evidentiary value, as far better than both secondhand witness testimony and the secondhand evidence of books. In the novel's representation of evidence, eyewitness testimony has been that source of knowledge upon which all other forms of evidence ultimately depend. For Stevens, loss of faith in the propensity of human nature to tell the truth thus eliminates the ability of anyone to know the true facts, or reconstruct the truth of the past. Yet just as Wortley shares Dr. Stevens's view of narrative totality, Stevens admits here the validity of Wortley's position that discrete facts, if proven true, can disrupt the apparent truth of even the most "ingenious and plausible" narrative.

In his defense of Mervyn, Dr. Stevens had reasoned that he "that listens to his words may question their truth, but he that looks upon his countenance when speaking, cannot withhold his faith."[113] Responding to what he perceives to be the naïve credulity of Dr. Stevens, Wortley says:

> It was time, replied my friend [Wortley], that your confidence in smooth features and fluent accents should have ended long ago. Till I gained from my present profession, some knowledge of the world, a knowledge which was not gained in a moment, and has not cost a trifle, I was equally wise in my own conceit; and, in order to decide upon the truth of any one's pretensions, needed only a clear view of his face and a distinct hearing of his words. My folly, in that respect, was only to be cured, however, by my own experience, and I suppose your credulity will yield to no other remedy. These are the facts. (249)

As we have seen, the debates over Mervyn's credibility and "character" consistently return to "the face of Mervyn." Wortley directly challenges Dr. Stevens's argument that Mervyn's face "is the index of an honest mind." He opposes the evidentiary value of direct testimony using the very logic Stevens had invoked earlier in its favor. Direct inspection of the witness's testimony reveals no truth, Wortley argues, only the skill of the liar's rhetorical performance, and the "folly" of the auditor's naïve confidence in his ability to judge testimony. Turning away from the interpretive aesthetics of testimony, Wortley emphasizes instead the truth of discrete facts (*vera*) as the only accurate access to the truth of an event.

Such a turn in the novel's central debate over evidence foregrounds the displacement of testimony by circumstantial evidence. What we can see in the novel's representation of this debate between Wortley and Stevens is a tension within the legal sphere itself in the late eighteenth century. As Alexander Welsh has observed, in the later eighteenth century, testimony was increasingly questioned as a reliable form of evidence, and its displacement by circumstantial evidence was signaled by the frequent use, in the courtroom and in legal treatises, of the phrase "circumstances cannot lie."[114] "Facts," in this formulation, were regarded less as events in dispute than as objective things, or conditions, over which neither defendants nor prosecutors, nor witnesses, had any narrative control. The assumption was that while witnesses might lie, "facts" (understood in this objective sense) did not. If the content of this debate between Dr. Stevens and Wortley reveals the epistemological tensions between testimony and circumstances, the form of Brown's novel can be seen also to enact this particular tension. It is as a mix of novel forms—of the first-person, testimonial form and the third-person, reportive account—that *Arthur Mervyn* reproduces, within the literary sphere, the epistemological problem of legal forms. As we will see, "the facts," independent of Mervyn's narrative, do ultimately decide the truth of the matter.

Wortley's account of these "objective" facts is itself complex, consisting of the embedded narrative testimonies of a Captain Williams, an old friend of Amos Watson (the man killed by Welbeck), and Mrs. Wentworth, the proprietor of the house rented by Welbeck before his disappearance. Both Williams and Mrs. Wentworth report a series of incidents at least as uncommon as those narrated by Mervyn, which would be considered incredible were they not also based on "intelligence respecting Mervyn, whose truth cannot be doubted" (249). The difference, of course, and the reason their truth cannot be doubted, is that characters other than the novel's central testifier, Mervyn, narrate these incidents. "What . . . more deeply absorbed our attention," Dr. Stevens says,

> was the testimony of Williams and Mrs. Wentworth. That which was mysterious and inscrutable to Wortley . . . was luminous to us. The coincidence between the vague hints, laboriously collected by these enquirers, and the narrative of Mervyn, afforded the most cogent attestation of the truth of that narrative. (251)

Once again the coincidence of facts, without prior collusion of witnesses, attests to the truth of testimony.

The "fact" contained in Mrs. Wentworth's testimony which proves to Wortley Mervyn's duplicity is that someone who Mervyn had claimed was dead—Mervyn says he witnessed the death—is reported to be still alive.

Mervyn's claim, Wortley asserts, "has since been confuted, in a letter just received from [Mrs. Wentworth's] brother in England. In this letter she is informed, that her nephew had been seen by one who knew him well, in Charleston; that some intercourse took place between the youth and the bearer of the news.... Thus, I hope you will admit that the duplicity of Mervyn is demonstrated" (250). Wortley's final word on this matter emphasizes the objective truth-value of discrete facts. It also assumes that even "ingenious and plausible" narratives can be proven false, when proven inconsistent with one of these true facts. Upon hearing Wortley's report of Mrs. Wentworth's testimony, Dr. Stevens says:

> The facts which you have mentioned... partly correspond with Mervyn's story; but the last particular is irreconcilably repugnant to it. Now, for the first time, I begin to feel that my confidence is shaken. I feel my mind bewildered and distracted by the multitude of new discoveries which have just taken place. I want time to revolve them slowly, to weigh them accurately, and to estimate their consequences fully. (250–51)

Even as he is reluctant to view Mervyn as duplicitous, Stevens's response reveals the same conception of truth in narrative (as opposed to truth revealed through narration). Despite his confidence in the evidence of oral testimony, and in his own ability to judge by direct observation the credibility of such testimony, Stevens admits Wortley's point, that the truth of discrete objective facts can undermine the apparent truth of even the most consistent and plausible testimony.

We should recall that the novel's turn toward an emphasis on the representation of facts as object-givens occurs while Mervyn is away from the scene of the narrative. That is to say, the novel has returned to its primary narrative frame, the narration of Dr. Stevens. With Mervyn's face—that index of an honest mind—no longer before him, Stevens's confidence in his credibility is more easily shaken. Accordingly, Stevens asks Wortley for time to consider his case: "Will you pardon me... if I defer commenting on your narrative till I have had an opportunity of reviewing it and comparing it with my knowledge of the lad, collected from himself and from my own observation" (251). Fulfilling the novel's structural logic of truth through embedded narrative, Stevens ends in the role of juror, in the most straightforwardly legal sense of the term: he must judge the matter of fact. In order to decide the truth of the *res facta*, Stevens must review and compare all the narratives of the facts considered together.

In its turn toward the objectivity of facts, the novel ultimately represents the truth of Mervyn's tale as decided by "facts" existing independently of Mervyn's testimony (both its narrative and its narration). Welbeck, Mervyn's suspected criminal co-conspirator, admits before the jury (the frame narrator Dr. Stevens) that after reading news of the money lost with the missing Amos Watson (whom Welbeck had killed and buried):

> I ventured to return.... I penetrated to the vaults of that deserted dwelling by night. I dug up the bones of my friend, and found the girdle and its valuable contents, according to the accurate description that I had read. I hastened back with my prize to Baltimore, but my evil destiny overtook me at last. I was recognized by emissaries of Jamieson, arrested, and brought hither, and here shall I consummate my fate and defeat the rage of my creditors by death. (351)

This narrative "fact" admitted by Welbeck finally confirms for Dr. Stevens the truth of Mervyn's narrative. In this crucial scene of testimony, the novel has returned to its original *mise-en-scène*: not Mervyn but Dr. Stevens, the novel's primary frame narrator, witnesses and narrates Welbeck's embedded narrative confession in this scene. And for the first time in the novel, Stevens must inform Mervyn of an unknown fact: "On leaving the prison, I hastened to inform Mervyn of the true nature of the scene which had just passed" (352). It is worth noting, then, in answer to critics who insist on the unreliable narration of Mervyn, that the novel's primary trial, of Mervyn's actions, is decided by the novel's frame narrator, Stevens, based upon facts existing independently of Mervyn's narration.

Dr. Stevens's character-function as frame narrator, and as writer of the novel's words, also ends here. After relating to Mervyn the true story behind "this extraordinary occurrence" (352)—significantly, Dr. Stevens here occupies the role of storyteller, and Mervyn, of auditor—Stevens literally hands over the role of narrator to Mervyn:

> No one is so skillful an advocate in a cause, as he whose cause it is. I rely upon your skill and address, and shall leave you to pursue your own way. I must leave you for a time, but shall expect to be punctually informed of all that passes. With this agreement we parted, and I hastened to perform my intended journey. (353)

In staging these scenes of testimony, Brown presents Stevens in that privileged role of an auditor who hears, from different characters' perspectives, many versions of the same sequence of overlapping facts. Connecting the novel's formal structure and its individual character-functions, Stevens exemplifies Brown's strategy of representing the ascertainment of truth. Once Dr. Stevens passes judgment in favor of Mervyn's innocence, his credible character, and the truth of his tale, Stevens's role as judge of the facts has been fulfilled. "The moment that the occasion is over," Dr. Stevens, like James Wilson's conception of the jury as an "abstract of the people" selected to exercise this discretionary power of judgment in the *trial per patrium*, "disappears among the general body of the citizens."

Mervyn began the novel as a wandering stranger, without family, home, or known "character." The first words Mervyn wrote within the world of the novel, as a "specimen of [his] penmanship," alluded to his condition as one "free in a double sense": "My poverty, but not my will consents" (50). This is why Mervyn's story had to be told through the framing narration of the respected citizen Dr. Stevens, and the trial of Mervyn's character staged through the embedded narratives of other respected citizens. Mervyn did not possess an unqualified "free will of his own"; he could not represent himself, so he must be represented.[115] Marking the successful assimilation of Mervyn's character into the civic community, the novel concludes with Mervyn taking up the pen once again, but now as "the skillful advocate" of his own cause, free to represent himself.

3

Fugitive Bonds

Contract and the Culture of Constitutionalism

> Dead letters! does it not sound like dead men?
> —Herman Melville, *Bartleby, the Scrivener*

The dominant critical account of Frederick Douglass interprets his writings as framed by his attempts to persuade Americans to adhere to the original founding principles, and to live up to the egalitarian promise of the American Revolution.[1] Similarly, accounts of Douglass's split with the Garrisonians, and their interpretation of the Constitution as a "pro-slavery compact," insert Douglass into a historical narrative of natural law interpretations of the Constitution, arguing that Douglass's embrace of political abolitionism was based on his belief in the universalist ideals of the founders. While this chapter does not discount the possibility that Douglass may have been motivated by the ideals of the Revolutionary founding, the focus of its analysis—Douglass's reading of the Constitution, and the history and context of his new interpretive strategy—highlights some of the limitations of such critical commonplaces, recovering both a more complex Douglass and his engagements with the antebellum labor history ignored in these accounts. Through reading Douglass's own reading practices, we can reinterpret the very historical narratives into which he has been inserted. This reading practice likewise provides new insight into the broader transformations in the "culture of constitutionalism" caused by the social struggle and political economic debates over slavery.[2]

Attention to Douglass's reading practice will also supplement another historical narrative, of the development of free labor ideology and its antislavery interpretation of the Constitution. In Eric Foner's account of free labor ideology and the rise of the Republican Party, it was the antislavery lawyer Salmon Chase who developed the interpretation of the Constitution that would provide the legal philosophy and unifying strategy for the development of political antislavery (a political abolitionism opposed to the moral abolitionism of the Garrisonians). According to Foner, "at the core of Chase's interpretation of the Constitution was his description of the founding fathers' intentions regarding slavery. Publicly and privately, [Chase] insisted, the founders deplored the institution and hoped for its early abolition."[3] Based on his argument that the "original intent" of the framers was in fact to limit slavery as a local institution of the then- existing slave states, Chase argued further that the 1793 Fugitive Slave Act, and later the Fugitive Slave Act passed with the 1850 Compromise, were both unconstitutional because the Constitution had not delegated to Congress such legislative authority. While Chase argued, against both the Garrisonians and slavery's defenders, for an opposite "original intent," he and the antislavery politics he helped shape retained the same category of "original intent" invoked regularly by slavery's defenders: in Chase's view, the Constitution's antislavery "original intent" could be ascertained by way of close study of the historical record of the framers' views on slavery. Chase catalogued the various statements of the founders to support this point. (He focused mainly on the writings of the slaveholding founder Thomas Jefferson: the natural law principles of the Declaration of Independence, and of the Northwest Ordinance, which barred slavery from the original territories of the United States.) According to Chase (and later, Abraham Lincoln), framers such as Jefferson intended to prevent the extension of slavery, and to finally secure abolition by the individual actions of the states.[4]

The story of the development of Douglass's political abolitionism is usually folded into this broader one. Yet if we look at Douglass's speeches and writings from this period, we discover a different and much more radical hermeneutic. Throughout his writings on the Constitution, Douglass does not merely argue, along with Chase, for an antislavery "original intent." As we have seen, Douglass began to complicate the very concept of "original intent" even before he announced his "Change of Opinion" in 1851. Douglass's 1849 editorial on Calhoun's "Southern Address" conceded the proslavery "intentions" of the Constitution's "slavery provisions" while arguing as well that the ambiguous language of those provisions left their meaning open to a radically different interpretation: "The language in each of the provisions to which the address refers, though doubtless *intended* to bolster up slavery and to respect slave property, has been so ambiguously worded as to bear a very different construction; and taken in connection with the preamble of that instrument, the very opposite of the construction given it by this wily band of slaveholders."[5] Douglass elaborated this point through the trope of the "man from another country," the figure for a legal hermeneutic which found the Constitution's "intentions" respecting slavery solely through a "strict construction" of its language. Through this figure of reading, Douglass suggested that the words of the so-called "fugitive slave clause" ran counter to that provision's widely accepted "original intent," and made the clause instead a provision for the recapture of fugitives from the labor bondage of indentured servitude and apprenticeship. The counterintuitive character of this interpretation of the most famous of the Constitution's slavery clauses was only heightened by the fact that it was Douglass, whose 1845 *Narrative of the Life of Frederick Douglass* had made him America's most famous fugitive slave, advancing it.

Douglass closed his 1849 editorial with an argument against the politics of compromise: "What Calhoun's address has to say on the subject of the original compromise entered into on the part of the free States with the slave States, every Northern man should ponder well; and draw from it a lesson that will forever preclude him from entering into another like it."[6] Less than a year later, northern and southern legislators entered into the Compromise of 1850 arranged by the "Great Triumvirate" of Henry Clay, Daniel Webster, and John Calhoun, and signed into law the Fugitive Slave Act. The Compromise of 1850 was the signal turning point in the growing Union crisis; the 1850 Fugitive Slave Act, requiring the participation of citizens of free states in the recapture of fugitive slaves, highlighted the structural link between the individual citizen's "moral" decisions regarding slavery and the formal-political community of the nation.

On 15 May 1851, then, Douglass published his "Change of Opinion" in the *North Star*. The Constitution, he now argued, could be "construed in the light of well-established rules of legal interpretation [and] be made consistent in its details with the noble purposes avowed in its preamble."[7] In this announcement, Douglass highlights the strategic importance of this new hermeneutic: "We found, in our former position, that, when debating the question, we were compelled to go *behind the letter* of the Constitution, and seek its meaning in the *history and practice* of the nation under it."[8] The advantage, Douglass argues, of finding legal intent exclusively in the letter of the law is that slaveholders can make no claims to the authority of the Constitution: "We hold it to be a system of lawless violence; that it *never was lawful, and never can be made so.*"[9] The stakes of this new model of interpretation are that political abolitionism can lay claim to the authority of the Constitution and the Union; and it presents slaveholders as illegal perpetrators of "a system of lawless violence."[10]

Throughout the decade after the 1850 Compromise, Douglass returned to the trope of a "man from another country" to underscore this opposition between "strict construction" and "original intent." In his 1854 address to a two-thousand-strong antislavery convention in Cincinnati, Ohio, for example, Douglass refers again to the question of "original intent" by citing Madison's record of *The Debates in the Federal Convention of 1787*: "Mr. Madison declared the framers were unwilling to admit that man could hold property in man. But what matters intentions in a matter that took place two hundred years ago? Where are we to find the intentions if not on the face of the instrument?"[11] Similarly, in his famous 1860 speech on the unconstitutionality of slavery delivered in Glasgow, Scotland, Douglass argues that it "would be the wildest of absurdities, and lead to endless confusion and mischiefs, if, instead of looking to the written paper itself, for its meaning, it were attempted to make us search it out, in the secret motives, and dishonest intentions, of some men who took part in writing it."[12] Criticizing both slavery's defenders and Garrisonian abolitionists for their shared interpretation of the Constitution's "original intent," Douglass adds: "What will the people of America a hundred years hence care about the intentions of the scriveners who wrote the Constitution?"[13] By divorcing *legislative* intention from the "original intent" of the framers, the trope of "a man from another country" likewise elevated the text over the political-cultural aura of the founders. Douglass concludes: "[It] should be borne in mind that the mere text, and only the text . . . was adopted as the Constitution. It should also be borne in mind that the intentions of those who framed the Constitution, be they good or bad, for slavery or against slavery, are to be respected so far, and so far only, as we find those intentions plainly stated in the Constitution."[14]

Douglass also uses the trope of the "man from another country" in this 1860 Glasgow speech (which also sold widely as a pamphlet) to return to that counterintuitive interpretation of the "fugitive slave clause" he had advanced as early as 1849. "But it may be asked," Douglass states,

> if this clause does not apply to slaves, to whom does it apply? I answer, that when adopted, it applies to a very large class of persons—namely, redemptioners—persons who had come to America from Holland, from Ireland, and from other quarters of the globe—like the Coolies to the West

Indies—and had, for a consideration duly paid, become bound to "serve and labour" for the parties to whom their service and labor was due. It applies to indentured apprentices and others who had become bound for a consideration, under contract duly made, to serve and labour. . . . The legal condition of the slave puts him beyond the operation of this provision. . . . He does not owe and cannot owe service. He cannot even make a contract. This provision, then, only respects persons who owe service, and they can only owe service who can receive an equivalent and make a bargain. The slave cannot do that, and is therefore exempted from the operation of this fugitive provision.[15]

Even after Justice Lemuel Shaw upheld the constitutionality of the 1850 Fugitive Slave Act in the 1851 *Sims Case* and sent Thomas Sims back into slavery, Douglass refers to the "fugitive slave clause" as "this fugitive provision" of the Constitution, and meditates further on the terms of contract and the true referent of the Constitution's letters. Douglass focuses here on both the common ground between the slave and the indentured servant—their labor bondage—and their distinguishing difference: the labor contract. "Redemptioners" (another name for indentured servants) and apprentices were the true objects of the fugitive labor provision because their bondage was voluntarily contracted, while the legal condition of the slave barred him from such agency.

Finally, Douglass uses this trope of a man from another country—that figure of reading that necessarily separates a law's legislative intention as found in its text from the supposed "original intent" of its framers—to refer to the Constitution itself as a contract, or, in his words, "a bond":

If the slaveholders entered into this contract as a bargain, they also knew from its face that this constitution was liable to be construed in favor of freedom, and [they are] like Shylock, who stipulated for one pound of the flesh of Antonio (forgetting the blood) and, when the bond became due, through malice demanded its fulfillment [and] is told by the shrewd judge he may take the flesh if he can get it without the blood. I take this to be as sound a principle in law as in a play.[16]

Just as Douglass uses throughout his writings and speeches on the Constitution the "man from another country" as the figure for his "strict construction" close reading practice (which could not see "slave" or "slavery" in the letter of the law), he would use this figure of the bond to describe the

Constitution itself. Signifying on both the Constitution as original bond of union and the slave as bondsman—whose pound of flesh served as the terms for the constitutional compromise between free and slave states—he likewise links the slaveholder to the figure of the nonlaboring, unproductive moneylender: "In all matters where laws are taught to be made the means of oppression, cruelty, and wickedness, I am for strict construction. I will concede nothing. It must be shown that it is so nominated in the bond. The pound of flesh, but not one drop of blood."[17] If the "man from another country" foregrounds the textual invisibility of the slave and the absent presence of the bondsman in the Constitution, the "letter of the bond" emphasizes the strategic political value of the strict constructionist interpretation of the Constitution as founding contract: if slaveholders, like the moneylender Shylock, demand what is due to them according to that contract, then antislavery politicians and judges should answer them as did Shakespeare's judge, by adhering strictly to the letter of the bond. This likening of the Constitution to Shylock's bond was a classic instance of Douglass's appropriation of forms, what Houston Baker has called the "mastery of form, and the deformation of mastery," wherein one step in the black subject's struggle for freedom is the mastering of the master's discourse.[18] In their defenses of slavery, southern politicians repeatedly asserted that their property rights in slaves were guaranteed as part of the original bond of the Constitution, and that the Constitution was founded upon this compromise over their property right in slaves. This position held that black subjects were no parties to the original compact of the Constitution, but rather were the bondsmen over whose flesh the contract was signed.

A Secret History of the National Bond

One of the intellectual legacies of the Civil War and the victory of free-labor ideology is that the conception of the Constitution's slavery-sanctioning "original intent" is now a critical commonplace. However, while this historicist conception legitimated by Story's Supreme Court in *Prigg v. Pennsylvania* was the dominant interpretation in its time, it did not go uncontested, as the reading practice of Douglass's "man from another country" reveals. In order to understand the significance of the *Prigg* decision—and the significance of Frederick Douglass's radical shift during "the American 1848"—we must first historicize this dominant historicism, and then analyze that other, repressed ideological current represented by Douglass's "man from another country," the radical political abolitionists.[19]

From where did the historicists of "original intent" derive their understanding of the Constitution's "necessary compromises" to protect slavery? Partial records of the intentions of the constitutional framers were available as early as 1788, when the essays penned during the ratification debates by Madison, Hamilton, and Jay (under the shared name of Publius) were published together as *The Federalist*. More knowledge of the framers' shared recognition of slavery and of the debates over the wording of the Constitution became available in 1821, when anti-Federalist editors published the *Secret Proceedings and Debates of the Convention Assembled at Philadelphia, in the Year 1787*.[20] In the years 1827–30, the Republican historian (and "states' rights" partisan) Jonathan Eliot published *The Debates in the Several State Conventions on the Adoption of the Federal Constitution*. Eliot's *Debates* remained the primary resource on the historical circumstances of the Constitution's ratification until the 1840 publication of the *James Madison Papers*, containing his record of *The Debates in the Federal Convention of 1787*.[21] Even more than Eliot's *Debates*, which gathered together the debates of the state ratifying conventions, Madison's record of the federal convention came to be considered the most authoritative account of what had occurred behind closed doors in Philadelphia, and thus the main source for those laying claim to knowledge of the framers' "original intentions."

Finally, while it did not initiate this originalism, the Supreme Court decision in *Prigg v. Pennsylvania* established as the dominant legal construction the historicist understanding of the Constitution's slavery-sanctioning "original intent." The *Prigg* decision became a defining event in the escalating Union crisis, as it ruled on both the constitutionality of the 1793 Fugitive Slave Act and the unconstitutionality of Pennsylvania's 1826 personal liberty law.[22] These two aspects of the decision, on the extent of federal authority to enforce the Constitution's fugitive labor clause, and on the right of free states to limit such enforcement, further nationalized the slavery debates.

Significantly, Pennsylvania's 1826 personal liberty law did not officially oppose either the Constitution's fugitive-from-labor clause or the 1793 federal Fugitive Slave Act; rather, it was "an act to give effect to the provisions of the constitution relative to fugitives from labor, for the protection of free people of color, and to prevent kidnapping." In addition to protecting the rights of alleged fugitive slaves (and making any attempted rendition slow and difficult), the object of the 1826 act was to guard the rights of black citizens of Pennsylvania, home to one of the largest and most politically organized free black populations in the nation. As the title of the act indicates, its provisions incorporated the abolitionist argument that the laws of the slaveholding states jeopardized the "privileges and immunities" of all black citizens.

Indeed, the 1826 act was itself a revision of an 1820 law, whose history illuminates the broader historical and hermeneutic stakes of the *Prigg* case. Ignoring the provision against kidnapping contained in Pennsylvania's 1780 gradual emancipation act, slave catchers from the bordering slaveholding states of Maryland and Virginia regularly entered Pennsylvania and charged free blacks with being fugitive slaves. This practice underscored the narrow limits of black freedom in a slavery-sanctioning republic: under the 1793 federal Fugitive Slave Act, local magistrates were obligated to assist slave owners or their agents, while they could not conduct a full investigation or admit the testimony of the alleged fugitive slaves. As early as 1801, the American Convention for Promoting the Abolition of Slavery reported an increase in the incidence of kidnapping; even Richard Allen, one of the most prominent leaders of the free black community in Philadelphia, was seized by a southern slave catcher armed with an arrest warrant. When, after the War of 1812, the demand for slaves rose in the South, kidnapping grew into an even larger problem, and Philadelphia's free black community and the Pennsylvania Abolition Society agitated for a strengthening of the kidnapping law. The 1820 law, the result of this struggle, increased the penalties for convicted kidnappers (to imprisonment at hard labor for up to twenty-one years), and required slave catchers to obtain writs of arrest and certificates of removal from higher court officials.[23] The 1826 act "to prevent kidnapping" under which the slave catcher Edward Prigg was convicted was a revision of this 1820 law, after Maryland slaveholders argued it threatened their right to recapture their "fugitives from labor."

Considering the decision's effect on the broader hermeneutic debate over the Constitution's "slave" clauses, it is significant that *Prigg v. Pennsylvania* was not itself a fugitive slave case, but rather an appeal to overturn the conviction of a slave catcher. Edward Prigg, acting as the agent of a Maryland slaveholder, had found "alleged fugitive from labor" Margaret Morgan and her children in Pennsylvania, and in accordance with Pennsylvania law filed for a warrant to have her brought before the court to confirm her identity and then to have issued a certificate of removal.

While the judge authorized the arrest warrant, when the alleged fugitive was brought before the court, he "refused to take further cognisance of said case." Prigg then took Margaret Morgan and her children back to Maryland without obtaining the required certificate of removal, and was convicted for violating Pennsylvania's 1826 act "to prevent kidnapping." Perhaps because it was not a fugitive slave case, *Prigg v. Pennsylvania* has received less critical attention than the 1851 *Thomas Sims* case decided by Lemuel Shaw and the 1857 *Dred Scott* case decided by Roger Taney. Yet it was the *Prigg* decision that established the legal precedent and the interpretation of the Constitution's "original intent" respecting slavery, which both Lemuel Shaw and Roger Taney would cite in their infamous decisions. Indeed, while Chief Justice Taney, the southerner and ally of John C. Calhoun, has been subject to a great deal of criticism for his *Dred Scott* opinion, in many ways his interpretation of the Constitution merely elaborated upon the hermeneutic principles of Chief Justice Story, "the avowedly antislavery New Englander," in *Prigg v. Pennsylvania*.[24]

In order to understand the cultural history of this historicism, we should note that the *Prigg* plaintiff's argument took for granted the slavery-protecting "original intent" of the fugitive-from-labor clause. Based on the historical context of a "conflict of law, of opinions and of interests between the northern and southern states" during the Constitution's adoption, Prigg's lawyers asserted: "That provision, it is well known, was the result of mutual concessions in reference to the whole subject of slavery.... [The] north agreed to recognise and protect the existing institutions of the south; and for that very purpose, the clause in question was engrafted upon the constitution. The history of the times proves, that the south regarded and relied upon it, as an ample security to the owners of slave property."[25] What is significant to the legal and cultural understanding of the *Prigg* decision and its ramifications is that this "history of the times" cited by the lawyers for Prigg to prove the fugitive labor clause's original intent was drawn directly from Justice Story's exposition of this clause in book 3 of his celebrated *Commentaries on the Constitution of the United States*. There, Story explained: "This clause was introduced into the constitution solely for the benefit of the slave-holding states, to enable them to reclaim their fugitive slaves, who should have escaped into other states, where slavery was not tolerated."[26] The plaintiff's argument that the fugitive slave clause was "the result of mutual concessions" was likewise drawn directly from Story's *Commentaries*, which had described all the so-called slave clauses as "necessary sacrifices," and "compromises" for the sake of the Union. Describing, for example, what he called "the real and . . . very exciting controversy" over the inclusion of (three-fifths of) the slave population in the taxation and representation clause, Story declared: "The truth is, that the arrangement adopted by the constitution was a matter of compromise and concession . . . a necessary sacrifice to that spirit of conciliation, which was indispensable to the union of states having a great diversity of interests. . . . [He] who wishes well to his country, will adhere steadily to it, as a fundamental policy. . . . The wish of every patriot ought now to be, *requiescat in pace.*"[27] The *Prigg* case appealing the conviction of a slave catcher came before the Supreme Court because the Commonwealth of Pennsylvania had not, like good patriots, let the supposed slavery "compromise" rest in peace. What any historical analysis of the *Prigg* ruling must take into account, therefore, is that the historicist conception of the Constitution's "original" slavery-sanctioning intent argued by the lawyers for the slave catcher Prigg was established as the dominant interpretation in judicial thought by Justice Story himself, well before the question came before his Supreme Court.

Story's majority opinion in *Prigg* begins with these twin historicist assumptions elaborated in his *Commentaries*: that the fugitive labor clause was originally intended to protect the slaveholders' property rights, and that it was a compromise necessary to the formation of the Union:

> Historically, it is well known, that the object of this clause was to secure to the citizens of the slave-holding states the complete right and title of ownership in their slaves, as property, in every state in the Union into which they might escape from the state where they were held in servitude. The full recognition of this right and title was indispensable to the security of this species of property in all the slave-holding states; and, indeed, was so vital to the preservation of their domestic interests and institutions, that it cannot be doubted, that it constituted a fundamental article, without the adoption of which the Union could not have been formed.[28]

The *Prigg* decision "was a unanimous reinforcement of the characterization of Fugitive Slave rendition as an article of compromise."[29] However, because the entirety of Story's ruling proceeds from this historicist conception of the intended object of the fugitive labor clause, we must analyze the form of this content to understand the ways in which this "original" historical situation was itself constructed by Story:

> By the general law of nations, no nation is bound to recognise the state of slavery, as to foreign slaves found within its territorial dominions, when it is in opposition to its own policy and institutions, in favor of the subjects of other nations where slavery is recognized. If it does it, it is as a matter of comity, and not as a matter of international right. The state of slavery is deemed to be a mere municipal regulation, founded upon and limited to the range of the territorial laws. This was fully recognized in *Somerset's Case*... which decided before the American revolution. It is manifest, from this consideration, that if the constitution had not contained this clause, every non-slave-holding state in the Union would have been at liberty to have declared free all runaway slaves coming within its limits, and to have given them entire immunity and protection against the claims of their masters; a course which would have created the most bitter animosities, and engendered perpetual strife between the different states.... The clause was accordingly adopted into the constitution, by the unanimous consent of the framers of it; a proof at once of its intrinsic and practical necessity. (41 U.S. 539, 612)

Story's narrative of the clause's historical origins is based on the imagined threat to the property rights of slaveholders posed by the famous *Somerset Case* "decided before the American revolution." This reference to *Somerset v. Stewart* (1772) reveals the presentist concerns of Story's historicism. For while abolitionists had long used the famous *Somerset* decision as precedent for their legal strategy, no reference to *Somerset* was made by the framers in their (altogether very brief) discussion of the fugitive-from-labor clause. Story's historical narrative took the prominence of the *Somerset* principle—that slavery, as the artificial creation of positive law was thus "limited to the range of the territorial laws"—from the slavery debates of his own time, and projected onto the minds of the framers this fear that escaped slaves might be "declared free" once they entered the legal boundaries of a nonslaveholding state.[30] This retroactively projected fear of the implications of the *Somerset* precedent then serves in Story's narrative as the primary motive behind the writing of the "fugitive slave clause," which then becomes the clause's sole "object and intent."

Significant also to our understanding of this historicism is that Story bases his view of the fugitive labor clause's historical "intrinsic and practical necessity" on a counterfactual history, on a past that never was: "if the constitution had not contained this clause, every non-slave-holding state in the Union would have been at liberty to have declared free all runaway slaves coming within its limits . . . a course which would have created the most bitter animosities, and engendered perpetual strife between the different states."[31] Narrating in the past conditional, Story discovers the origins of the fugitive labor clause in an unreal past—"if the constitution had not contained this clause"—and in the sequence of events, ending in perpetual strife, this alternative history would have engendered. Story grounds the fugitive labor clause's original intent, and its historical necessity as an article of compromise, in a counterfactual history proceeding from the clause's absence, in a possible past that, according to Story, inevitably would have occurred if not for its presence. Story thus legitimates the dominant slavery-sanctioning construction of the fugitive clause by claiming the history based on such a construction to be better than that turbulent alternative history imagined by him.

Story's recourse to counterfactual history highlights again the presentist concerns of this historicism. As with his reference to *Somerset*, Story projects the federal judiciary's concern over "the bitter animosities" engendered by the slavery debates of his own time onto the minds of the founders, and imagines them in that historical moment, with all their foresight, to have recognized what would have happened if not for this compromise to protect the slaveholders' property rights in their fugitive slaves. Similarly, Story takes the absence of extended debate over the fugitive rendition clause (in contrast, for example, to the long debates over the three-fifths clause and the migration and importation clause) as indicative of the "unanimous consent of the framers," which in turn serves as positive "proof at once of its intrinsic and practical necessity."[32]

Proceeding from this historical context constructed to explain the clause's "well known" object and intent, Story also ruled the fugitive clause to be self-executing:

> The clause manifestly contemplates the existence of a positive, unqualified right on the part of the owner of the slave, which no state law or regulation can in any way qualify, regulate, control or restrain. . . . If this be so, then all the incidents to that right attach also. The owner must, therefore, have the right to seize and repossess the slave, which the local laws of his own state confer upon him, as property. . . . Upon this ground, we have not the slightest hesitation in holding, that under and in virtue of the constitution, the owner of a slave is clothed with entire authority, in every state in the Union, to seize and recapture his slave, whenever he can do it, without any breach of the peace or any illegal violence. In this sense, and to this extent,

this clause of the constitution may properly be said to execute itself, and to require no aid from legislation, state or national.[33]

Interpreting the clause as a guarantee of the slaveholder's right to "seize and recapture his slave" in every state of the Union, Story ruled that "the slaveholder, in short, carried the laws of his own state with him when he pursued a fugitive into a free state."[34]

This granting of the *extraterritoriality* of the slaveholder's right to recapture his slave resounded throughout the antislavery movement because it "had the effect ... of compelling free states to accept the slave-state principle that a [black person] or mulatto was a slave unless he could prove otherwise."[35] Ostensibly addressing only the slaveholder's right of remedy as one of the "incidents" attached to his right of property, this aspect of the decision reinforced the *racialization* of legal-formal freedom: even the black citizens of free states would be presumed fugitive slaves. We should recall here David Walker's famous statement on the limitations of black freedom in a nation that sanctioned racial slavery: "If any of you wish to know how 'free' you are, let one of you start and go thro' the southern and western States of this country, and unless you ... have your free papers (which if you are not careful they will get from you) if they do not take you up and put you in jail, and if you cannot give evidence of your freedom, sell you into eternal slavery, I am not a living man."[36] By declaring "the owner of a slave clothed with entire authority in every state in the union" and nationalizing the presumption of slavery, Story thus stamped every free black person in the Union with the "badge of the slave."[37]

Further, in declaring Congress's 1793 Fugitive Slave Act constitutional, Story dismissed the argument made by counsel for the Commonwealth of Pennsylvania that the 1793 act violated the personal rights of free blacks, guaranteed to them as citizens by the privileges and immunities clause (Article IV, Section 2) and by the due-process clause of the Fifth Amendment. Coupled with the nationalization of the presumption of slavery, the Court's disregard for this argument further attenuated the already precarious character of the formal freedom of black citizens, for under it, those claimed as "alleged fugitives" were denied fundamental constitutional protections guaranteed to all citizens.

The Story Court's *Prigg* decision thus not only underscored the truth of David Walker's insight that the freedom of black Americans was "the most servile and abject kind," it also declared unconstitutional Pennsylvania's attempts to guard this already precarious formal freedom.[38] Long before Chief Justice Taney in *Dred Scott v. Sanford*, Chief Justice Story's *Prigg* opinion (with which Taney concurred) wrote a narrative of the Union whose only problem was the escape of slaves, not the kidnapping of black citizens. Indeed, Story's narrative of the "necessity" of the constitutional "compromise" over the fugitive slave clause ignores entirely the existence of free blacks and the long history of infringements of their citizenship rights. The Story Court thus reinforced the historical narrative of the Constitution's slavery "compromises" by erasing black citizenship from the nation's history, and the legal fact of black enslavement displaced the historical fact of black freedom.

While proceeding from what the history of black citizenship revealed to be a partial historicism, Story's construction of the fugitive labor clause's "original intent" solidified the cultural authority of the "historical-necessity thesis," that the constitutional compact would not have been ratified without such slavery compromises.[39] This narrative constructed within the legal sphere became the dominant narrative in the wider culture. As I have noted, Story had elaborated this thesis in his *Commentaries on the Constitution*, and he popularized it further through his *A Familiar Exposition of the Constitution* (1840), designed for wide circulation as the nation's first civics textbook.[40]

However, it was Story's employment of this historicist conception in the 1842 *Prigg* decision, placing "the full weight of Constitutional legitimacy behind the clause," that would "split antislavery legal forces."[41] On one side of this split stood Wendell Phillips and the Garrisonians, who accepted this "original intent" interpretation of the Constitution as a bond of compromise, and subsequently declared the moral obligation "to declare the contract at an end" and break from such a "covenant with death, and agreement with hell."[42] On the other side of this split, political abolitionism was itself divided. As I have noted, moderate antislavery constitutionalists such as Salmon Chase also accepted the historicist conception of compromise, yet argued for the Constitution's antislavery "original intent." As I discuss in the next section, radical antislavery constitutionalists rejected this form of historicism altogether as an abuse of history, declaring Story and the Court to be "nearly as false to the history of the clause as they are to its law," and argued for the unconstitutionality of slavery on the basis of "strict construction."[43]

Following the 1842 *Prigg* decision's unanimous reinforcement of the historical-necessity thesis, Wendell Phillips in 1844 presented evidence for this view in *The Constitution: A Pro-Slavery Compact; Selections from the Madison Papers*, a compilation of all those extracts from *Eliot's Debates* and the *Madison Papers* having to do with slavery (references to which Phillips, Justice Story's former law student at Harvard, most likely obtained from Story's *Commentaries* and his *Prigg* opinion). Phillips's *A Pro-Slavery Compact* was presented as an answer to those political abolitionists such as Gerrit Smith and William Goodell (among the radical constitutionalists), and Salmon Chase (among the moderates), who were, according to Phillips, ignoring or selectively citing the historical record to claim antislavery intentions for the Constitution. "Now these pages prove," Phillips asserted, "the melancholy fact that willingly, with deliberate purpose, our fathers bartered honesty for gain and became partners with tyrants."[44] In the introduction, I analyzed Madison's record of *The Debates in the Federal Convention of 1787* in order to trace what they reveal about the role of the bondsman in the constitution of the legal-political subject, the citizen. Here what is noteworthy for cultural and legal history is the particular rhetorical battle cited by Phillips, and the broader discursive situation signaled by the publication of *A Pro-Slavery Compact*. With the circulation of Madison's *Notes on the Federal Convention* through Phillips's *A Pro-Slavery Compact*, the views of the framers became widely available, leaving the chambers of Story's Court, and as a consequence the political debate over constitutional recognitions of slavery became even more complicated by the debates over "original intent." In this way, the hermeneutic question of discovering the "letter and the spirit" of the law, while not new to legal history, first emerged as a problem for the United States' culture of constitutionalism in the midst of these debates over the constitutionality of slavery.

"As False to History as They Are to the Law"

Much has been written of the anticonstitutionalist Garrisonians and of the moderate antislavery constitutionalists, most likely because their conception of the framers' "original compromise" over slavery accords with the dominant post–Civil War understanding.[45] Less attention has been given to the "strict construction" position of the radical antislavery constitutionalists, which in its adherence to the words of the text alone and in its rejection of (a certain form of) historicism, may appear rather counterintuitive. In *Justice Accused*, Robert Cover characterizes the radical antislavery constitutionalists as "Constitutional utopians" and dismisses them as a "handful of relatively unimportant antislavery thinkers."[46] Taking Lysander Spooner's 1845 *The Unconstitutionality of Slavery* as "the most complete of the arguments for the utopians," Cover describes it as substantively reliant on natural law theory, and "amputated from societal context." Agreeing with William Lloyd Garrison's condemnation of it ("The important thing is not the words of the bargain, but the bargain itself"), Cover, as with most legal historians of the antebellum debates over slavery, accepts the dominant view of the Constitution's slavery-sanctioning original intent articulated by Justice Story: "The position that slavery, itself, was unconstitutional was so extreme as to appear trivial."[47] According to Cover, the true purpose of the argument made by these "radical" utopians "was not to prove slavery unconstitutional (whatever that means in a confessedly utopian context) but to prove that antislavery men may become judges and may use their power to free slaves."[48]

Cover's characterization of these "Constitutional utopians" as a "handful of relatively unimportant antislavery thinkers" is misleading in several ways. First, its historical claim is incorrect. William Goodell's 1844 pamphlet *Views of American Constitutional Law*, introducing the principal ideas of the radical constitutionalists, circulated widely in more than thirteen thousand copies, with a second edition published in 1845, and Goodell was at the center of their political organizing.[49] The publication of Goodell's *Views* signaled a major political split within the antislavery ranks; and Wendell Phillips, recognized as the legal mind of the Garrisonians, responded to its claims (and the claims of other political abolitionists) with *The Constitution: A Pro-Slavery Compact; Extracts from the Madison Papers*. Lysander Spooner's 1845 *Unconstitutionality of Slavery*, which extended the constitutional arguments of Goodell's *Views*, was also extremely popular, so much so that Wendell Phillips wrote a detailed series of responses to it in the American Anti-Slavery Society's newspaper, the *National Anti-Slavery Standard*, and republished these in extended book form as *A Review of Lysander Spooner's Essay on the Unconstitutionality of Slavery* (1847).[50] Indeed, while Spooner was not as central an activist figure as Phillips, Goodell, or Chase, his constitutional hermeneutic influenced many in the antislavery movement, such as the one-time Garrisonian Frederick Douglass, who cited Spooner in his 1851 "Change of Opinion" and throughout his writings on the Constitution thereafter—and, more importantly, incorporated both the substance and the form of the constitutional hermeneutic articulated by Spooner and Goodell.

Also, Cover's dismissal of the argument of the radical antislavery constitutionalists as wholly reliant upon natural law theory ignores its sustained engagements with constitutional hermeneutics more generally and with the legal "construction" of the slave clauses in particular. Lysander Spooner's argument for "strict construction" of the letter as opposed to an imagined "original intent" derived from "contemporaneous exposition," and his rereading of the Constitution's "slave" clauses, had profound effects on the language of antislavery debate and the development of political abolitionism, as well the development of free-labor ideology. As we will see, these interpretations also reveal a great deal about the changing conceptions of social and civic personhood caused by the struggles over both slave and "free" waged labor. Finally, then, the critical dismissal of Spooner and the "utopians" fails to grasp the complexity of transformations in legal-political thought wrought by the wide spectrum of debates in the antislavery struggle. Law and labor historians (and, following their lead, literary critics), by reading through the lens of this dominant historicism—of the Story Court; of the disunionist Garrisonians; and of "free soil, free labor" politicians such as Chase and Lincoln—ignore those historical contingencies involved in that crisis of constitutional interpretation, and its transformation of conceptions of social and civic personhood, produced by the slavery debates. Goodell, Spooner, Douglass, and others who argued this more "radical" position on the unconstitutionality of slavery were committed to persuading others that their interpretation of the letter and the spirit of the Constitution was the correct one, and to the belief that although the Constitution had been given, since its moment of inscription, a proslavery construction, it could likewise be given an antislavery construction. This was precisely what Douglass suggested in his 1849 critique of Calhoun's "Southern Address." To appreciate the radical contingency of history itself, we should remember that in 1844 (the year of Goodell's *Views* and Phillips's *A Pro-Slavery Compact*) and 1851 (when Douglass published his "Change of Opinion"), the Civil War was over a decade away, and the question of slavery's constitutionality was very far from being answered. Indeed, we should recall that this question of the Constitution's "original intent" regarding slavery was never answered in theory, and instead decided by the violence of America's Civil War. We can retain Cover's naming of these "radical Constitutionalists" as "utopian," then, but in that political sense of a position which imagines an alternative to the dominant ideological closures of the present. It is in this sense that I read the radical antislavery constitutionalists, and Fredrick

Douglass's adaptations of them, as political tactics innovated to meet the contingencies of the American 1848.

The antislavery constitutionalists' intervention was to demonstrate both the legal and the historical mistakes of the dominant historicism represented by Story's Supreme Court. As Spooner argues in "A Defense for Fugitive Slaves" (1850), the historicist interpretation of the fugitive labor clause's "original intent," which Chief Justice Story used as the basis of his *Prigg* ruling, contradicted Story's own principles of legal interpretation. Instead of finding legislative intention in the words of the law, Story "discard[ed] all other rules of interpretation ... resorting to history to make the clause apply to the slaves. And yet no judge has ever scouted more contemptuously than Story the idea of going out of the words of a law, or the constitution, and being governed by what history may say were the intentions of the authors."[51]

To demonstrate the extent of Story's deviation in *Prigg* from his own rules of interpretation, Spooner quotes from Story's extensive remarks in his *Commentaries on the Constitution* "as to the absurdity of relying on 'history' for the meaning of the constitution" or any other legal instrument:

> He [Story, in his *Commentaries*] says: "Such a doctrine would be novel and absurd. It would confuse and destroy all the tests of constitutional rights and authorities.... Besides, what possible means can there be of making such investigations? The motives of many of the members may be, nay, must be, utterly unknown, and incapable of ascertainment by any judicial or other inquiry." 2 *Story's Comm.*, 534[52]

This aspect of Story's own critique of "original intent" was epistemological: the intentions of a law cannot be located in the imagined "motives" of the legislators because such motives "must be utterly unknown, and incapable of ascertainment." As Story elaborated, if the Constitution's meaning were grounded in the unknowable intentions of such individuals, the "constitution would thus depend upon processes utterly vague, and incomprehensible; and the written intent of the legislature upon its words and acts, the *lex scripta*, would be contradicted or obliterated by conjecture, and parole declarations, and fleeting reveries, and heated imaginations. No government on earth could rest for a moment on such a foundation. It would be a constitution of sand heaped up and dissolved by the flux and reflux of every tide of opinion."[53] Because the stability of government requires certainty in the meaning of its laws, Story here contrasts the uncertainties of individual memory with the certainty of the written instrument, of the *lex scripta*. What necessarily follows is that "every act of the legislature [and, for the same reason, every clause of the Constitution] must, therefore, be judged of from its objects and intent, as they are embodied in its provisions."[54] The object and intent of a law—its signifying "spirit"—are to be found solely in the words of its text.

Story's *Commentaries* likewise emphasized his opposition to the "absurd doctrine" of locating *legislative* intention—the intentions of the law—in the minds of its drafters, even if historical records of their expressed intentions existed. Spooner quotes Story's arguments against using the recorded debates of either the state ratifying conventions (as contained in Eliot's *Debates*) or the federal convention (as contained in the *Madison Papers*):

> *The constitution was adopted by the people of the United States*; and it was submitted to the whole, upon a just survey of its provisions, as they stood *in the text itself*. . . . And there can be no certainty either that the different state conventions, in ratifying the constitution, gave the same uniform interpretation to its language. . . . It is not to be presumed that even in the convention which framed the constitution . . . the clauses were always understood in the same sense, or had precisely the same extent of operation. Every member necessarily judged for himself; and the judgment of no one could, or ought to be, conclusive upon that of others. . . . *Nothing but the text itself was adopted by the people.*—1 Story's Comm. on Const., 287 to 392.[55]

In quoting Story's opposition to the use of the recorded history of individual framers' intentions to determine *legislative* intent, Spooner separates the authority of the Constitution as a written document from the aura of the founders; he is also addressing those historicists among the Garrisonians, free-soilers, and slaveholders who cited these historical records as evidence of the framers' original "compromise" over slavery.

Because it was the Story Court's *Prigg* decision that established the dominance of the "historical-necessity thesis" in the slavery debates, Spooner sought to demonstrate the extent to which Story's ruling was a "fraud," in defiance of the very rules of construction Story himself insisted upon throughout his *Commentaries*. As Story stated unequivocally in his *Commentaries*, the Constitution must be construed according to the words of its text because "nothing but the text itself was adopted by the people," and the imagined motives of the framers have nothing to do with the meaning of this written document. Spooner was well aware that Story opposed (at least in theory) the use of historical circumstances or motives in determining the "object and intent" of a law, as Spooner had cited Story's *Commentaries* as legal authority throughout his systematic explanation of "strict construction" in *The Unconstitutionality of Slavery*.[56] Yet in order to rule in favor of the slaveholders' extraterritorial property rights in the *Prigg* case, Justice Story, the "avowedly anti-slavery New Englander," had disregarded his own rules of interpretation, searching outside the letter of the Constitution's text to find its intentions, and using a history written by slaveholders to determine the slavery-sanctioning "spirit" of its law.

Spooner concludes this criticism of Story's failure of jurisprudential principle with a critique of its "false" history: "Story and the court, in saying that history tells us that the clause of the constitution in question was intended to apply to fugitive slaves, are nearly as false to the history of the clause as they are to its law."[57] Citing those records of the debates so favored by the historicists of "original intent," Spooner points out:

> In the national convention, "Mr. Butler and Mr. Pinckney moved to require 'fugitive slaves and servants to be delivered up like criminals.'" "Mr. Sherman saw no more propriety in the public seizing and surrendering a slave or servant than a horse."—*Madison Papers*, 1447–8. In consequence of this objection, the provision was changed, and its language, as it now stands, shows that the claim to the surrender of slaves was abandoned, and only the one for servants retained.[58]

Reinterpreting the fugitive labor clause's much-cited original scene of inscription, Spooner focuses on that ellipsis between the proposal of the provision and its final written form: the slaves' literal disappearance from the final language of the law registers the abandonment of the slaveholders' claim to their "surrender," while the remaining language of servitude ("held to service or labor") demonstrates the retention of the original claim to the rendition of fugitive servants.

This alternative reading of the clause's historical "circumstances" is a legal-cultural history from below, recovering what the dominant historicism of Story ignores—the intertwined material histories of slavery and indentured servitude as related forms of labor bondage—and focuses on the *agency of the letter* in the constitution of legal subjects. In their argument for "strict construction," the radical antislavery constitutionalists were pursuing those very rules of construction that Justice Story had detailed so thoroughly in the *Commentaries* (even as he made exception to these rules in this same study when it came to the Constitution's "intentions" regarding slavery). Yet what also becomes evident is that this was not merely a difference in rules of interpretation, but rather differing conceptions of history: of its material economic determinations and of how such determinations were made visible or invisible, according to the historian's narrative point of view. Whereas Story could only see escaped slaves in the fugitive labor clause (despite the glaring absence of the word from its letter), Spooner focused on the bonds of labor shared by slaves and indentured servants, and on the significant differences in the legal language describing their subjection and labor exploitation: "service" is not slavery. In the case of the Constitution's so-called slave clauses, the difference that matters is that between the property in labor and the property in persons.

Bonds of Labor

Adhering to those rules of legal interpretation detailed by Story in his *Commentaries* (yet disregarded by Story when it came to the slaveholder's extraterritorial property rights in the *Prigg* case), the radical antislavery constitutionalists argued for the "strict construction" of the Constitution as a written instrument. Because the Constitution's clause for the rendition of fugitive labor became, after *Prigg*, the provision most cited by both proslavery forces and Garrisonian abolitionists as one of its slavery "guarantees," Goodell's *Views on American Constitutional Law* and Spooner's *The Unconstitutionality of Slavery* both begin their arguments with an analysis of its language.

Reading the letter of the fugitive labor clause from the perspective of "strict construction," Goodell first focuses on the terms "service or labor." Quoting from the slaveholding states' own laws defining the slave, Goodell argues: "The phrase 'held to service or labor' does not describe the legal condition of the slave. He is held as '*property*,' '*goods and chattels personal*'; but the law knows nothing, and has nothing to say or to prescribe, concerning his service or uselessness."[59] Spooner argues similarly: "'Held to service or labor,' is no legal description of slavery. Slavery is property in man. It is not necessarily attended with either 'service or labor.... The 'laws' take no note of whether a slave 'labors' or not."[60] The dominant slavery-sanctioning argument of "necessary compromise" was articulated as a defense of the slaveholder's rights of property in the slave. Answering this claim, Goodell and Spooner point to the fact that while slave laws define the slave as property, they say nothing of the "use" value of this property, "nothing concerning his labor or his idleness."[61] Indeed, as Goodell points out, this legal distinction between slaves as chattel property and slaves as laborers was demonstrated by the slave market itself, in the selling of slave women for sex: "The highest priced slaves, those commanding incomparably the largest sums of money in the market, are 'held,' bought and sold for other purposes than labor, purposes altogether incompatible with it!" Goodell argues further that while the slave may be defined in law as property, such a condition does not entail any obligations to "service or labor": "The phrase supposes a *legal obligation* to labor which cannot rest on the slave. The law requires no labor of him, whatever his *master* may do."[62] And as Spooner elaborates: "If the slave refuses to labor, the law will not interfere to compel him. The law simply recognizes the master's right of property in the slave.... Having done that, it leaves the master to compel the slave.... In short, it recognizes no obligation, on the part of the slave, to labor, if he can avoid doing so."[63] While the law may protect the slaveholder's property rights in the slave, it leaves the slaveholder to force the slave to labor. We should recall in this context Henry Highland Garnet's revolutionary call, in his 1843 "Address to the Slaves," for America's 3 million slaves to immediately "cease to labor for tyrants who will not remunerate you."[64] As Garnet, Goodell, and Spooner understood, a slave's labor was distinct from his person. In Garnet's "Address," this distinction became the basis of his conception of slave agency: slaves could refuse to labor for those who owned their persons, even if this refusal meant facing death.

Goodell and Spooner pursue the implications of this absence in slavery law, of the slave's "legal obligation" to labor by turning to the other key terms of the fugitive labor clause: "'On *claim* of the party to whom such service or labor may be *due*.'—Nothing can be legally *due* from a slave to his master.... 'The slave can make no contract,' and hence, nothing can be '*due*' from him."[65] And Spooner, highlighting again that the relation of master and slave is one of property ownership: "the laws "will enforce no 'claim' of a master, upon his slave, for 'service or labor.'"[66] Just as slave laws recognize the slave as property yet say nothing of the slave's obligations to "service or labor," the terms of the Constitution's fugitive labor clause, while saying nothing of property in man, recognize only *contractual* claims to debt, to service or labor legally owed.

Goodell and Spooner here build upon the "rise of contract" as that legal form central to the law's definition of freedom. Even if one were to concede the slaveholders' point, following James Madison's oft-quoted argument in *The Federalist No. 54*, that slaves were recognized by positive law "in the mixed character of persons and property," the fact remained that slaves were considered "incapable of contract" by the slaveholders' own laws.[67] As George Stroud noted in his extensive survey of the laws of the American slave states, this legal principle—that the slave was incapable of contract—predominated in the laws of all the slave states.[68] Such a legal disability made them likewise incapable of "debt": "Master and slave can not be creditor and debtor.... This [fugitive] clause ... proceeds upon the basis of *self ownership* in the person held to labor, and makes its provisions applicable only to a debtor in law, who, in order to *owe* the creditor, must own himself."[69] While free-labor ideology developed by defining the freedom of wage labor in contrast to the visible bondage of slavery, radical antislavery constitutionalism drew upon these constitutive terms of "free labor" to present the slave as standing outside the relations of contract, whose parties were persons bound by obligation and debt, and thus outside those bonds described in the Constitution's fugitive labor clause. Capitalizing on both the absence of slavery's terms of subjection and the presence of words instead descriptive of freely contracting subjects, the strict construction of the fugitive labor clause revealed that "all such language is inapplicable to the slave."[70]

Yet in the context of the debate over the Constitution's meaning, this negative critique regarding the fugitive labor clause's inapplicability to the slave was necessary but insufficient; a more probable referent for the clause's terms must be posited. If this constitutional clause did not bind the slave, if the fugitive slave eluded its reach, to whom would it apply? Goodell's answer again invokes the bonds of contract, and in doing so recovers that third term I have traced throughout the present study, the *supplement* to both slavery and free labor: "The clause does describe a condition, familiarly known among us ... persons 'from whom such service or labor may be due' because they *may* have contracted to perform it, or because due to parents or guardians; ... persons who may wish to 'escape' from the obligations believed to be resting on them.... Such is the condition of the apprentice, the minor, the contractor of job work, the debtor, who is held to service or labor by the terms of his own voluntary agreement."[71] Here the fugitive is not a slave escaping from the bondage of a master, but a servant escaping the obligations of a contract. Indentured servitude mediates the legal distinctions between slavery and free labor because it is a form of labor bondage whose subjects are recognized in law as "free"; indeed, such servitude is legally binding solely because its subjects are recognized as free, self-owning persons capable of contract, understood to have bound themselves "by voluntary agreement" and thus owing "service or labor."

The local significance of indentured servitude and apprenticeship to Goodell's argument is that it offered an alternative referent for the words of the fugitive rendition clause. Insofar as the terms of the clause entail contract, obligation, and debt, this alternative referent also made greater textual sense than the proslavery interpretation, which must not only ignore this language but also assume intentions ulterior to the text of the law. According to "strict construction," then, this interpretation must be taken as the fugitive labor clause's true *legislative intent*: "'Strict construction' will not permit the supposition that the Constitution means a slave, when its framers, whatever their intentions might be, took such special care not to say that they meant it, but actually said the contrary."[72] The broader significance of this claim to the historical and theoretical concerns of this chapter arises from its insight that the legal "contrary" of the slave is the servant, escaping obligations and debts that can only pertain to a "free" person. Even more than free-labor ideology's wage laborer, the indentured servant, as the figure of the *free* bondsman, serves to delimit the attributes and disabilities of personhood ascribed to the slave. If free-labor ideology developed in contrast to the unfree labor of chattel slavery, the legal condition of this latter unfreedom was itself defined as the conceptual "contrary" of the formally free labor of indentured servitude.

Goodell's reading of the clause is also revealing of the conception of "race" in these antebellum constitutional debates. In a footnote to his positing of servitude as that labor form described in the fugitive clause, Goodell adds: "This view of the subject [that the clause refers to indentured servants] is moreover confirmed and additional force is given to the idea that the peculiar condition of the slave is not described in the clause, when we remember that no allusion is made to *the color* commonly supposed to be the badge of the slave, and of those that may be claimed as such."[73] As a supplement to the positive claim that the clause's true referent is indentured servitude, this point illuminates another aspect of the dialectic of visibility operating in the law. In one of the earliest uses of the phrase "the badge of the slave" in the context of U.S. racial formations, Goodell cites "color" as that "commonly supposed" evidence of whether a person was a slave. "Color" became "the badge of the slave" because under the racial slavery of the United States it was the most visible form of evidence. As such, it demonstrates how "race," an aspect of social personhood ostensibly distinct from the legal personhood of the citizen, became in the antebellum era structurally linked to this legal form. Black citizens, while formally free, became always-already identified as slaves because they shared this "badge of the slave." As we observed in *Prigg v. Pennsylvania*, Justice Story's majority *Prigg* decision had extended this racialization of civic freedom by affirming the extraterritoriality of the slaveholder's right of recapture and thus effectively nationalizing the presumption of slavery based on color.

Further, those aspects of citizenship composing the formal freedom of black Americans—rights of property, of mobility, of *habeas corpus*, of trial by jury, of testimony—were all abridged by the laws enacted to protect slavery. Consider, for example, the first clause of Article IV, Section 2: "The citizens of each State shall be entitled to all the privileges and immunities of citizens, in the several States."[74] Goodell reads this clause to argue that the "laws of all, or nearly all the slave States, or the regulations and ordinances of cities within those States and under State authority, are in *direct violation* of the above provision of the Constitution, so far as free citizens of color are concerned."[75] As he points out, "many of the 'citizens' in some of the States, are free people of color. They are recognized as citizens by the Constitution and Laws of the States wherein they reside. Large numbers of them are legal voters and vote at Presidential as well as State elections. They are eligible, and are sometimes elected to office." The slave states are in direct violation of the Constitution because their laws deny the black citizens of free states "all privileges and immunities of citizens in the several states" to which they are "entitled" by this founding law. Free blacks "can not visit the slave States without being subjected to violations of their rights as citizens. . . . If they visit the Southern seaports in coasting vessels, as seamen, they are seized and put in prison."[76]

In addition to these southern laws designed specifically for free blacks, the rights of black citizens were violated by the laws designed for slaves: "Any such citizen of a free State, visiting a slave State, is liable to be seized on suspicion of being a fugitive from slavery . . . and unless able . . . to make satisfactory proof of his freedom, sold into perpetual slavery."[77] While not intended for free blacks, the "fugitive slave" laws violated the rights of black citizens by restricting their freedom of mobility throughout the United States (and subjecting them to the possibility of enslavement) solely because they were of "the color commonly supposed to be the badge of the slave." This was especially true after the *Prigg* ruling on the extraterritoriality of the slaveholder's right of recapture, entailing the nationalization of the slave states' laws presuming any black person to be a slave. Such slave laws thus underscore not only the tenuous nature of the "privileges and immunities" of black citizens but also the precariousness of their formal freedom itself, revealing it to be what Olaudah Equiano had called a "but nominal liberty" and "a mockery of freedom," and what David Walker had called "the very dregs . . . the most servile and abject kind" of freedom.[78]

While Goodell's argument that indentured servants were those fugitives named in the clause proceeded from an interpretation of the terms "held to service or labor" as indicating a labor form "familiarly known" to his contemporaries in the 1840s, Spooner gives greater legal precision and historical support to the "strict construction" argument by grounding his interpretation in the meanings of the clause's terms as they were legally defined and "commonly understood" during the historical moment of the Constitution's ratification: "The proper definition of the word 'service' . . . is the labor of a servant. And we find, that at and before the adoption of the Constitution, the persons recognized by the State laws as 'servants,' constituted a numerous class. The statute books abounded with statutes in regard to 'servants.'"[79] And whereas Goodell referred only to the apprenticeship and contract labor still prevalent in the 1840s to explain application of the clause, Spooner refers explicitly to indentured servitude and bases the "original" signification of the fugitive labor clause in the history of indentured servitude as a widespread labor form:

> Many seemed to have been indented as servants by the public authorities, on account of their being supposed incompetent, by reason of youth and poverty, to provide for themselves. Many were doubtless indented as apprentices by their parents and guardians, as now. The English laws recognized a class of servants—and many were brought here from England, in that character. . . . Many indented and contracted themselves as servants for the payment of their passage money to this country.[80]

These claims for the historical signification of the fugitive clause's terms of labor are essential to an accurate understanding of radical antislavery constitutionalism and its role in the transformation of legal conceptions of enslaved and free personhood during the Union crisis. They did not deny the nation's history of recapturing fugitive slaves, but argued that "the fact that slavery was tolerated ... is no evidence of its legality," and through a historically grounded "strict construction" demonstrated its unconstitutionality.[81] This strict construction was not an absolute textualism or empty formalism, "amputated from societal context"; on the contrary, it strove to demonstrate that its interpretation was more historically accurate than the opposing (and dominant) slavery-sanctioning construction.[82] As we saw in *Prigg v. Pennsylvania*, this slavery-sanctioning interpretation looked past the letter of the law to the historical circumstances surrounding the writing of the fugitive labor clause, and then used this (imagined) historical "context" to determine its "original intent." In contrast, strict construction's close reading of the letter of the law reveals the historical signification of its words, thus recovering the repressed material history of that labor bondage which stood between chattel slavery and free labor.

Immediately following this grounding of the clause's terms in the historical context of indentured servitude's recognition as "a prominent subject of legislation," Spooner points out that the Constitution itself confirms this historical truth: "Indeed, no other evidence of their number is necessary than the single fact, that 'persons bound to service for a term of years,' were especially noticed by the constitution of the United States, (Art 1, Sec. 2,) which requires that they be counted as units in making up the basis of representation."[83] While the meaning of "service" in the fugitive labor clause was debatable, its meaning in the important representation (and taxation) apportionment clause was not; all sides agreed that "those bound to service" in the apportionment clause referred to indentured servants. The Constitution's recognition of indentured servants as political economic subjects (counting them for the purposes of representation and taxation) thus serves, like the contemporaneous state statute books and English laws, as historical evidence of the "prominence" of indentured labor at the time of the Constitution's adoption. Further, the undisputed fact that the phrase "those *bound* to service for a term of years" in the representation apportionment clause refers to indentured servants would make Spooner's interpretation of "*held* to service or labor" in the fugitive-from-labor clause, as likewise referring to indentured servants, the most historically probable and textually coherent. As Spooner elaborates in "A Defense for Fugitive Slaves":

> The word "held" being, in law, synonymous with the word, "*bound*," the description, "person *held* to service or labor," is synonymous with the description in another section, (Art. 1, Sec. 2) to wit, "those *bound* to service for a term of years."... In fact, everybody, courts and people, admit that "persons *bound* to service for a term of years," as apprentices, and other indented servants, are to be delivered up under the provision relative to 'persons *held* to service or labor.[84]

In a closing footnote to this alternative labor history of the fugitive rendition clause, Spooner cites the debates of the constitutional convention as further evidence of the historical recognition of indentured servitude:

> In the convention that framed the constitution, when this clause was under discussion, "servants" were spoken of as a distinct class from "slaves." For instance "Mr. Butler and Mr. Pickney moved to require 'fugitive slaves *and servants* to be delivered up like criminals.'" Mr. Sherman objected to delivering up either slaves or servants.—*Madison Papers*, p. 1447-8.[85]

Even from the erroneous perspective of the proslavery argument that "intentions" expressed in the debates of the convention should determine the *legislative intent* of the law, their resulting interpretation of it would be incorrect. For what the records of these debates show is that the framers understood the legal difference between "service" and slavery; underscoring once again the partial historicism of the original intentionalists, who, searching through these very debates in their hunt for the slave, ignore the presence of the servant. Further, if those very records cited by the original intentionalists show that the framers distinguished between servants and slaves during discussion of the clause's wording, the "language finally adopted shows that they at last agreed to deliver up '*servants*,' but *not 'slaves'*—for as the word 'servant' does not mean 'slave,' the word 'service' does not mean slavery."[86] In Spooner's interpretation of this historical scene of inscription, the slave and the servant both may have been the proposed subjects of the fugitive labor clause, but in that ellipsis between the proposal's original motion and the "language finally adopted," the slave disappeared, leaving only the fugitive servant as that laborer subject to its law. As we saw, Spooner would use this same historical point in his 1850 critique of the Story Court's "false history" in *Prigg v. Pennsylvania*. This history from below made visible what indentured servitude shared with slavery—the condition of servile labor—as well as what distinguished it from slavery: the principle of property. Whereas slaves were recognized in law as property, servants were recognized as self-owning, and thus able to sell the only property they held in their personhood, their labor.

The Letter and the Spirit

Inspired most likely by the *Prigg* case, Goodell presented his *Views of American Constitutional Law* in the rhetorical frame of a trial adjudicating a contract dispute, with the two opposing interpretations of the Constitution (proslavery and antislavery) represented as claimants.[87] Through this rhetorical frame, Goodell situates his antislavery interpretation within the prevailing cultural conception of the Constitution as the "original contract." H. Jefferson Powell has described the cultural currency of this view of the Constitution, and suggests that "the notion of the constitutional compact served as a metaphor for the Constitution's ultimate subordination to the people and thus for the legitimacy of popular authority regarding the Constitution's interpretation."[88] The Garrisonians likewise invoked this conception of the Constitution as the founding contract ("a covenant with death and an agreement with hell"), arguing for its end. Yet Goodell's employment of this concept shifted the terms of the debate away from the imagined or recorded "original intentions" of the parties to that contract, to the intent of the law as it was found in the words of the written instrument itself. Goodell does so in order to highlight the contradictions of the proslavery constitutional interpretation, which he locates in their distinction between "the letter of the law" and "the spirit of the law." The slaveholders' argument

> commonly begins by insisting that the *minutest specifications* of the document shall be strictly and literally complied with, that not one iota or tittle of the detailed provisions of the Constitution [referring to the "slavery clauses"] shall be suffered to fail, though the known and openly avowed *end and object, the main purpose and spirit* of the instrument [as announced in the Constitution's "Preamble"], which gave it existence, should be nullified, should suffer defeat, and be relinquished.... The *dead letter* construction shall be held [by them] omnipotent here. But let it be shown that the "words of the bond" do not happen, exactly to specify, to describe, much less to *name* the very "peculiar" thing claimed to be guaranteed or compromised, behold! The dead-letter construction is repudiated, at once, and

supposed and *conjectural* intentions TO SECURE SLAVERY start up in its place, and become Constitutional Law![89]

When in favor of slavery, the "dead letter construction" of the Constitution prevails; but when this mode of construction cannot find slavery named in the letter of its law, it turns to "*supposed* and *conjectural* intentions" as the true "spirit" of the law; it is this very selective, contradictory mode of interpretation which Goodell's *Views* takes as its point of departure. The rhetorical purchase of such a framing of the debate quickly becomes clear. Elaborating the distinction between "strict construction" and "supposed intentions," Goodell extends the constitutional contract metaphor, alluding to another infamous "contract" with wide cultural currency: the bond of Shylock, the usurer ("the words of the bond"). This opening allusion to "the words of the bond" is extended further at the end of Goodell's "strict construction" reading of the so-called slave clauses:

> For illustration's sake, let the slave power stand before the Court, in the person of Shakespeare's . . . Shylock, demanding his pound of flesh, from the . . . merchant of Venice, to be cut out of his very vitals, "according to the bond!" The plea was a "strict construction" plea, and the Court was a "strict construction" court. The sentence accordingly had to be rendered in favor of the plaintiff! The pound of flesh was his "due." . . . But hold! Rejoins the Judge. "One pound" is the judgment of the Court "according to the bond." At your peril, cut not a fraction less or more![90]

Goodell's allusion to the "words of the bond" announces the "strict construction" interpretation as a political strategy. Inserting the "claimants" of the constitutional contract debate into this famous scene, it signals its own legal tactic as drawn from classical rhetoric: the appropriation of the very mode of argument insisted upon by the opponent, the slaveholder. Spooner would also incorporate this concept of strict construction of "the words of the bond" into his argument on *The Unconstitutionality of Slavery*. Arguing for a national interest in "the freedom of all the States"—as opposed to the arguments of Garrisonian secessionists; of "states' rights" slavery defenders; and of moderate "free soil" political abolitionists, all of whom would leave slavery where it existed—and pointing to those freedoms of republican government "incompatible with slavery," Spooner asks, "Is this such a union as we bargained for? Was it 'nominated in the bond,' that we should be cut off from these the common rights of human nature? If so, point to the line and letter, where it is written."[91]

The key point in Goodell's and Spooner's use of the bond as image of "strict construction" is one of political abolitionist legal strategy: if the slaveholders insisted, like Shylock, on what was their due "according to the bond," then all judges who were opposed to slavery should act as did the judge in Shakespeare's play, and construe the law strictly according to its letter. The circulation of this bond image, which Douglass raised to a tropological level throughout his speeches and writings on the unconstitutionality of slavery, highlights the prevalence of that conception of the Constitution as the founding contract, as well as the central point of divergence for these competing interpretations of that document: the "original intentions" of the parties to the bond, as opposed to the "strict construction" of the language of the bond itself.

These differing hermeneutic models produced radically differing interpretations of the "slave clauses," which led to yet another significant figure of language to describe the political implications of the "strict construction" hermeneutic. Quoting in full the fugitive labor rendition clause of Article IV, Section 2, Goodell asks, "Who, unacquainted with the facts that have taken place, with the past and daily passing history of this country, would ever have conceived that *these words* described the case of a fugitive slave, and required his delivery to the slaveholder?"[92] Similarly, after quoting the three-fifths representation clause, Goodell declares, "And who, among the *uninitiated* could have divined that either a 'compromise' or a 'guarantee' of slavery, was bound up in these *words*? Nothing is *said* about *slavery* or *slaves*. And since nothing is *said*, how can 'strict construction' admit the plea that something was *intended*?"[93] Even before analyzing the words of these "slavery" provisions, Goodell presents a figure of reading: the "uninitiated," one "unacquainted with ... the history of this country," who therefore would find it inconceivable that slavery was part of the "intended" meaning of the words of these clauses. In his *Unconstitutionality of Slavery*, Spooner also elaborates on this image for the "strict construction" reading practice: "Everybody must admit that the constitution itself contains no language, from which *alone* any court, that were either strangers to the prior existence of slavery, or did not assume its prior existence to be legal, could legally decide that the constitution sanctioned it."[94]

In contrast, originalists used this figure of "the stranger" to the nation's slaveholding history to argue that the very ambiguity of the language of the slave clauses was itself evidence of the original historic compromise. In his "Address at North Bridgewater" (1844), John Quincy Adams asserted:

> The reluctance with which the freemen of the North submitted to the dictation of these [slaveholders'] conditions, is attested by the awkward and ambiguous language in which they are expressed. The word slave is most cautiously and fastidiously excluded from the whole instrument. *A stranger, who should come from a foreign land*, and read the Constitution of the United States, would not believe that slavery or a slave existed within the borders of our country. There is not a word in the Constitution apparently bearing upon the condition of slavery, nor is there a provision but would be susceptible of practical execution if there were not a slave in the land.[95]

Adams refers to the same hypothetical reader employed by Goodell and Spooner, the "stranger," "unacquainted with . . . the history" of slavery in the United States; yet Adams does so from the perspective of the dominant historicist understanding of the Constitution's "original intent," to underscore what he calls that "delusive ambiguity of language and of principle" which guided its writing.

Of literary historical interest is that Adams's "Address" appears in Phillips's *A Pro-Slavery Compact*, with which Douglass, the one-time Garrisonian, was deeply familiar, just as he would become familiar with Goodell's *Views of American Constitutional Law* and Spooner's *Unconstitutionality of Slavery* after his independence from the Garrisonians. If Douglass developed Goodell's allusion to Shylock's "bond" to describe the constitutional compact, his "man from another country" was likewise an adaptation of the "stranger, who should come from a foreign land," as the figure of "strict construction." The point here is not merely to recover the various sources incorporated into Douglass's literary style (though for cultural historians this is important as well).The more significant point is that Douglass's adaptations of the rhetoric and the constitutional claims of Goodell and Spooner were mediated by his exposure to them while still a Garrisonian. Douglass was singular in that he had held both of these opposing views at the center of the constitutional crisis over slavery: he had begun his abolitionist activism as a Garrisonian, and was criticized by them as an apostate after publishing his "Change of Opinion."[96] Douglass was thus in a position to incorporate these varying and explicitly opposed intellectual strands into the rhetoric of his antislavery constitutionalism.

Reading both sides of these debates over constitutional interpretation, the former fugitive slave Douglass saw in "the "uninitiated" and the "stranger ... from a foreign land" the image of the African American bond slave, and so transformed this rhetorical figure into the trope of the "man from another country," that reader whose vision saw through the law's ambiguous forms of appearance, and recognized the utopian possibilities of the Constitution's dialectic of visibility.

Throughout the 1850s, Douglass would link these two tropes of reading—"the man from another country" and the constitutional "bond"—to play on the ambiguous relation between the act of interpretation and the object of interpretation. Both highlight as well that his reading practice is precisely that: a strategic play of signification, a tactical rhetorical shift attending his political abolitionism. Rather than understanding Douglass's rhetoric as the result of changed political ideals, we should recognize the ways in which his political philosophy changed according to the strategic interpretive practices and rhetorical tactics that he developed within the contingencies of his political moment. We should recognize, in other words, the extent to which Douglass's political praxis determined his change in theory. As we have seen, these strategic interpretive practices preceded his change in political opinion: in 1849, while still subscribing to the Garrisonian interpretation of the Constitution's slavery-sanctioning original intent, Douglass used the "man from another country" to separate the Constitution's *legislative intent* as a strictly construed text from the "original intent" of its imagined historical context. It is because he approached the text of the Constitution as would the "man from another country"—occupying a position of distance from the nationalist aura of the Constitution as monumental origin—that Douglass could in 1851 interpret the Constitution as an antislavery document, and thus consider it "the first duty of every American citizen ... to use his *political* as well as his *moral* power for [slavery's] overthrow."[97]

In an 1860 speech, Douglass reveals the link between his strategic political abolitionist interpretation of the Constitution and the forms of resistance developed by the slave, and those who wore "the badge of the slave." In this speech, published as a pamphlet entitled *The Constitution of the United States: Is It Pro-Slavery or Anti-Slavery?*, Douglass writes:

> They have given the Constitution a slaveholding interpretation.... But it does not follow that the Constitution is in favor of these wrongs because the slaveholders have given it that interpretation.... I am therefore for

drawing the bond of the Union more closely.... What they most dread, that I most desire. I have much confidence in the instincts of the slaveholders. They see that the Constitution will afford slavery no protection when it shall cease to be administered by slaveholders.[98]

Readers of the 1845 *Narrative of the Life of Frederick Douglass, an American Slave* will recognize the line: "What they most dread, I most desire." The line comes from that exemplary moment in the 1845 *Narrative* when Douglass becomes aware of the importance of literacy. Describing his response to Master Auld's lecture to Mrs. Auld on the dangers of teaching a slave to read, Douglass writes: "The very decided manner with which he spoke, and strove to impress his wife with the evil consequences of giving me instruction, served to convince me that he was deeply sensible of the truths he was uttering.... What he most dreaded, that I most desired. What he most loved, that I most hated. That which was to him a great evil... was to me a great good."[99] Douglass narrates the episode as both a scene of initiation and a scene of reading: Douglass the uninitiated slave interprets the address of one slaveholder to another, and learns a lesson unintended by his master. In the very manner through which Master Auld delivers his injunction, Douglass recognizes the significance of that knowledge prohibited the slave. If this scene from Douglass's 1845 *Narrative* is read as exemplary of the significance of literacy, it must also be understood for the dialectic of master and slave upon which this moment of Douglass's initiation turns. Engaging in the political struggle over the future of slavery in the Union, Douglass applied this dialectic to all slaveholders. If in the first instance it was a question of literacy, in the national crisis of the American 1848 it is a much larger-scale concern: it is a matter of mastering the discourse of the slaveholders to recast the terms of the slavery debate; and to transform the culture of constitutionalism. In both instances, such mastery is a necessary part of the struggle for freedom; and what they together confirm is that for Douglass, the realm of ideas—what the slaveholding history of the national founding meant, and what its founding law would mean—is the result of material struggle in the "ever-present now."[100]

The slavery debates thus led to two interconnected transformations in the mid-nineteenth century, whose histories I have traced through Douglass's conversion to political abolitionism. First, there is a transformation in the reading practice itself, focusing as it does on the conception of the national bond of the Constitution and the "strict construction" reading of this text as opposed to its imagined "original intent"; and, second, as a result of this reading practice, a transformation in the conceptions of subject personhood and bound labor as they are inscribed in the Constitution. Douglass's reading uncovers the ideological work of the bondsman as absent presence in the Constitution: as that shadow figure which delimits the formal inscription of the abstract citizen-subject in the law. As Douglass's "man from another country" reveals, in the modern racial state the individual subject is visible primarily as *legible*: as he is inscribed as a "person" in the letter of the law.[101] Thus what Douglass's trope highlights also is that literature becomes the space for the other appearances of these "persons"; literature does not merely represent or express an already-existing historical "context"; it is the space through which the ambiguities of the political subject—its *subjectivation* through the letter and its *subjection to* the law—will be articulated. In 1881, three decades after publishing his "Change of Opinion," Douglass writes in *The Life and Times of Frederick Douglass* that the Constitution "was in its letter and spirit an anti-slavery instrument, demanding the abolition of slavery as a condition of its own existence as the supreme law of the land."[102] As Douglass first recognized in the midst of the American 1848, this spirit was the object of a struggle over the signification of the letter.

4

Hereditary Bondsman

Frederick Douglass and the Spirit of the Law

Frederick Douglass's "man from another country" was a double figure, representing both the perspective of the "stranger from a foreign land," unaware of the peculiar history of the Constitution and so seeing slavery nowhere named in the letter of its law, and the perspective of the African American bondslave, who read its letters as part of the discourse of the master.[1] A year after he published his "Change of Opinion," Douglass delivered his most famous address, "What to the Slave Is the Fourth of July?"[2] Throughout the address, Douglass extends this double perspective of the "man from another country," linking it to his own view of the national holiday, and of the state of the Union following the 1850 Compromise. Douglass begins by remarking upon the "distance between this platform and the slave plantation from which I escaped," identifying immediately with the point of view of the fugitive slave.[3] This point of view is then articulated as the distance between himself and his audience: "It is the birthday of your National Independence, and of your political freedom. This, to you, is what the Passover was to the emancipated people of God."[4] Likewise, throughout the address, Douglass refers to the nation's founders as "your fathers," suggesting to his audience that "you feel, perhaps, a much deeper interest" in "the causes which led to this anniversary than your speaker."[5] Rather than embracing the nation and the patriotic celebration of its founding, Douglass distances himself from both, as one who stood "identified with the American bondman."[6]

Douglass was not concerned with "the intentions of those scriveners who wrote the Constitution," but rather, as he announced in his "Change of Opinion," with "the ever-present now."[7] This becomes Douglass's explicit concern in "What to the Slave Is the Fourth of July?": "My business, if I have any here to-day, is with the present. The accepted time of God is the ever-living now. . . . We have only to do with the past only as we can make it useful to the present and to the future. To all inspiring motives, to noble deeds which can be gained from the past, we are welcome. But now is the time, the important time."[8] As he turns to the present, then, Douglass again emphasizes the distance between the slave's point of view on the Fourth of July and his audience's perspective on the occasion: "Fellow-citizens; above your national, tumultuous joy, I hear the mournful wail of millions! whose chains, heavy and grievous yesterday, are, to-day, rendered more intolerable by the jubilee shouts that reach them."[9] Even as he remarks upon this ideological distance between their respective points of view, however, Douglass claims to address his "fellow-citizens," and does so throughout the speech. Douglass's recurring claim to citizenship, in an address that so emphatically disclaims patriotic attachment to the memory of the nation's founding or "your fathers," articulated the double perspective Douglass now represented. African Americans, slave and free, were not considered parties to the "original contract" of that founding past; yet in "the ever-present now," free African Americans such as Douglass could claim the rights of citizens, according to Douglass's new reading of the Constitution. This point of view is articulated throughout the address as the "ever-living now's" perspective of "distance" from the founding past, and from the letter of the law inscribed in that past.

Employing that "scorching irony" as a point of view which he asserted was needed "at a time like this," Douglass declared that "the existence of slavery in this country brands your republicanism as a sham, your humanity a base pretence, and your Christianity as a lie."[10] As we have seen, the trope of a "man from another country" separated the Constitution's legislative intention—the law's meaning in the "ever-present now"—from the "original intent" of those long-dead scriveners who framed the law, and so elevated the letter of the law over the political-cultural aura of the founders. Douglass concludes this famous address to his "fellow-citizens" with this very distinction between writer and text, between imagined intentions and inscribed meanings. After his detailed denunciations—of state and federal law, of the internal slave trade, and of the American church, Douglass closes with the contemporary debates over the constitutionality of slavery:

> But it is answered in reply to all this, that precisely what I have now denounced is, in fact, guaranteed and sanctioned by the Constitution of the United States; that the right to hold and to hunt slaves is a part of that Constitution framed by the illustrious Fathers of the Republic.

> *Then*, I dare to affirm, notwithstanding all I have said before, your fathers stooped, basely stooped
> "To palter with us in a double sense;
> And keep the word of promise to the ear,
> But break it to the heart."
> And instead of being the honest men I have before declared them to be, they were the veriest imposters that ever practiced on mankind.[11]

Douglass paraphrases Macbeth's address to the witches, whose ambiguously worded prophecies seemed, in a literal interpretation, to promise him success, but in spirit intended otherwise.[12] Douglass cites these lines to emphasize his own ironic perspective on the national founding, whose "illustrious Fathers" his audience now celebrated. As Douglass highlights, the logical conclusion of the national consensus recently codified by the 1850 Compromise—that slavery was "guaranteed and sanctioned by the Constitution of the United States"—was that the illustrious framers "stooped" to hide their true intentions. According to this dominant interpretation of the Constitution, the founding was a compromise of religion and morality with calculating interest; and rather than name honestly the slavery they "intended" to sanction and protect, the founders instead cunningly used euphemism and indirection, employing ambiguous words "to palter with us in a double sense."

Throughout the decade before the Civil War, Douglass continued to employ this double perspective, marking his ideological distance from the national community while simultaneously laying claim to American citizenship. In "A Nation in the Midst of a Nation," for example, Douglass returned to the "peculiar relation subsisting between" him and the white audience he addressed.[13] While his white audience, and, indeed, the "Hungarian, the Italian, the Irishman, the Jew, and the Gentile, all find in this land a home," African Americans, slave and free, were denied this right: "Here, upon the soil of our birth, in a country which has known us for centuries . . . we are esteemed less than strangers and sojourners—aliens are we in our native land."[14] Black Americans were "esteemed" aliens by the nation, and denied the equality and rights granted any "white man," no matter how recently that man from another country had immigrated: "The fundamental principles of the Republic to which the humblest white man, whether born here or elsewhere, may appeal with confidence . . . are held inapplicable to us."[15] It was this national color-line, solidified with the 1850 Compromise, that led directly to the formation of a black nation within the nation: "This people, free and slave, are rapidly becoming a nation, in the midst of a nation which disowns them, and for weal or woe this nation is united. The distinction between the slave and the free is not great, and their destiny seems one and the same."[16] Throughout this address, Douglass reasserts his own identification with this developing race-consciousness: "I am not ashamed to be numbered with this race. I am not ashamed to speak here as a negro."[17]

Yet even as Douglass illuminated this peculiar "national" status of enslaved and free African Americans, he continued to assert his claim to the rights of U.S. citizenship. In his celebrated 1854 speech in Chicago on the Kansas-Nebraska Act, for example, Douglass claimed his right to speak as one with his identity as an American citizen: "I have a right and duty to perform here. That right is a constitutional right, as well as a natural right. It belongs to every citizen of the United States."[18] In "A Nation in the Midst of a Nation," Douglass's point was that black Americans were "esteemed less than strangers"—they were considered by the rest of the nation "aliens" in their "native land." This is the very point of view Douglass combats as he claims his right to speak on the Kansas-Nebraska Act, expressing his new reading of the Constitution: "The Constitution knows but two classes: Firstly, citizens, and secondly, aliens. I am not an alien; and I am, therefore, a citizen."[19] In both speeches, Douglass's self-identifications are tied to his speaking point of view: he spoke simultaneously "as a negro," one of that nation in the midst of a nation, and "as a citizen."

Historians and literary scholars have remarked upon the "double character" of the slave, recognized in law as both property and person.[20] After his shift to political abolitionism and radical antislavery constitutionalism, Douglass articulated the double character of African American citizenship. Douglass stages this double character of African American citizenship throughout his 1855 autobiography, *My Bondage and My Freedom*.

A Type of His Countrymen

In the last two decades, scholars have argued that the 1855 *My Bondage and My Freedom* is a more sophisticated literary work than the 1845 *Narrative*, and "tells us far more about Douglass as a slave, and about slave culture generally, than does the *Narrative*, whose main virtue now, as in Douglass's own day, is pedagogical: it is easily absorbed and taught."[21] Despite this emerging critical consensus, the version of Frederick Douglass presented in the 1845 *Narrative* continues to be taken as representative of the historical figure.[22] I would add that in preferring the 1845 *Narrative* over the 1855 *My Bondage and My Freedom*, readers remain attached to Douglass's identity as *fugitive* slave, and as adherent to Garrisonian abolitionism. Douglass frames *My Bondage and My Freedom* with this very point, emphasizing in its concluding chapter the political significance of his changed interpretation of the Constitution: "Here was a radical change in my opinions, and in the action logically resulting from that change. To those with whom I had been in agreement and in sympathy, I was now in opposition. What they held to be a great and important truth, I now looked upon as a dangerous error."[23] Continuing to read the 1845 *Narrative* as exemplary, historians and literary scholars ignore the multiple ways in which Douglass's political engagements in the decade between the 1845 *Narrative* and the 1855 *My Bondage and My Freedom* influenced his changed self-representation in the 1855 autobiography. As Douglass declared in his 1854 address "The Claims of the Negro Ethnologically Considered": "A man is worked upon by what he works upon. He may carve out his circumstances, but his circumstances will carve him out as well."[24] As we saw in chapter 3, Frederick Douglass articulated his changed views on political abolitionism, constitutionalism, and national union through a greater focus on the historical role of labor in slavery as an economic system—a focus which corresponded to Douglass's own recognition of the transforming character of labor exploitation and the corresponding changes in the language of class struggle in antebellum America.

Those commentators who have addressed Douglass's revisionary autobiography have focused on the theme of literary self-fashioning, and its attendant questions of "authority," "authenticity," and "authorial" independence.[25] In this chapter, I argue that Douglass's transformed political views—specifically, his political abolitionism—led to significant changes in both the content and the form of his literary self-representation, from revisions of formative episodes in his life to changes in his narrative point of view: a point of view expressing that estranged, double perspective of the African American citizen, esteemed an alien in his native land. I focus in particular on Douglass's representations of the family and of slave women, to describe his transformed understanding of the relation between gender, race, and the slave's subject-formation; and on Douglass's depictions of his "Apprenticeship Life," to describe his transformed understanding of the political-economic interdependence of slave labor, "free labor," and the formal freedoms of American citizenship.

My Bondage and My Freedom is neither a fugitive slave narrative nor a conventional slave autobiography wherein the slave narrator relates the horrors of slavery through the facts of his individual experience. Rather, as Dr. James McCune Smith emphasizes in his introduction to *My Bondage and My Freedom*, the aim of this 1855 text was to present, in the figure of Frederick Douglass as "a Representative American man—a type of his countrymen," "the justice, safety and practicability of Immediate Emancipation" (*MB* 17–18). *My Bondage and My Freedom*, organized in two parts entitled "Life as a Slave" and "Life as a Freeman," thus stages Douglass's movement from bondage to freedom, in order to demonstrate the practicability of both immediate emancipation and the assimilation of the formerly enslaved into the social and civic life of the nation. Throughout the 1855 text, Douglass uses his own life as representative, continually emphasizing that his own individual situation was not unique, but rather one shared by all slaves. As Douglass states in his letter included in the "Editor's Preface," "I have never placed my opposition to slavery on a basis so narrow as my own enslavement, but rather upon the indestructible and unchangeable laws of human nature, every one of which is perpetually and flagrantly violated by the slave system" (*MB* 6).

Departing from the sentimental conventions of the slave narrative, *My Bondage and My Freedom* instead focuses on Douglass's intellectual development: his coming into consciousness, first of his social being as a slave, and then of his natural right to freedom. Douglass's description of his early childhood in the first three chapters of *My Bondage and My Freedom* is tied not only to his critique of the slave system but to his positive claims regarding mankind's natural right of liberty—a natural rights discourse in contrast to the positive laws of slavery.

Douglass uses the narration of his childhood and the slave child's developing point of view to depict what he refers to as the "abolition" of the family under slavery. Stating that "Nor, indeed, can I impart much knowledge concerning my parents," he immediately broadens this particular point about his individual experience: "A person of some consequence here in the north, sometimes designated father, is literally abolished in slave law and practice" (*MB* 30). Douglass later elaborates the significance of the word "abolition" when he describes first hearing the term in association with those fighting slavery (*MB* 121), but its primary signification in this first chapter entitled "The Author's Childhood" is already clear: it emphasizes the ways in the very structure of the family was destroyed by the peculiar institution of slavery. Douglass refers to the term "father" as a "designation" rather than as a natural relation. Douglass will emphasize this point throughout these early chapters as he narrates his developing consciousness of his social being as a slave. Douglass likewise never names his father; and after introducing the father-figure as "a designation" of some importance in the North, Douglass proceeds to identify that absent figure with another "mysterious personage," his master:

> Living here, with my dear old grandmother and grandfather, it was a long time before I knew myself to be a slave. I knew many other things before I knew that. . . . [B]ut as I grew larger and older, I learned by degrees the sad fact, that the "little hut," and the lot on which it stood, belonged not to my dear old grandparents, but to some person who lived at a great distance off, and was called, by grandmother, "OLD MASTER." I further learned the sadder fact, that not only the house and lot, but that grandmother herself, (grandfather was free,) and all the little children around her, belonged to this mysterious personage, called by grandmother, with every mark of reverence, "Old Master." . . . I was told that this "old master," whose name seemed ever to be mentioned with fear and shuddering, only allowed the children to live with grandmother for a limited time, and that in fact as soon as they were big enough, they were promptly taken away, to live with the said "old master." . . . The absolute power of this distant "old master" had touched my young spirit with but the point of its cold, cruel iron, and left me something to brood over after the play and in moments of repose. . . . I dreaded the thought of going to live with that mysterious "old master," whose name I never heard mentioned with affection, but always with fear. (*MB* 33)

In this account of how he first became conscious of his social being as a slave, Douglass emphasizes the slave child's point of view. As Douglass notes, "early I learned that the point from which a thing is viewed is of some importance" (*MB* 38). Douglass intertwines the description of this developing consciousness of his social identity as a slave with a representation of the symbolic identity of the master: "Old Master"—a designation he uses six times in this relatively short passage—names a function, rather than a specific individual (and the young Douglass does not learn the actual name of this "Old Master" until much later in *My Bondage and My Freedom*). Douglass reinforces the symbolic identity of "Old Master" through the mystery which surrounded this name: describing how he first came to hear the term as a child, Douglass emphasizes that the "name seemed ever to be mentioned with fear and shuddering," and "with every mark of reverence." Douglass thus depicts the slave child's developing self-consciousness as directly bound up with the symbolic identity of the master. The born slave comes into consciousness of his social being through the recurring name of this distant, mysterious figure, a point Douglass registers at the end of this narration with the image of the sword: "the absolute power of this distant 'old master' had touched my young spirit with but the point of its cold, cruel iron" (*MB* 33). Douglass stages the slave child's first awareness of his social identity as the first touch of that weapon which is the sign and symbol of worldly rulers. Douglass underscores the significance of his childhood point of view at the end of this chapter: "And such a boy, so far as I can now remember, was the boy whose life in slavery I am now narrating" (*MB* 35). In one of the text's many self-reflexive moments, Douglass steps back from the narrative here, speaking of this younger self in the third person to remark upon the temporal and existential distance between that point of view he has just narrated—the point of view of the born slave—and the perspective of the free man now writing the pages of the text.

Douglass extends this representation of the interdependent relation between the slave's self-consciousness and the figure of "Old Master" in the next chapter:

> I was A SLAVE—born a slave and though the fact was incomprehensible to me, it conveyed to my mind a sense of my entire dependence on the will of *somebody* I had never seen; and, from some cause or other, I had been made to fear this somebody above all else on earth. Born for another's benefit, as the *firstling* of the cabin flock I was soon to be selected as a meet offering to the fearful and inexorable *demigod*, whose huge image on so many occasions haunted my childhood's imagination. (*MB* 37)

Once again the still-unnamed and unseen "Old Master" is a symbolic figure: godlike, disembodied, a haunting specter. Douglass emphasizes that as a child he could not fully comprehend the meaning of his status as a slave; yet he understood this slave identity as necessarily bound to the identity of this "fearful and inexorable" Other: it signified "my entire dependence on the will of somebody I had never seen." In these early chapters narrating his developing self-consciousness, Douglass introduces the slave's "point of view" on the dialectic of master and slave, the recognition of his slave identity as dependent upon the will of the master.

In chapter 3, "The Author's Parentage," Douglass again emphasizes the absence of the father, that person "abolished in slave law and practice" (*MB* 30): "I say nothing of *father*, for he is shrouded in a mystery I have never been able to penetrate. Slavery does away with fathers, as it does away with families" (*MB* 41). In his description of the absent father-figure, Douglass employs the very terms he had used to describe the "distant," "mysterious personage" of "Old Master." Even before he states, "My father was a white man, or nearly white. It was sometimes whispered that my master was my father" (*MB* 42), Douglass thus presents these two figures as structurally identical: both master and father are absent, mysterious personages. Indeed, Douglass introduces the unconfirmed "whisper" that his master and his father were one and the same man with the broader point that the family, an institution central to the economic and ideological life of the republic, had been "abolished"(*MB* 40) such that "the order of civilization is reversed" (*MB* 41).

The moral argument against slavery as destructive of familial bonds was a convention of antislavery writings, reliant on the tropes of sentimental literature. In *My Bondage and My Freedom*, however, Douglass links this conventional moral criticism of slavery to a sustained critique of racial classification itself:

> The name of the child is not expected to be that of its father, and his condition does not necessarily affect that of the child. He may be the slave of Mr. Tilgman; and his child, when born, may be the slave of Mr. Gross. He may be a *freeman*; and yet his child may be a *chattel*. He may be white, glorying in the purity of his Anglo-Saxon blood; and his child may be ranked with the blackest slaves. Indeed, he *may* be, and often *is*, master and father to the same child. He can be father without being a husband, and may sell his child without incurring reproach, if the child be by a woman in whose veins courses one thirty-second part of African blood. (*MB* 41–42)

Douglass invokes here the language of the increasingly popular pseudosciences of race and ethnography, extending his critique of slavery's effects on the family to a critique of racial classification in a slaveholding nation. He emphasizes the arbitrary character of "race," whose classifications depend ultimately on slave law: the father "may be white, glorying in the purity of his Anglo-Saxon blood; and his child may be ranked with the blackest slaves" (*MB* 42). The child of a "white" man of pure "Anglo-Saxon blood" was classified as black because the laws of slavery dictated that the child of a slave woman followed the condition of the mother. Douglass will return to the arbitrariness of this racial classification, and its basis in slave law, several times throughout the text: "I knew of blacks who were *not* slaves; I knew of whites who were *not* slaveholders; and I knew of persons who were *nearly* white, who were slaves. *Color*, therefore, was a very unsatisfactory basis for slavery" (*MB* 69). Again recalling his childhood point of view on the unnatural basis of slavery, Douglass emphasizes the disjunction between physiognomy and a "racial" classification dictated by slave law. Thus, in Douglass's account, the whisper "that my master was my father" does not need to be proven true—Douglass adds that "I cannot say that I ever gave it credence"—for the material fact remains "that, by the laws of slavery, children, in all cases, are reduced to the condition of their mothers" (*MB* 46). It is this historical reality of "slave law and practice" (*MB* 30) which subtends Douglass's construction of the image of his mother, and the narrative of his relationship to that image.

A Slave in Form

In his description of the identity of the unknown white father, and this figure's symbolic identity with the master, Douglass had invoked with irony the language of racial classification, contrasting "the purity of [the father's] Anglo-Saxon blood" with the "one thirty-second part of African blood" coursing "in the veins" of the slave mother (*MB* 42). Douglass pursues this critique of contemporary race science in his reconstruction of his mother's image, and engages directly with the ethnography of his time:

> Her personal appearance and bearing are ineffaceably stamped upon my memory. She was tall, and finely proportioned; of deep black, glossy complexion, had regular features, and, among other slaves, was remarkably sedate in her manners. There is in *Prichard's Natural History of Man*," the head of a figure—on page 157—the features of which so resemble those of my mother, that I do often recur to it with something of the feeling which I suppose others experience when looking upon the pictures of dear departed ones. (*MB* 42)

As a slave, Douglass has no daguerreotype or photograph, no material image of his mother—the image is stamped instead upon his memory.

Significantly, Douglass suggests that this image of her resembles an illustration in Prichard's book of natural science.

Readers have puzzled over Douglass's comparison of his mother's features with this image of an Egyptian prince.[26] To understand the narrative significance of Douglass's representation of his mother here, we must historicize the allusion itself. James Prichard's 1813 *Research into the Physical History of Man* advanced the theory of monogenesis, arguing for the original unity of the human species, and for the natural equality of the different "races" of man. Prichard's 1843 *Natural History of Man* reiterated the argument for monogenesis, and emphasized that the same interior "mental" and "intellectual" nature was shared by all the classified "races." Prichard's work was important to Douglass and other abolitionists because it countered the increasingly popular racist ethnography of proslavery writers such as Josiah Nott and George Gliddon, who argued in *The Types of Mankind* for the theory of polygenesis—that the races of mankind had different origins and different genetic lineages—and for the natural inferiority of "the Negro."

This broader debate over the origins and the natural equality of mankind had direct implications for the slavery debates. In 1854, as he was writing *My Bondage and My Freedom*, Douglass gave his famous address "The Claims of the Negro Ethnologically Considered," in which he argued forcefully against the racist ethnography of Samuel Morton, Louis Agassiz, Josiah Nott, and George Gliddon. As Douglass argued in his address, they "reason[ed] from *prejudice* rather than from *facts*," to construct a "scientific" basis for black enslavement.[27] Douglass cites the rise of this theory of polygenesis at the very beginning of the address:

> There was a time when, if you established the point that a particular being is a man, it was considered that such a being, of course, had a common ancestry with the rest of mankind. But it is not so now. This is, you know, an age of science, and science is favorable to division.... There is, therefore, another proposition to be stated and maintained, separately, which in other days, (the days before the Notts, the Gliddens, the Agasiz[es], and Mortons, made their profound discoveries in ethnological science), might have been included in the first.[28]

With characteristic irony, Douglass makes clear from the outset how he regarded their theory. Pointing to modern scientific advancements and the increase of human knowledge—"when time and space, in the intercourse

Fig. 48.

Head of Rameses.

In this figure, it is observed that "the general expression is calm and dignified; the forehead is somewhat flat; the eyes are widely separated from each other; the nose is elevated, but with spreading nostrils; the ears are high; the lips large, broad, and turned out, with sharp edges; in which points there is a deviation from the European countenance."†

  * See Mr. Martin's " Natural History of Mammiferous Animals," &c. 8vo. Plates. London, 1841.
  † Ibid.

Figure 1. Head of Rameses, from James C. Prichard, *Natural History of Man* (1848), 157. Courtesy of Image Collection Library, University of Massachusetts, Amherst.

of nations, are almost annihilated ... when nationalities are being swallowed up and the ends of the earth brought together"—Douglass remarks, "it is strange, that there should be a phalanx of learned men—speaking in the name of *science*—to forbid the magnificent reunion of mankind in one brotherhood."[29] Rather than dismiss them outright, however, Douglass proceeds to deconstruct each of the major claims of this scientific theory, to reveal the racial prejudice motivating it.

Focusing on Samuel Morton and "his very able work, *Crania Americana*" as representative of this school of thought, Douglass argues that "his contempt for Negroes is ever conspicuous" throughout.[30] For example, Morton (and his followers Nott and Gliddon) repeatedly asserted that the ancient Egyptians were "Caucasian." Addressing this point, Douglass cites the recognition of Egypt as "one of the earliest abodes of learning and civilization," the "fact ... not denied by anybody" that "Greece and Rome—and through them Europe and America—have received their civilization from the ancient Egyptians," and declares:

> But Egypt is in Africa. Pity that it had not been in Europe, or in Asia, or better still, America! Another unhappy circumstance [for their theory] is, that the ancient Egyptians were not white people; but were, undoubtedly, just about as dark in complexion as many in this country who are considered genuine negroes; and that is not all, their hair was far from being of that graceful lankness which adorns the fair Anglo-Saxon head.[31]

Douglass focuses on complexion and hair because these were aspects of physiognomy that ethnographers such as Morton, Gliddon, and Nott used to classify the different "types of mankind," which they then ranked in racial hierarchy, with "the Negro" as "the lowest type."[32] Douglass likewise uses those physiognomic traits to draw a direct link between ancient Egyptians and modern African Americans. This debate—over the original unity of mankind, and the natural equality of the "races"—is the political historical context for Douglass's description of his mother's "personal appearance and bearing," and for his emphasis in that description on her "deep black, glossy complexion" (*MB* 42).

In "The Claims of the Negro Ethnologically Considered," Douglass also praises Prichard's *Natural History of Man*, in whose pages Douglass found that image of the Egyptian prince, "the features of which so resemble those of" his mother (*MB* 42). Significantly, Douglass's praise for Prichard's *Natural History* appears in his critique of the racist portraits of "Negro" heads contained in Nott and Gliddon's *Types of Mankind*:

> It is the province of prejudice to blind; and scientific writers, not less than others, write to please, as well as to instruct, and ... sacrifice what it true to what is popular.... [It] is fashionable now, in our land, to exaggerate the differences between the negro and the European. If, for instance, a phrenologist or naturalist undertakes to represent in portraits, the differences between the two races—the negro and the European—he will invariably present the highest type of the European and the lowest type of the negro. The European face is drawn in harmony with the highest ideas of beauty, dignity, and intellect.... The negro, on the other hand, appears with features distorted, lips exaggerated, forehead depressed—and the whole expression of the countenance made to harmonize with the popular idea of negro imbecility and degradation.[33]

Prichard's *Natural History of Man*, and George Combs's *The Constitution of Man*, Douglass notes, were the only exceptions to this "fashion" in modern ethnography, of "reasoning ... from *prejudice* rather than from *facts*."[34]

In his introduction to *My Bondage and My Freedom*, Dr. James McCune Smith highlights the political significance of Douglass's pointed allusion to Prichard's *Natural History*, making mocking reference to Nott and Gliddon as he discusses Douglass's African ancestry and "negro blood" (*MB* 23): "The head alluded to [by Douglass] is copied from the statue of Ramses the Great, an Egyptian king of the nineteenth dynasty. The authors of the 'Types of Mankind' give a side view of the same on page 148, remarking that the profile, 'like Napolean's is superbly European!'" (*MB* 23). Just as commentators have been confused by Douglass's allusion to Prichard's text, they have missed the irony in Smith's reference to Nott and Gliddon. Here, Smith quotes directly from the description of Ramses II in Nott and Gliddon's *Types of Mankind*, which compared the features of Ramses II to those of the "European" Napoleon.

As Smith's mocking reference to *Types of Mankind* observes, Nott and Gliddon insisted—against facts—that the Egyptian king Ramses II (along with Egypt's ruling elite more generally) was of the "Caucasian" race. Likewise, as with Douglass's reconstruction of his mother's image, Smith's allusion to this image ties the racist ethnography of Nott and Gliddon to the immediate concerns of proslavery thought in the United States: "The great 'white race' now seeks paternity, according to Dr. Pickering,

156 *Hereditary Bondsman*

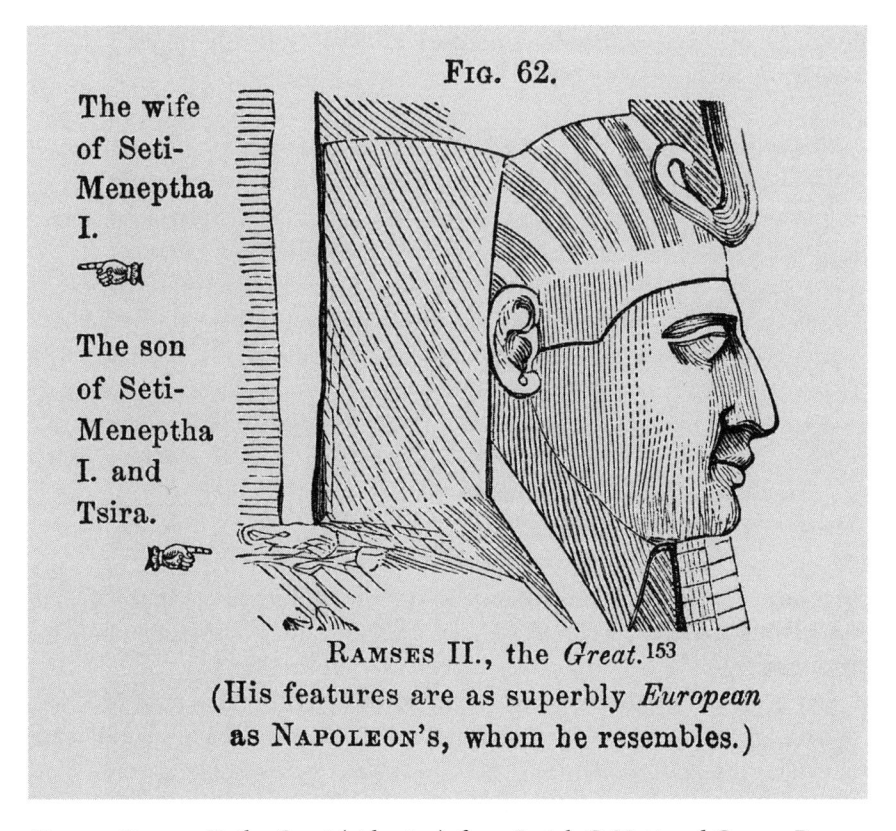

> Fig. 62.
>
> The wife of Seti-Meneptha I.
>
> The son of Seti-Meneptha I. and Tsira.
>
> Ramses II., the *Great*.¹⁵³
> (His features are as superbly *European*
> as Napoleon's, whom he resembles.)

Figure 2. Ramses II, the Great (*side view*), from Josiah C. Nott and George R. Gliddon, *Types of Mankind* (1854), 148. Courtesy of Image Collection Library, University of Massachusetts, Amherst.

in Arabia—'Arida Nutrix' of the best breed of horses &c. Keep on gentlemen; you'll find yourselves in Africa, by-and-by. The Egyptians, like the Americans, were a mixed race, with some negro blood circling around the throne, as well as in the mud hovels" (*MB* 23–24). Both Douglass's allusion to Prichard's *Natural History of Man* in the description of his mother's features and Smith's mocking reference to the competing theory of *Types of Mankind* emphasize that it was the political struggle over slavery that gave rise to the latter's "scientific" claims for polygenesis, inherent racial difference, and the natural inferiority of "the Negro."

In Douglass's account of his "parentage," racial classification thus becomes a matter of both social and individual identification; and for

Douglass, his "racial" identity is an active political affiliation. Reconstructing the memory of his mother, Douglass uses the image from Prichard's *Natural History of Man* to align himself with his mother's "race." For regardless of Douglass's own "color," and regardless of the "race" of Douglass's "Anglo-Saxon" father, "by the laws of slavery" Douglass was "reduced to the condition" of his slave mother (*MB* 46). Douglass thus goes further in this affiliation with his mother's "race," then, when he notes

> that she was the only one of all the slaves and colored people in Tuckahoe who [could read].... I am quite willing, and even happy, to attribute any love of letters I possess, and for which I have got—despite of prejudices—only too much credit, not to my Anglo-Saxon paternity, but to the native genius of my sable, unprotected, and uncultivated mother—a woman who belonged to a race whose mental endowments it is, at present, fashionable to hold in disparagement and contempt. (*MB* 46)

Douglass alludes here once again to the fashionable scientific racism of Morton, Nott, and Gliddon. As Douglass noted in "The Claims of the Negro Ethnologically Considered": "an intelligent black man is always supposed to have derived his intelligence from his connection with the white race. To be intelligent is to have one's negro blood ignored."[35] After staging the symbolic identification of his unknown white father with the mysterious figure of "Old Master," Douglass identifies himself as black, affiliating with the oppressed and maligned race of the slave, through this representative image of his long-lost mother.

Douglass extends this sustained attention to the figure of the slave mother to the depictions of his formative encounters with other slave women throughout the early chapters of *My Bondage and My Freedom*. One of the most famous scenes from Douglass's 1845 *Narrative of the Life of Frederick Douglass, an American Slave* is the whipping of Aunt Hester. As readers have noted, that scene followed the sensational conventions of slave autobiography and sentimental literature in its depiction of a slave woman as passive victim, and stood in stark contrast to the masculinist model of violent slave resistance Douglass would present in his equally famous battle with the slave-breaker Covey.[36] Paul Gilroy, in his reading of the battle with Covey as a staging of the master-slave dialectic "from the slave's point of view," acknowledges the "distinctly masculinist resolution of slavery's inner oppositions" presented in the battle with Covey, yet suggests, in response to feminist critiques of Douglass, that this "idea of masculinity is largely defined against the infantilism on which the institutions of plantation slavery rely rather than against women."[37] Gilroy's attempt to "counter any ambiguity around this point"—namely, whether Douglass's critique of slavery "cannot be separated from the distinct mode of masculinity with which it has been articulated"—leads him to supplement his interpretation of that battle with a reading of the well-known historical and literary accounts of the Margaret Garner case.[38] While the story of Margaret Garner and her act of infanticide certainly contributes to a critical understanding of "representations of death as agency" in African American literature, its circulation cannot sufficiently answer feminist critiques of the "masculinist" model of resistance presented in the 1845 *Narrative*.[39] Yet we do not need to go too far afield to answer this critique, for Douglass himself clarifies the ambiguity in the 1855 *My Bondage and My Freedom*.[40]

In *My Bondage and My Freedom*, Douglass describes another scene of violence against a slave woman, "the whipping of a woman belonging to Colonel Lloyd, named Nelly" (*MB* 70). Appearing immediately after the whipping of Aunt Esther, this scene of Nelly's whipping serves explicitly as the narrative supplement to the depiction of Esther, and implicitly as the feminist counterpoint to that masculinist model of resistance represented in Douglass's battle with Covey. Insofar as both scenes involve the young Douglass witnessing the whipping of a slave woman (Esther by the master, Nelly by the overseer), the two scenes are structurally similar; and Douglass introduces his narration of Nelly's whipping with direct reference to the preceding account of Esther's whipping (*MB* 69). Yet in contrast to the "revolting and shocking" (*MB* 67) spectacle of Esther's whipping, whose narration is framed in the sentimental terms of sorrow and pity—a point underscored by Douglass's own response: "From my heart I pitied her" (*MB* 67)—Douglass frames the narration of Nelly's whipping as an exemplary "lesson" in the value of slave resistance.[41] Indeed, Douglass's subtitles for the account of Nelly's whipping—"Combat between an Overseer and Slavewoman"; and "The Advantage of Resistance" (*MB* 68)—underscore this scene's representative function.

Whereas Esther is described as a "suffering victim" (*MB* 67) begging for mercy from her master, Nelly is described as a "vigorous and spirited woman" (*MB* 70), "sternly resisting" (*MB* 93) the overseer as he attempts to whip her, "combating" against him throughout the scene. "She nobly resisted," Douglass adds, "and unlike most of the slaves, seemed determined to make her whipping cost Mr. Sevier as much as possible. The blood on his (and her) face attested her skill, as well as her courage and dexterity in using her nails" (*MB* 71). At the conclusion of Esther's whipping, the "suffering victim ... could scarcely stand, when untied" and "poor Esther" exits the narrative in passive, silent defeat (67). Emphasizing once again the slave child's point of view—"I could distinctly see and hear what was going on, without being seen by old master" (*MB* 67)—Douglass frames the meaning of this scene of Esther's suffering through the description of his own response as powerless witness: "I was hushed, terrified, stunned, and could do nothing" (*MB* 67). In the 1845 *Narrative*, this whipping scene is famously identified as "the blood-stained gate," the entrance into the hell of slavery, from whose depths Douglass would not emerge until his transformative battle with Covey.[42] In the 1855 *My Bondage and My Freedom*, the whipping of Esther is no longer central or formative, and is instead framed as one among the many common "heart-rending incidents" which "led [Douglass], thus early, to inquire into the nature and history of slavery" (*MB* 68). Further, in contrast to the "pitiful" conclusion of "poor Esther's" suffering, at the conclusion of "spirited" Nelly's struggle Douglass emphasizes that Nelly "was whipped—severely whipped; but she was not subdued, for she continued to denounce the overseer, and to call him every vile name" (*MB* 72). Douglass's description of Nelly focuses on the distinction between the body and the spirit, between the slave's physical punishment and her continued defiance: "she was whipped, but she was not subdued" (*MB* 72). It is this distinction between outer form and inner spirit which Douglass elaborates in the "lesson" he learned from witnessing this "Combat between an Overseer and Slavewoman."

And it is at the close of this scene of struggle, which Douglass "watched with palpitating interest," long before his own battle with Covey, that Douglass asserts he first learned "the advantage of resistance":

> He had bruised her flesh, but had left her invincible spirit undaunted. Such floggings are seldom repeated by the same overseer. They prefer to whip those who are most easily whipped. The old doctrine that submission is the best cure for outrage and wrong, does not hold good on the slave plantation. He is whipped oftenest, who is whipped easiest; and that slave who has the courage to stand up for himself against the overseer, although he may have many hard stripes at the first, becomes, in the end, a *freeman*, even though he sustain the *formal relation* of a slave. "You can shoot me but you can't whip me," said a slave to Rigby Hopkins; and the result was that he was neither whipped nor shot. If the latter had been his fate, it would have

been less deplorable than the living and lingering death to which cowardly and slavish souls are subjected. (*MB* 72, emphasis added)

Douglass articulates this lesson in the advantages of slave resistance as a series of oppositions between inner truth and outer form: an invincible, undaunted spirit within the bruised flesh, becoming "in the end, a freeman, even though he sustain the formal relation of slave" (*MB* 72). The terms Douglass uses here to describe the lesson he learns from Nelly's resistance are the very same ones he will use later in *My Bondage and My Freedom*, to describe the significance of his own decision to resist a whipping from the slave-breaker Covey. Calling "the battle with Mr. Covey . . . the turning point in my 'life as a slave'" (*MB* 180), Douglass concludes that later scene with a new self-consciousness:

> I was no longer a servile coward, trembling under the frown of a brother worm of the dust, but, my long-cowed spirit was roused to an attitude of manly independence. I had reached the point, at which I was *not afraid to die*. This spirit made me a freeman in *fact*, while I remained a slave in *form*. When a slave cannot be flogged he is more than half free. . . . While slaves prefer their lives, with flogging, to instant death, they will always find Christians enough, like unto Covey, to accommodate that preference. (181, emphasis in original)

These are the very lessons in "The Advantage of Slave Resistance" which, as Douglass highlighted, were first taught him by the slave woman Nelly.

Striking the Blow

Douglass concludes his reflections on the significance of his resistance to Covey with a quotation from Byron's *Childe Harold's Pilgrimage*: "Hereditary bondsmen! know ye not, / Who would be free, themselves must strike the blow?" (*MB* 182).[43] In their original poetic context, the lines address Greece's "bondage" under the Ottoman Empire, enjoining the Greeks to fight for their own independence: "By their right arms the conquest must be wrought? / Will Gaul or Muscovite redress ye? no! / True, they may lay your despoilers low, / But not for you will Freedom's altars flame."[44] The success of Douglass's 1845 *Narrative* made him the most famous fugitive slave in America, and raised fears of his recapture. As Douglass notes in

My Bondage and My Freedom, with characteristic irony: "The writing of my pamphlet, in the spring of 1845, endangered my liberty, and led me to seek refuge from republican slavery in monarchical England" (269). Dr. James McCune Smith suggests in his introduction to *My Bondage and My Freedom* that Douglass would have heard Byron's lines throughout "his sojourn in England," Scotland, and Ireland: "And one stirring thought, inseparable from the British idea of the evangel of freedom, must have smote his ear from every side: 'Hereditary bondsman! / know ye not / Who would be free, themselves must strike the blow?" (*MB* 16). Like other invocations of Byron's call for "hereditary bondsmen" to "themselves . . . strike the blow" for their freedom, Smith invokes the poetic lines to underscore the importance of African American agency in the cause of "radical abolitionism" (*MB* 10). Dr. Smith links this call for the agency of African American "hereditary bondsmen" to Frederick Douglass's decision to publish his own newspaper: "The result of this visit was, that on the return to the United States, he established a newspaper. This proceeding was sorely against the wishes and the advice of the leaders of the American Anti-Slavery Society, but our author had fully grown up to the conviction of a truth which they had once promulgated, but now forgotten, to wit: that in their own elevation—colored men have a blow to strike 'on their own hook,' against slavery and caste" (*MB* 16). Introducing the changed figure of Frederick Douglass in *My Bondage and My Freedom*, Smith thus links Byron's call for hereditary bondsmen's self-liberation not only to the abolition of slavery but also to the "elevation" of the "free colored people" (*MB* 16). Describing free African Americans as "the half-freed colored people of the free states," Smith writes:

> Ward and Garnet, Wells Brown and Pennington, Loguen and Douglass, are banners on the outer wall, under which abolition is fighting its most successful battles, because they are living exemplars of the practicability of the most radical abolitionism; for, they were all of them born to the doom of slavery, some of them remained slaves until adult age, yet that have not only won equality to their white fellow citizens, in civil, religious, political and social rank, but they have also illustrated and adorned our common country by their genius, learning and eloquence. (*MB* 10)

Smith thus frames Douglass's writing, and in particular Douglass's role as the editor and publisher of his own newspaper, as necessarily tied to broader national debates over black agency and the practicability of emancipation. As Smith and Douglass both note, the recurring argument against immediate emancipation was that the enslaved were incapable of freedom, or (at best) unprepared for it.

Douglass's quotation of Byron's lines in the 1855 *My Bondage and My Freedom* thus signals another transformation in his political views and in his self-representation. For Douglass had heard these lines invoked before his 1846 "sojourn in England" (*MB* 16), when he attended the 1843 National Negro Convention in Buffalo, New York. Henry Highland Garnet, in his "Address to the Slaves of the United States of America" delivered at the 1843 convention, had declared: "Brethren, the time has come when you must act for yourselves. It is an old and true saying, that 'if hereditary bondmen would be free, they must themselves strike the blow.' You can plead your own cause, and do the work of emancipation better than any others."[45] Citing the historical lessons of "Denmark Vezie, of South Carolina, ... patriotic Nathaniel Turner, ... Joseph Cinque, the hero of the Amistad, ... and Madison Washington, that bright star of freedom," Garnet called for "Resistance! Resistance! Resistance!" throughout the slaveholding states. Garnet was a leading black abolitionist aligned with Gerritt Smith.[46] As a political abolitionist, Garnet focused on the collective labor power of the slaves: "We do not advise you to attempt a revolution of the sword, because it would be INEXPEDIENT. Your numbers are too small, and moreover the rising spirit of the age, and the spirit of the gospel, are opposed to war and bloodshed. But from this moment cease to labor for tyrants who will not remunerate you. Let every slave throughout the land do this, and the days of slavery are numbered."[47] Indeed, Garnet links this form of slave resistance—the refusal of labor—to an understanding of "death as agency": "Inform them [your lordly enslavers] that all you desire is Freedom, and that nothing else will suffice. Do this, and for ever after cease to toil for the heartless tyrants, who give you no reward but stripes and abuse. If they then commence the work of death, they, and not you, will be responsible for the consequences. You had far better all die—die immediately, than live slaves, and entail your wretchedness upon your posterity.... If you must bleed, let it all come at once—rather, die freeman, than live to be slaves."[48] Although Garnet's "Address to the Slaves" did not explicitly call for armed slave revolt, many in attendance opposed adopting his "Address" as an official publication of the convention, objecting to it as "war-like" and encouraging "insurrection."[49] Frederick Douglass, in 1843 still an adherent to Garrisonian abolitionism and moral suasion, was one of those who spoke against the adoption of Garnet's "Address," and among the "small majority" that voted to reject it (eighteen voted in its favor; nineteen opposed it).[50] In his 1855 *My Bondage and My Freedom*, however, Douglass quotes these same lines, marking his intellectual and political transformations of the intervening decade.

Douglass no doubt heard the call for "hereditary bondsman" to themselves "strike the blow" throughout his 1845–46 lecture tour of England, Scotland, and Ireland, as Dr. James McCune Smith suggests in his introduction" to *My Bondage and My Freedom*. Byron's poems were regularly excerpted in British periodicals, and these lines calling for self-liberation circulated widely, in different political contexts. A writer in the British working-class periodical *Radical Reformer's Gazette* (1832–33), for example, quoted the lines as the heading to an article on the condition of the poor in Birmingham, England.[51] Perhaps most famously, Daniel O'Connell, the leader of the Irish movement for the repeal of the Union with England, applied Byron's lines to the long-standing oppression of Ireland by the British, and claimed them for the political motto of his campaign. During his 1845–46 tour, Frederick Douglass lectured in Ireland at the invitation of the Hibernian Anti-Slavery Society, forming friendships with Daniel O'Connell and other Irish independence and antislavery activists. In *The Life and Times of Frederick Douglass*, Douglass recalled the power of O'Connell's oratory to inspire his audience: "His eloquence came down upon the vast assembly like a summer thunder-shower upon a dusty road.... [O'Connell] held Ireland within the grasp of his strong hand, and [he] could lead it whithersoever he would."[52] Douglass's citation of Byron's lines—"Hereditary bondsmen, know ye not / Who would be free themselves must strike the blow!"—thus register another significant change in Douglass's views during the decade between the 1845 *Narrative of the Life* and the 1855 *My Bondage and My Freedom*. By 1855, Douglass's audience had broadened considerably, to include the Irish independence movement as well as the large working-class antislavery movement throughout Great Britain. If, as James McCune Smith suggests, Byron's lines articulate the importance of African American agency in the cause of abolition, Douglass's invocation of the lines also aligns the black American freedom struggle with these other international movements against oppression.

Throughout *My Bondage and My Freedom*, Douglass draws comparisons between the condition of African American slaves and the condition of the Irish under British oppression. The most significant instance of this comparative view occurs in Douglass's revision of his famous account of those "songs of the slave [that] represent the sorrows, rather than the joys, of his heart" (*MB* 75). As Douglass emphasized in both the 1845 *Narrative* and the 1855 *My Bondage and My Freedom*, the words of these slave songs were "jargon to others, but full of meaning to themselves" (*MB* 74). In *My Bondage and My Freedom*, however, as he describes the "tinge of deep melancholy" in these "outbursts of rapturous sentiment," Douglass adds: "I have never heard any songs like those anywhere since I left slavery, except when in Ireland. There I heard the same *wailing notes*, and was much affected by them. It was during the famine of 1845–6" (*MB* 74, emphasis in original). Following W. E. B. Du Bois's account of "The Sorrow Songs" in *The Souls of Black Folk*, literary scholars have focused on Douglass's 1845 discussion of the uniqueness of the African American slave songs.[53] Yet in 1855, Douglass uses these same songs to suggest a similarity between the African American slaves' oppression under American slavery and the social degradation of the Irish under British colonization and occupation. Significantly, Douglass locates this similarity in the *"wailing notes."* The words of the slave songs—"jargon to others but full of meaning to themselves"—refer to the slaves' unique experience of America's peculiar institution, but the sounds of the songs, "speak[ing] to the heart and to the soul of the thoughtful" (*MB* 75), "told a tale of grief and sorrow" (*MB* 74), with which those who had experienced a like oppression could identify.

Apprenticeship Life

Among the most famous of Douglass's speeches from his tour of Great Britain was the oft-reprinted and widely circulated "Reception Speech" (1846) at Finsbury Chapel. Douglass opened that speech with a strident argument against the use of the term "slavery" as a metaphor for other forms of oppression:

> I have found persons in this country who have identified the term slavery with that which I think it is not, and in some instances, I have feared, in so doing, have rather (unwittingly, I know) detracted much from the horror with which the term slavery is contemplated. It is common in this country to distinguish every bad thing by the name of slavery. Intemperance is slavery; to be deprived of the right to vote is slavery, says one; to have to work hard is slavery, says another. . . . I do not wish for a moment to detract from the horror with which the evil of intemperance is contemplated—not at all;

nor do I wish to throw the slightest obstruction in the way of any political freedom that any class of persons in this country may desire to obtain. But I am here to say that I think the term slavery is sometimes abused by identifying it with that which it is not.[54]

In this 1846 speech, Douglass argued that the constant use of "slavery" as metaphor was an abuse of the term, which threatened to weaken if not evacuate entirely the "horror" of the word. He follows this critique by emphasizing the legal distinction specific to slavery, the slave's condition as property:

> Slavery in the United States is the granting of that power by which one man exercises and enforces a right of property in the body and soul of another. The condition of the slave is simply that of a brute beast. He is a piece of property—a marketable commodity, in the language of the law, to be bought or sold at the will and caprice of the master who claims him to be his property; he is spoken of, thought of, and treated as property.[55]

For Douglass, what defined slavery was the chattel principle, the slave's legal status as property; and throughout the remainder of this famous speech, Douglass emphasized the multiple legal and social implications of the chattel principle and its "incidents." Douglass's argument in the 1846 "Reception Speech" is unsurprising; Garrisonians often argued against the use of the slavery metaphor. As David Roediger has suggested, "a consistent lesson taught by abolitionism was that chattel slavery was a category of oppression much harsher than any other."[56]

Historians and literary scholars have described the abolitionist critique of the recurring use of slavery as a metaphor for other forms of oppression, citing Douglass's 1846 "Reception Speech" as exemplary. They have overlooked, however, the historical fact that by 1855 Douglass reverses this position on the use of the white slavery metaphor. And Douglass does so in the very period during which such slavery metaphors were "eclipsed" in the political language of organized labor.[57]

If Douglass opened his 1846 London "Reception Speech" in Garrisonian fashion, criticizing the "white slavery" metaphor and emphasizing the uniqueness of black chattel slavery, in *My Bondage and My Freedom* he uses this very metaphor to describe the condition of the white wage laborers of the South. Douglass's most sustained description of southern wage workers as "white slaves" occurs as he introduces the scene of his own brutal beating at the hands of his white "fellow-apprentices" (*MB* 228). The narrative context of Douglass's use of the "white slavery" metaphor to describe wage labor is especially important to our understanding of the change in Douglass's politics, and his identification of the antislavery movement with the rising "free labor" politics of both moderate and radical political abolitionism: "The facts, leading to this barbarous outrage upon me, illustrate a phase of slavery destined to become an important element in the overthrow of the slave system, and I may, therefore state them with some minuteness. That phase is this: *the conflict of slavery with the interests of the white mechanics and laborers of the south*. In the country, this conflict is not so apparent; but, in cities, such as Baltimore, Richmond, New Orleans, Mobile, &c., it is seen pretty clearly" (*MB* 226). Before depicting the beating itself (which he had described in the 1845 *Narrative*), Douglass frames the narrative significance of this event in his "apprenticeship life," emphasizing first that the social conditions surrounding it—"the spirit of the times, at Gardiner's shipyard, and, indeed, in Baltimore more generally, in 1836" (*MB* 229)—were illustrative of a broader historical "phase of slavery." Douglass identifies this historical phase as the contradiction between the political economy of slavery and the economic "interests of the white mechanics and laborers of the South." Moreover, Douglass directly links this economic "conflict of interests" to the national antislavery struggle, suggesting that this historical phase is "destined to become an important element in the overthrow of the slave system." Moving beyond the conventional antislavery argument that slavery was a crime against morality and religion, Douglass engages the political economic argument, and his focus on this "conflict of interests" draws upon the rising "free labor" discourse shared by both moderate and radical political abolitionism:

> The slaveholders, with a craftiness peculiar to themselves, by encouraging the enmity of the poor, laboring white man against the blacks, succeeds in making the said white man almost as much a slave as the black slave himself. The difference between the white slave, and the black slave, is this: the latter belongs to *one* slaveholder, and the former belongs to *all* the slaveholders, collectively. The white slave has taken from him, by indirection, what the black slave has taken from him, directly, and without ceremony. Both are plundered, and by the same plunderers. The slave is robbed, by his master, of all his earnings, above what is required for his bare physical necessities; and the white man is robbed by the slave system,

of the just results of his labor, because he is flung into competition with a class of laborers who work without wages. The competition, and its injurious consequences, will, one day, array the nonslaveholding white people of the slave states, against the slave system, and make them the most effective workers against the great evil. (*MB* 226)

According to Douglass, the core of this "conflict of interests" is the competition on the labor market between free labor and slave labor, and the necessary effect of this competition on the white laborer's wages: "the white man is robbed by the slave system, of the just results of his labor, because he is flung into competition with a class of laborers who work without wages." Like Marx, who argued that "the veiled slavery of wage-labourers... needed the unqualified slavery of the New World as its pedestal," and that the wage laborer's "appearance of independence is maintained by... the legal fiction of contract," Douglass focuses on the condition of labor exploitation shared by white and black workers, and the "difference" between them as a form of appearance: "the white slave has taken from him, by indirection, what the black slave has taken from him, directly, and without ceremony."[58] Relying on Douglass's 1845 *Narrative*, historians have argued that for Douglass slavery was "more than an economic category."[59] This should not lead us to ignore the fact that for Douglass it was also an economic category. Douglass and other black abolitionists repeatedly emphasized that slaves were laborers. As we have seen, this was the basis of Henry Highland Garnet's call, in his 1843 "Address to the Slaves," for the slaves throughout the South to "themselves... strike the blow" against slavery by "ceas[ing] to labor for tyrants who will not remunerate" them.[60] Douglass, writing now as a political abolitionist, likewise argued that insofar as both enslaved and "free" waged workers were laborers, they both were subject to exploitation, and that this condition bound them together, in shared interests against "the slave system."

Modern readers may find Douglass's prediction that the shared interests of white wage laborers and black slaves "will, one day, array the nonslaveholding white people of the slave states, against the slave system, and make them the most effective workers against the great evil," to be a utopian one. After all, Douglass advances this claim as he introduces the brutal beating he suffers at the hands of his white "fellow-apprentices" (*MB* 228). And within modern labor history, the critical focus of "whiteness studies" has been on the racism of the "white" working class. Yet the seemingly utopian character of Douglass's prediction is precisely his point: radical political abolitionists worked to link abolitionism to the "free labor" ideology developed among the working class. When Douglass refers to "the character of the men, and the spirit of the times, at Gardiner's shipyard, and indeed, in Baltimore generally, in 1836" (*MB* 229), he alludes to the "year of the strikes," when thousands of wage laborers staged labor strikes across the skilled trades.[61] Just as Douglass had developed his representations of slave women to reflect his engagements with the women's rights movement, and just as he had elaborated the elements of social oppression which the enslaved African American and the colonized Irish shared in common in order to identify the black freedom struggle with the Irish independence movement; Douglass here addresses the "antislavery rank and file."[62] Modern historians can never know whether this historical "phase of slavery" would have led to Douglass's predicted outcome, would have "array[ed] the nonslaveholding white people of the slave states, against the slave system, and make them the most effective workers against the great evil." The Civil War forever changed the course of this history, just as it did the debates over the constitutionality of slavery. Like his "white slavery" metaphor, Douglass's prediction was based upon what he argued were the shared political economic interests of white wage workers and black slaves against the slave system, and as such it registers his active engagements with the other social struggles of this period. For Douglass, of paramount importance were the contingencies of the "ever-present now," and the shaping of the undecided future.

Douglass extends the "white slavery metaphor," moreover, to analyze racism as an ideology developed by the ruling class:

> At present, the slaveholders blind them to this competition by keeping alive their prejudice against the slaves, *as men*—not against them *as slaves*. They appeal to their pride, often denouncing emancipation, as tending to place the white man, on an equality with Negroes, and, by this means, they succeed in drawing off the minds of the poor whites from the real fact, that, by the rich slave-master, they are already regarded as but a single remove from equality with the slave. (*MB* 226–27)

Douglass's use of the "white slavery" metaphor was thus doubly resonant. Even as he employed the term to underscore the common condition of labor exploitation shared by white wage workers and black slaves, Douglass was fully aware of its uses by slavery's defenders. Douglass wrote *My Bondage and My Freedom* as the popularity of the proslavery critique of "free labor" was at its height, and he here alludes directly to the arguments of that critique. In George Fitzhugh's 1854 *Sociology for the South; or, the Failure of Free Society* (parts of which Fitzhugh delivered in lectures and debates with abolitionists in the northern states), Fitzhugh argued that "slave society" was superior to the "free society" of wage labor: "Three-fourths of free society are slaves, no better treated, when their wants and capacities are estimated, than negro slaves. The masters in free society, or slave society, if they perform properly their duties, have more cares and less liberty than the slaves themselves."[63] Fitzhugh's positive defenses of "slave society" underscored the insight of Douglass's argument that the southern ruling elite of "the rich slave-master" did in fact already regard wage laborers "as but a single remove from equality with the slave" (*MB* 227). Fitzhugh famously argued further that in the society of "free labor," wage laborers were worse off than slaves, the former being "free" to starve, while slaves, according to Fitzhugh's paternalist fantasy of the slaveholding South, would be cared for as part of the slaveholder's plantation "family": "In fact, the ordinary wages of common labor are insufficient to keep up separate domestic establishments for each of the poor, and association or starvation is in many cases inevitable. . . . With negro slaves, their wages invariably increase with their wants. The master increases the provision for the family as the family increases in number and helplessness."[64] When Douglass depicted his beating in the 1845 *Narrative*, he focused solely on that white working-class racism which David Roediger (following W. E. B. Du Bois's point in *Black Reconstruction*) has described as "the wages of whiteness." Yet Douglass revises this scene significantly in the 1855 *My Bondage and My Freedom*, and, rather than blame the working class for American racism, he emphasizes that this "race prejudice" was an ideology fostered by the ruling class of the South, the wealthy slaveholders: "The impression is cunningly made, that slavery is the only power that can prevent the laboring white man from falling to the level of the slave's poverty and degradation. To make this enmity deep and broad, between the slave and the poor white man, the latter is allowed to abuse and whip the former, without hindrance" (226–27). Long before whiteness studies, Douglass turned to "the dialectics of race and class," using the metaphor of "white slavery" to critique the exceptional character of class formation in the United States.[65]

As with Douglass's changed views of the Constitution, political abolition, and disunion, his shift from the Garrisonian claims of his 1846 "Reception Speech" to the arguments of the 1855 *My Bondage and My*

Freedom are articulated in the language of labor and class struggle. It is thus equally significant that Douglass's analysis of the dialectics of race and class appears in the chapter that Douglass pointedly entitles "Apprenticeship Life." The chapter title describes that period in which Douglass worked as a slave alongside free black and white wage workers in the shipyards of Baltimore. After Douglass is brutally beaten by his white "fellow-apprentices" at Gardiner's shipyard, his Master Hugh withdrew him from employment by Gardiner; taking him to another shipyard. Douglass describes this as a continuation of the "apprenticeship" training he had begun at Gardiner's: "The best [Master Hugh] could now do for me, was to take me into Mr. Price's yard, and afford me the facilities there, for completing the trade which I had began to learn at Gardiner's" (*MB* 232). Slavery's defenders asserted that Africans and African Americans were incapable of exercising liberty, even if it were granted them. In *Sociology for the South*, Fitzhugh began his chapter entitled "Negro Slavery" with a distillation of this very proslavery argument: "The negro is improvident; will not lay up in summer for the wants of winter; will not accumulate in youth for the exigencies of age. He would become an insufferable burden to society. Society has the right to prevent this, and can only do so by subjecting him to domestic slavery.... At the North he would freeze or starve."[66] As we have seen, while free-labor ideology developed by defining the "freedom" of wage labor in contrast to the visible bondage of black chattel slavery, radical political abolitionism drew upon the constitutive terms of "free labor" to argue that the slave stood outside the relations of contract, and thus outside those bonds described in the Constitution's "fugitive labor" clause. In *My Bondage and My Freedom*, Douglass employs these very terms of the "law of contract" to describe his "apprenticeship" into the world of wage labor: "Here I rapidly became expert in the use of caulking tools; and, in the course of a single year, I was able to command the highest wages paid to journeymen calkers in Baltimore.... After learning to calk, I sought my own employment, made my own contracts, and collected my own earnings; giving Master Hugh no trouble in any part of the transactions to which I was a party" (*MB* 232). Douglass focuses on the relative value of his labor, and the market "equality" of slave and free labor: even while a slave, Douglass could command the highest wages paid to journeymen caulkers. Comparing himself to these free workers, Douglass likewise emphasizes that while still a slave he was already participating in the world of "free labor": seeking his own employment, making his own contracts, and collecting his earnings. Though still "a slave in form"

(*MB* 181), Douglass was exercising all those attributes of the self identified with "free" personhood which, as we have seen, came to be identified with the rights, privileges, and duties of national citizenship: self-will, legal agency, and that "discipline" and "responsibility" required of the contracting individual. Indeed, this widespread practice—of smaller slaveholders allowing their slaves to work like "free" wage laborers by seeking their own employment, making their own contracts, and collecting their earnings—contradicted the slaveholders' own arguments against abolition and emancipation. Douglass's depictions of his participation in the world of "free labor" while still a slave in form thus reinforce the broader "representative" function of *My Bondage and My Freedom*. In detailing his "apprenticeship" into those attributes of personhood recognized, by abolitionists and slaveholders alike, as necessary to the exercise of freedom and citizenship, Douglass demonstrated "the practicability of the most radical abolitionism" (*MB* 10) and "irrefutable evidence of the justice, safety, and practicability of Immediate Emancipation" (*MB* 17).

5

"If Man Will Strike"

Moby-Dick *and the Letter of the Law*

The seal of the General Society of Mechanics and Tradesman, founded in New York in 1785, depicts an arm wielding a hammer, with the accompanying motto: "By Hammer and Hand All Arts Do Stand." This emblematic image circulated throughout the antebellum years in self-representations of newly organized journeymen and wage workers, appearing in pamphlets, broadsides, newspapers such as the *Working Man's Advocate* and the *Champion of American Labor,* and emblazoned on banners carried in union parades and protest rallies.[1]

Melville introduces this image into the world of *Moby-Dick* during one of Ishmael's early moments of narrative prolepsis. In "Knights and Squires" (chapter 26), as Ishmael alludes to the "abasement of poor Starbuck's fortitude" to be revealed in the "coming narrative"—the first instance of which soon occurs in Starbuck's famous debate with Ahab in chapter 36, "The Quarter-Deck"—Ishmael describes that nobility of "man, in the ideal" which he as a writer aspires to depict: "But this august dignity I treat of, is not the dignity of kings and robes, but that abounding dignity which has no robed investiture. Thou shalt see it shining in the arm that wields a pick or drives a spike; that democratic dignity which, on all hands, radiates without end from God; Himself! The great God absolute! The centre and circumference of all democracy!"[2] After invoking this image from the world of popular labor organizing as representative of "that democratic dignity" which his "coming narrative" will treat, Ishmael extends the image into his artist's apostrophe to the "great democratic God . . . the Spirit of Equality": "If, then, to meanest mariners, and renegades and castaways, I shall hereafter ascribe high qualities, though dark; weave round them tragic graces . . . if I shall touch that workman's arm with some ethereal light; if I shall spread a rainbow over his disastrous set of sun; then against all mortal critics bear me out in it, thou

Figure 3. The seal of the General Society of Mechanics and Tradesmen, designed in 1785. Courtesy of Image Collection Library, University of Massachusetts, Amherst.

just Spirit of Equality, which hast spread one royal mantle of humanity over all my kind!" (103–4). Ishmael's apostrophe to "the Spirit of Equality" transfers this "ideal" vision of the workman's arm, as object of his artistic representation, to the writing arm of the literary artist: "Bear me out in it, thou great democratic God! who didst not refuse to the swart convict, Bunyan, the pale, poetic pearl; Thou who didst clothe with doubly hammered leaves of finest gold, the stumped and paupered arm of old Cervantes" (104). In this self-reflexive narrative prolepsis introducing the novel's principal cast of characters, the image of the workman's arm thus serves to identify the labors of the writer with the labors of working-class democracy. As Ishmael likewise inserts himself into this history of everyman writers, his identification of "that workman's arm" with the writer's "paupered arm" brings together the expression of Ishmael's artistic aspirations and his own social identification: to Ishmael, these meanest mariners, renegades, and castaways are "all my kind" (103).

After its introduction in "Knights and Squires" (chapter 26), this image of the workman's arm will recur throughout *Moby-Dick*, linking together the novel's most famous chapters—"The Quarter-Deck," "The Doubloon," "The Candles," "The Symphony," and the concluding chapter, "The Chase—Third Day."[3] If the image, in Ishmael's apostrophe to the "Spirit of Equality," identifies the labors of the writer with the labors of workingmen, it recurs throughout *Moby-Dick* to link Ishmael's artistic ambitions to the ambitions of the novel's other prime mariner, renegade, and castaway, "that man [who] makes one in a whole nation's census—a mighty pageant creature, formed for noble tragedies," Captain Ahab (73).

Indeed, "that workman's arm" which Ishmael will first "touch . . . with some ethereal light" (103) belongs to Captain Ahab, as Ahab prepares to announce on the quarterdeck his true mission to the *Pequod*'s crew: "Receiving the top-maul from Starbuck, [Ahab] advanced towards the main-mast with hammer uplifted in one hand, exhibiting the gold with the other" (138). Viewed alone, this image of Ahab's arm wielding a hammer supports the critical argument that the scenes of labor on the *Pequod* depict the "industrial apparatus of nineteenth-century America," locating the novel's descriptive realism within the social struggles of what Michael Rogin has described as "the American 1848."[4] Yet Melville does more than cite the emblem of popular labor organizing at the beginning of "The Quarter-Deck" scene. As Ahab announces to the *Pequod*'s crew the "prime but private purpose" of their voyage, Ahab punctuates his declaration by nailing the doubloon to the mainmast, promising it to the one who first sights the white whale. If the image of Ahab "with hammer uplifted in one hand" cites the emblematic self-representations of mechanics and tradesmen, Ahab's action as he makes his announcement invokes another aspect of labor history specific to the antebellum rise of organized labor: by nailing the doubloon to the mainmast, Ahab literally "strikes the mast" (138).

Common sailors, journeyman, mechanics, and other wage workers of the nineteenth century were familiar with the etymology of the labor "strike": to "strike" in the sense of a collective work stoppage derives from the nautical phrase "strike the mast." "Strike" as a nautical term originally meant: "To lower or take down (a sail, mast, yard, etc.)."[5] The nautical term first became identified with collective work stoppages in the late eighteenth century, when sailors began to "strike the mast" in acts of protest, refusing to work and preventing their ships from sailing, as in this example from the *Annual Register* of 1768: "A body of sailors ... proceeded ... to Sunderland ... and, at the cross there read a paper, setting forth their grievances.... After this they went on board the several ships in that harbour, and struck (lowered down) their yards, in order to prevent them from proceeding to sea."[6] The sailors' literal act of "striking" became identified as a symbolic act, announcing their refusal to work until their collective demands were met. "Strike," in both its original transitive form—as short for "strike the mast" or "strike mast"—and its verbal nominative form (as "*a strike*") became identified with organized work stoppages in England by the turn of the nineteenth century, as in this 1793 usage: "The poor seldom strike, as it is called, without good reason.... The colliers had struck for more wages."[7] In the industrializing United States, this latter meaning of the term became especially prevalent during the rise of journeymen's associations in the 1820s. With the increasing labor radicalism of the 1820s and 1830s, there was a rapid rise in collective work stoppages called "strikes," as part of the campaign for the ten-hour day. Almost every year between 1830 and 1836 saw thousands of journeymen mechanics and tradesmen involved in successful work "strikes"; and by 1836, the ten-hour day had been won by much of the working class.[8] As the anti-union *New York Herald* noted in early 1836, "These are truly *striking* times."[9] The increasing currency of the term "strike" to describe a protest refusal of work was even registered by Ralph Waldo Emerson, a thinker far removed from the world of labor struggles and the "meanest mariners" of Ishmael's kind. In "The Transcendentalist," Emerson cited the phrase to describe the Transcendentalists' own rejection of the dictates of the market:

> It is a sign of our times, conspicuous to the coarsest observer, that many intelligent and religious persons withdraw themselves from the common labors and competitions of the market and the caucus, and betake themselves to a certain solitary and critical way of living.... They hold themselves aloof: they feel the disproportion between their faculties and the work offered them..... They are *striking work*, and crying out for somewhat worthy to do![10]

The nautical history of this protest language was likewise invoked by William Lloyd Garrison and the Executive Committee of the American Anti-Slavery Society, in their 1844 *Address* calling for a revolt against the ship of state: "Up, then, with the banner of revolution! . . . Secede, then, from the government. Submit to its exactions, but pay it no allegiance, and give it no voluntary aid. . . . Circulate a declaration of DISUNION FROM SLAVEHOLDERS, throughout the country. Hold mass meetings—assemble in conventions—*nail your banners to the mast!*"[11]

Throughout *Moby-Dick*, Ishmael explains the meanings and etymologies of terms specific to seafaring and the world of whaling—"loomings," "the mast-head," "crow's nest," "the line," and "gam," to name a few. For those readers less familiar with the nautical history of the labor "strike" as a form of protest, Melville emphasizes the common sailors' understanding of Ahab's act on the quarterdeck at the end of chapter 99, "The Doubloon," in the words of seemingly mad Pip: "Here's the ship's navel, this doubloon here, and they are all on fire to unscrew it. But, unscrew your navel, and what's the consequence? Then again, if it stays here, that is ugly, too, for when aught's nailed to the mast it's a sign that things grow desperate" (335).

"The Quarter-Deck" chapter is narrated as a theatrical scene, complete with stage directions ("*Enter Ahab: Then, all*"), whose central set-piece is the debate between Ahab and Starbuck. Thus incorporating theatrical forms, the chapter's introductory narration frames the broader narrative significance of Ahab's famous quarterdeck speech. Before Ahab makes his announcement and nails the doubloon to the mast, he summons the crew: "[Ahab] ordered Starbuck to send everybody aft. 'Sir!' said the mate, astonished at an order seldom or never given on ship-board except in some extraordinary case. 'Send everybody aft,' repeated Ahab. 'Mast-heads, there! Come down!'" (137). With Starbuck's astonishment, Melville emphasizes the extraordinary character of Ahab's command. It is so extraordinary because the captain himself has ordered the crew away from their work. Ahab even calls the mastheads down from their stations, the most important in the business of whaling, as Ishmael had explained in the preceding chapter, "The Mast-Head." Immediately after ordering the crew to cease work and "strike mast"—to strike in the original nautical sense—Ahab announces the "prime but private purpose" of their voyage, to hunt the white whale (178). And Ahab punctuates this announcement by "striking the mast" as he nails the doubloon to it, thereby invoking the sailors' understanding of this act: "when aught's nailed to the mast it's a sign that things grow desperate" (335). Like the sailors' act of labor protest originating the term, Ahab's literal act is simultaneously a symbolic one, for with his announcement Ahab breaks his contract with the owners of the *Pequod*. Melville underscores this radical meaning of Ahab's act soon after "The Quarter-Deck" scene, in Ishmael's "Surmises" (chapter 46).

In "Surmises," Ishmael speculates upon the possible reasons motivating Ahab to "continue true to the natural, nominal purpose of the Pequod's voyage," after having revealed to the crew his own private purpose, to hunt the white whale. Ishmael's final surmise sheds light on the narrative context through which we are to understand Ahab's famous speech from the stage of the quarterdeck: "Having impulsively, it is probable, and perhaps somewhat prematurely revealed the prime but private purpose of the Pequod's voyage, Ahab was now entirely conscious that, in so doing, he had indirectly laid himself open to the unanswerable charge of usurpation; and with perfect impunity, both moral and legal, his crew if so disposed, and to that end competent, could refuse all further obedience to him, and even violently wrest from him the command" (178). Through the retrospective voice of Ishmael, Melville emphasizes a narrative fact ignored in critical interpretations of *Moby-Dick* as a political allegory, and of Ahab as a figure of political coercion, as a mad "dictator" or "totalitarian."[12] Such interpretations, which have long predominated in critical and popular readings of *Moby-Dick*, all agree that "Ahab's demand for freedom enslaves his crew."[13] As Michal Rogin has suggested, however, "as a political allegory *Moby-Dick* remains, paradoxically, above politics," such that its representations cannot be simply translated back into any specific historical referents.[14]

There is also a literary-formal problem with readings of the novel as political allegory, and of the *Pequod* as representative of the ship of state: *Moby-Dick* is a shipwreck narrative, and the *Pequod* a whaling ship. Melville announces this formal point in the "Extracts" from the *Narrative of the Shipwreck of the Whale Ship Essex* (14), and discusses the "narrative in this book" (170) *Moby-Dick* in direct relation to the popular literary genre of shipwreck narratives in "The Affidavit" (chapter 45). As a private whaler, the *Pequod*, with a crew of thirty "*Isolatoes*" drawn from the distant continents of the globe forming "an Anacharsis Clootz deputation from all the isles of the sea," was very different from the man-of-war, a large military vessel and literal ship of state (107). In *White-Jacket; or, the World in a Man-of-War*, Melville explicitly describes the man-of-war and its rigid hierarchy as representative of state and society:

> For a ship is a bit of terra firma cut off from the main; it is a state in itself; and the captain is its king. It is no limited monarchy, where the sturdy

> Commons have a right to petition, and snarl if they please; but almost a despotism, like the Grand Turk's. The captain's word is law; he never speaks but in the imperative mood. When he stands on his Quarter-deck at sea, he absolutely commands as far as eye can reach..... He is lord and master of the sun.[15]

The man-of-war was a massive ship (a seventy-four) carrying a crew of five hundred men, whose society was so large that they could be aptly compared to "the people" (*White-Jacket* 225). And, as Samuel Otter has shown, it is in *White-Jacket* that Melville so powerfully stages the analogy between "the world in a man-of-war" and the state and society of antebellum slavery.[16] Melville emphasizes these distinctions between ships and their social spaces throughout his sea novels. This distinction between the private vessel and the man-of-war would be central to the social and legal order depicted in *Billy Budd*, for example: Melville begins the plot with Billy's removal from the merchantman *The Rights of Man* to the "seventy-four outward bound, H.M.S. *Bellipotent*."[17]

Likewise, the prospects for success of a mutiny on the *Pequod* were much greater than any attempted mutiny on those "ships of state" the *Neversink* and the *Bellipotent*. Melville emphasizes this point as well in Ishmael's surmises as to Ahab's reasons for continuing the "nominal purpose" of their voyage: "I will not strip these men, thought Ahab, of all hopes of cash—aye, cash. They may scorn cash now; but let some months go by, and no perspective promise of it to them, and then this same quiescent cash all at once mutinying in them, this same cash would cashier Ahab" (*Moby-Dick* 178). Moreover, through Ishmael's surmises, Melville emphasizes that Ahab "was now entirely conscious" that with the announcement of his "private purpose" he had released the crew from his command, and that the crew could "refuse all further obedience" to him "with perfect impunity, both moral and legal," which is to say that any "rebellion" against Ahab would not be considered a criminal mutiny (140). Melville reminds us, in other words, that Ahab cannot force the crew to follow him. Speaking from the elevated stage of the quarterdeck, Ahab must instead recruit them to join with him in his cause; he must persuade them to make his individual private purpose their shared collective one.

That these are Ishmael's surmises as to Ahab's rationale for pursuing the *Pequod*'s nominal purpose is likewise significant to an understanding of Melville's representation of Ishmael as a figure of the artist, finding symbolic significance in Ahab's mad hunt. What Ishmael and Ahab recognize is that in the very announcement of his vengeance as the "prime but private purpose" of the *Pequod*'s voyage, Ahab breaks his contract with the ship's owners—thus the "unanswerable charge of usurpation" to which "he had indirectly laid himself open" (178). And in Ahab's appeal to the ship's crew to join him in his private purpose, Ahab asks that they, too, violate their labor contracts. Ahab's announcement is thus also a call to "strike" in that other sense, as a collective refusal to continue working for the owners of the *Pequod*. And by calling upon his crew to join with him in violation of the contract with the ship's owners, Ahab calls upon them to join him in what was considered under antebellum law to be a "criminal conspiracy."

U.S. courts had long used the common-law definition of "conspiracy" to criminalize journeyman's associations and labor combinations; outlawing strikes with landmark conspiracy convictions at Philadelphia in 1806 and New York in 1810.[18] Under the broad terms of this conspiracy doctrine, "any confederacy affecting public trade or public health, public morals or public peace, to effect some unlawful object might be the subject of indictment for conspiracy."[19] This broad conspiracy doctrine was successfully applied against striking workingmen until the landmark decision of Massachusetts Chief Justice Lemuel Shaw, Melville's father-in-law and the man to whom he had dedicated *Typee*, in the case of *Commonwealth v. Hunt* (1842). A conspiracy, Shaw wrote in his precedent-setting opinion, "must be a combination of two or more persons, by some concerted action, to accomplish some criminal or unlawful purpose, or to accomplish some purpose, not in itself criminal or unlawful, by criminal or unlawful means." Shaw ruled that an association of journeyman mechanics could not be considered a "criminal conspiracy" based on the mere fact of their combination, or on their collective agreement to refuse to work for an employer (to go on "strike"). Instead, criminality lay in the "purpose" and "the means" of the association: "The legality of an association will . . . depend upon the means to be used for its accomplishment."[20]

While establishing the significant legal precedent distinguishing journeymen's associations from "criminal conspiracy punishable by law," Shaw's emphasis on the "means" used by these associations to advance their interests maintained an important element of conspiracy doctrine, which could still be applied against labor strikes: "If a large number of men, engaged for a certain time, should combine together to violate their contract . . . it would surely be a conspiracy to do an unlawful act."[21] As Shaw emphasized in his decision, the journeymen in *Commonwealth v. Hunt* had not contracted with their employer; and so their collective refusal to continue working for him—their threatened labor strike—was not illegal.[22]

Each and every member of the crew of the *Pequod* had contracted with the ship's owners. Melville emphasized this point in chapter 16 ("The Ship") with the comic scenes of Ishmael "signing the papers" (77) and in chapter 18 ("His Mark") with Queequeg copying onto the contract "an exact counterpart of a queer round figure which was tattooed upon his arm (85). Ahab breaks his contract with the *Pequod*'s owners when he announces "the prime but private purpose" of the voyage, and thereby releases the crew from his legal command. If the crew allies with Ahab in his private purpose, they "combine together to violate their contract" and join with him in a "criminal conspiracy."

Ahab's act of nailing the doubloon to the mast simultaneously marks Ahab's rejection of that contract which originally bound him and initiates the collective bond that will replace the law of contract: the oath the crew swears to hunt the whale, forming an "indissoluble league" (142). Introducing the dramatic quarterdeck debate between Ahab and Starbuck with the representative image of the workingman's arm and hammer, and with Ahab's signifying act, the scene's opening narration thus frames their debate within the historical context of labor conspiracies, workers' strikes, and Ahab's rejection of the law of contract. Immediately before Ahab makes his famous declaration—"If man will strike, strike through the mask!"—Ahab "strikes the mast," and he does so by striking through the surface of the doubloon, that gold coin whose monetary value depends upon its symbolic meaning in the market.

In this scene introducing Ahab's "mad" purpose, Melville thus situates Ahab's monomania within a collective class discourse, a class *langue* which, as Fredric Jameson has argued, is dialogical in structure.[23] Melville will make the essentially antagonistic form of the dialogical explicit in the debate between Ahab and Starbuck. Melville stages many dialogues between Ahab and Starbuck throughout the novel; these other dialogues, however, are private exchanges whose contents are known only to Ahab and Starbuck (and to Ishmael the storyteller). In contrast, "The Quarter-Deck" debate occurs in front of the crew. Starbuck "cried out" for all to hear his objections to Ahab's purpose (139). Unlike the private exchanges between them later in the novel, this first dialogue between Ahab and Starbuck is a scene of rhetorical battle, taking place on the symbolic stage of the quarterdeck, that space by the mainmast reserved for the captain and his officers.

As first mate, Starbuck is the one who would lead any opposition to Ahab's proposal to violate the contract with the *Pequod*'s owners.

In his first attempt at opposition, Starbuck invokes the very business contract Ahab proposes they break, and speaks that legal contract's conception of quantitative market value:

> I am game for his crooked jaw, and for the jaws of Death, too, Captain Ahab, if it fairly comes in the way of the business we follow; but I came here to hunt whales, not my commander's vengeance. How many barrels will thy vengeance yield thee even if thou gettest it, Captain Ahab? it will not fetch thee much in our Nantucket market. (139)

In his response to Starbuck, Ahab appropriates Starbuck's market-based metaphor for value and extends it excessively, to catachresis:

> "If money's to be the measurer, man, and the accountants have computed their great counting-house the globe, by girdling it with guineas, one to every three parts of an inch; then, let me tell thee, that my vengeance will fetch a great premium *here!*"
> "He smites his chest," whispered Stubb, "what's that for? methinks it rings most vast, but hollow." (139)

That Melville includes Stubb's remark on Ahab's actions as Ahab speaks these lines underscores the public character of this debate as a scene of "cultural persuasion," and points to another, "lower layer" of meaning in Ahab's response to Starbuck.[24] As Melville emphasizes in "The Ship" (chapter 16), "Ahab's above the common; Ahab's been in colleges, as well as 'mong the cannibals" (78). With Ahab's excessive play on Starbuck's mundane metaphor of market value, Melville places Ahab in a long history of master rhetoricians. Ahab's opening response—"If money's to be the measurer, man . . ."—puns on the maxim of the ancient Sophist Protagoras: "Man is the measure of all things, of all things that are, that they are, and of all things that are not, that they are not" (DK80b1).[25] This maxim (*homo-mensura*), associated since Plato with a radical relativism, was understood to mean that the knowledge of qualities, such as "value," are contingent rather than absolute truths, relative to each individual knower. Against Starbuck's Nantucket-market reason, which posits "money to be the measurer" of all things, Ahab invokes Protagoras's famous maxim in both word and deed: Ahab "smites his chest," pointing to himself as he declares where his "vengeance will fetch a great premium." To Ahab, man is the measure.

Starbuck's second point of opposition—"'Vengeance on a dumb brute!' cried Starbuck, 'that simply smote thee from blindest instinct! Madness! To be enraged with a dumb thing, Captain Ahab, seems blasphemous'"— occasions Ahab's performance of another philosophical maxim attributed to Protagoras: "About the gods, I am not able to know whether they exist or do not exist, nor what they are like in form" (DK80b4). This second maxim was understood as expressive of a radical agnosticism; and linked to the relativism of the first maxim (man is the measure). Both maxims were linked to a final one, through which the teachings of the ancient Sophists were associated by Plato with the insidious sophistry of "rhetorical man."[26] Protagoras was also known for claiming that through *orthoepeia*—the mastery of "the correct use" of words—he could "make the weaker cause the stronger" (DK80b6), and win any debate. In Ahab's response to Starbuck's second point of opposition, Melville associates Ahab—or rather depicts Ahab associating himself—with these three maxims of the ancient Sophists, while interweaving the language of ancient philosophy with the language of the modern market:

> Hark ye yet again,—the little lower layer. All visible objects, man, are but as pasteboard masks. But in each event—in the living act, the undoubted deed—there, some unknown but still reasoning thing puts forth the mouldings of its features from behind the unreasoning mask. If man will strike, strike through the mask! How can the prisoner reach outside except by thrusting through the wall? To me, the white whale is that wall, shoved near to me. Sometimes I think there's naught beyond. But 'tis enough. He tasks me; he heaps me; I see in him outrageous strength, with an inscrutable malice sinewing it. That inscrutable thing is chiefly what I hate; and be the white whale agent, or be the white whale principal, I will wreak that hate upon him. (140)

Ahab again appropriates the terms of Starbuck's objection (that vengeance on a dumb brute is madness, and seemingly blasphemous). This appropriation of the terms of his opponent underscores the representation of this scene as one of rhetorical battle, the essentially antagonistic character of the dialogic mode. In Ahab's view, man's knowledge of the world is structured as a distinction between surface and substance, between a phenomenal reality—what one perceives and thereby mistakes for objective reality—and a noumenal truth, a truth lying in the "little lower layer" beyond phenomenal apprehension. Yet the series of metaphors employed by Ahab takes this vision further, linking perceived reality to the world of deceptive artifice: phenomenal reality masks truth.

The corollary to this metaphor of the pasteboard mask is Ahab's conception of the "event": because "all visible objects," including the white whale, are but as "unreasoning masks," intentional agency (what Starbuck believes to be the "blindest instinct" of a dumb brute) is not to be found in such visible objects. It is only in moments of action—"in each event—in the living act, the undoubted deed"—that whatever "unknown but still reasoning thing" begins to reveal the contours, "the mouldings," of its truth. It is through an inversion of this representation of agency—"the living act, the undoubted deed"—that Ahab will counter Starbuck's characterization of his hunt for vengeance as "madness." Ahab can "make the weaker cause the stronger" by staging a corresponding transformation in the figurations of individual agency. In Ahab's figuration of agency, man must "strike through" the unreasoning mask of phenomenal reality, to reach that "unknown but still reasoning thing" behind it. This universal man is then identified with the figure of the prisoner confined by that phenomenal reality of visible objects, now identified as a wall. In the final elaboration of these metaphors—"to me, the white whale is that wall, shoved near to me"—Ahab recalls the first maxim (man is the measure of all things), while inserting himself into this universalist narrative. Ahab becomes representative of universal man striking through the mask, identified further with the prisoner liberating himself from his prison walls. Through this series of metaphors for visible phenomena as opposed to noumenal truth, Ahab elevates the meaning of his own "living act," his strike at the white whale, as standing for universal man's act of self-liberation. The meaning Starbuck would ascribe to the hunt—madness, blasphemy—has been overwhelmed by this now heroic meaning.

Ahab likewise answers the charge of "madness" by setting aside the question of the white whale's intentional agency—whether it be "blindest instinct" or "inscrutable malice"—altogether: "That inscrutable thing is chiefly what I hate; and be the white whale agent, or be the white whale principal, I will wreak that hate upon him" (140). In his figuration of the white whale itself, Ahab returns here to the language of the market contract. In nineteenth-century contract law, the "principal" named the primary merchant or business owner; and his "agent" was that employee fully authorized to act—contract to buy and sell in the marketplace—in the name of the principal. Thus authorized to act, the agent's "intention" and "will" were considered those of the principal. With the rapid antebellum expansion of the market, spurred by the cotton boom, commercial litigation increasingly required clarification of this "law of agency." As described in Joseph Story's 1839 *Commentaries on the the Law of Agency*, antebellum contract law understood the modern "law of principal and agent" as similar to the older "law of master and servant." This older law represented a status-based liability derived from traditional feudal conceptions of the legal identity of master and servant: the bound servant had no unqualifiedly "free will" of his own, and so the master remained responsible for the actions of his servant. According to the antebellum law of agency, the liability of a principal for the contracts of his agent rested on grounds similar to this liability of a master for the torts of his servant. The actions of the "agent" were considered the actions of his employing "principal," and thus bound the principal in all cases.[27]

To Ahab, it matters not whether the white whale is "agent" or "principal," the servant or its master. As he sets aside the question of intelligent, intentional agency in Moby-Dick, Ahab does more than counter Starbuck's charge of "Madness! To be enraged with a dumb thing." As with the symbolic meaning of Ahab's act of "striking the mast," Ahab's invocation of the language of contract and its law of agency to characterize the white whale locates the historical origins of his "rage" in the market itself, that "intangible" thing which Moby-Dick "personified, and made practically assailable" (156). Under the market's "freedom of contract," free men remained the servants of unseen masters. As pasteboard mask, the white whale is the face of the unseen forces ruling over men, and as wall it gives form to the invisible prison of the market world, that "great counting-house the globe," girdled with guineas.

Ahab rails against the "inscrutable" (140), the "intangible" (156), and the "personified impersonal" (382) throughout *Moby-Dick*. To Ahab, "all the things that most exasperate and outrage mortal man, all these things are bodiless, but only bodiless as objects, not as agents" (420). Melville emphasizes the white whale's role as the embodiment, the "incarnation," of all these bodiless forces. As Ishmael describes in "Moby Dick" (chapter 41), Ahab "at last came to identify with him, not only all his bodily woes, but all his intellectual and spiritual exasperations. The White Whale swam before him as the monomaniac incarnation of all those malicious agencies which some deep men feel eating in them, till they are left living on with half a heart and half a lung" (156). Once again figuring Ishmael in the role of storyteller, drawing symbolic significance from Ahab's hunt, Melville imagines Ahab as Prometheus, the Titan who, with hammer in hand, defied the gods. Finally, Ahab's reflections on the meaning of "the living act, the undoubted deed" have already been framed by a very specific "living act" of his own: Ahab invokes the market contract law of agency after he has struck through the surface of the doubloon, that phenomenal symbol of the market, nailing it to the mast as he announced his strike.

"When Aught's Nailed to the Mast"

Throughout the series of chapters depicting the business of whaling, Ishmael reflects upon the different aspects of whaling as representative of the condition of man in modernity: the hunt for whales for the Nantucket market as representative of man's appropriation of nature; the voyages in this hunt as representative of man's attempt to master the sublime space of the ocean, that last space unconquered by capitalism; and the transformation of the body of the whale into oil and other commodities as representative of the socialized labor process under industrial capitalism.

The paired chapters "Ambergris" and "The Castaway" together stage the link between the labors of the *Pequod* and the working world of Melville's America. In "Ambergris," Ishmael takes the description of this "very curious substance" (317) as occasion to discuss the origins of value in human labor. Remarking on the importance of ambergris "as an article of commerce" (317), Ishmael describes the great monetary value of ambergris, and the many "precious" commodities into which it is made. The origins of the valuable ambergris are unknown, however, to its consumers: "Who would think, then, that such fine ladies and gentleman should regale themselves with an essence found in the inglorious bowels of a sick whale! Yet so it is" (317). While "the precise origin of ambergris remained . . . a problem to the learned" (317), its source is known to the common sailor: the commodity's "value" originates in human labor, and man's appropriation of nature.

Melville extends these reflections on the origins of the commodity's exchange-value into "The Castaway." After Pip's jump from Stubb's whaleboat leads to the loss of a whale, Stubb orders Pip never to jump again: "Stick to the boat, Pip, or by the Lord, I wont pick you up if you jump; mind that. We can't afford to lose whales by the likes of you; a whale would sell for thirty times what you would, Pip, in Alabama. Bear that in mind, and don't jump any more" (321). While given in a "plain business-like, but still half-humorous manner," Stubb's "peremptory command" draws explicit equation between the monetary value of whales and the monetary value of slaves. Ishmael elaborates Stubbs's meaning for us: "Hereby perhaps Stubb indirectly hinted, that though man loves his fellow, yet man is a money-making animal, which propensity too often interferes with his benevolence" (321). In the midst of these chapters depicting the laborious business of whaling, Melville reminds us that the "Nantucket market" for which the *Pequod* sailed remained inextricably tied to the American slave market.

This series of chapters depicting the labor of whaling and reflecting on the origins of value culminates in chapter 99, "The Doubloon." Melville returns here to that piece of gold nailed to the mast by Ahab in "The Quarter-Deck," to reflect on the multiple valences of the concept of "value," and on the interpretive processes through which "wonders" come to be read as "signs," natural and man-made phenomena taken for significant, meaningful symbols. The focus of chapter 99 is the doubloon as a symbolic text, and the chapter proceeds by staging the many attempts to interpret the doubloon's "signs."

While Melville does not stage Ishmael's reading of the doubloon in the same way he stages the readings of other characters, he characterizes Ishmael's perspective in Ishmael's opening narration of the chapter:

> But one morning, turning to pass the doubloon, [Ahab] seemed to be newly attracted by the strange figures and inscriptions stamped upon it, as though now for the first time beginning to interpret for himself in some monomaniac way whatever significance might lurk in them. And some certain significance lurks in all things, else all things are little worth, and the round world itself but an empty cipher, except to sell by the cartload, as they do hills about Boston, to fill up some morass in the Milky Way. (331–32)

As Ishmael introduces Ahab's action, Ishmael's narrative point of view becomes intertwined with Ahab's imagined point of view. Melville suggests a parallel between Ishmael's and Ahab's perspectives through the repetition of those terms Ishmael uses to narrate Ahab's actions— "beginning to interpret for himself in some monomaniac way whatever significance might lurk in them"—in Ishmael's own reflections upon perceiving Ahab's action: "And some certain significance lurks in all things." With this repetition, Melville also introduces the chapter's focus on the relation between interpretation, finding "significance" in things, and valuation, finding the "worth" of things.

The parallels between their perspectives are underscored further as Ishmael elaborates the trope of "signification" as both an act of interpretation and an act of valuation: "else all things are little worth, and the round world itself but an empty cipher, except to sell by the cartload, as they do hills about Boston, to fill up some morass in the Milky Way." Ishmael's elaboration of the trope of signification introduces the metaphor of the cipher, identifying the round shape of the world with the shape of the "zero," now emptied of its contents. The metaphor has multiple valences: as one great zero, the round world itself is of "little worth"—that is, of little quantitative value—and also of little significance, little meaning. In addition to the numerical character, the round world as empty cipher raises the other meaning of "worth," which is to "interpret": a cipher is also a "symbolic character, a hieroglyph" to be deciphered. As "The Doubloon" chapter returns to that piece of gold nailed to the mast in "The Quarter-Deck," Ishmael's language here explicitly echoes Ahab's famous lines in response to Starbuck's first objection to his hunt for Moby-Dick: "If money's to be the measurer, man, and the accountants have computed their great counting-house the globe, by girdling it with guineas, one to every three parts of an inch; then let me tell thee, that my vengeance will fetch a great premium *here!*" (139). Just as in Ahab's elaborate catachresis, wherein the globe itself is figured as a great counting-house, and its equator, wrapped in gold coins, is used to highlight Ahab's perspective on value—a qualitative one, as opposed to Starbuck's quantitative market conception—Ishmael's metaphor here identifies the round shape of the earth with the numerical figure zero to raise the link between qualitative and quantitative value; and it highlights Ishmael's ironic perspective on that market-oriented quantitative conception: it is an empty cipher "except to sell by the cartload, as they do hills about Boston, to fill up some morass in the Milky Way." This sense of "cipher" figures the world as of "little worth" in the sense of monetary value: good only to be sold for its dirt, filling up holes in the universe.

Extending this image of the round world, Ishmael turns to an extensive description of the doubloon itself as "raked somewhere out of the heart of gorgeous hills whence, east and west, over golden sands, the headwaters of many a Pactolus flow. And though now nailed amidst all the rustiness of iron bolts and the verdigris of copper spikes, yet, untouchable and immaculate to any foulness, it still preserved its Quito glow" (332).

The end rhymes of these lines—"Pactolus flow . . . Quito glow"—emphasize both images, identifying each with the other: its "Quito glow," the brightness of the doubloon, still shining immaculate after this long voyage, finds its original source in the "headwaters of many a Pactolus flow." In the legend of King Midas, the Pactolus was the river in which Midas washed his hands to remove the gift that had become his curse. Yet as Ishmael notes further, the "precious" doubloon retained its "Quito glow" because "it was set apart and sanctified to one awe-striking end; and however wanton in their sailor ways, one and all, the mariners revered it as the white whale's talisman" (332). Thus "set apart and sanctified," the doubloon has been removed from circulation, removed from its original signification as universal equivalent, and its "significance" (its meaning and its "worth") transformed in the hunt for Moby-Dick. Becoming "the white whale's talisman," it comes to stand for the whale, now perceived by the sailors in superstitious and religious senses as a supernatural force. The central theme of this chapter, as highlighted here in the transformation of the "worth" of the coin from market symbol to talismanic symbol, is the intangible, qualitative conception of "value"—the other meaning of "worth"—as opposed to that quantitative, monetary conception of the Nantucket market. For Ishmael as for Ahab, man is the measure.

Ishmael emphasizes also that the "mariners revered it as the white whale's talisman," which is to say that the meaning of the doubloon has been transformed by the viewers. While still a money-form of value in any other context, through the hunt it has undergone a transvaluation, becoming instead a symbolic object to be interpreted, and the principal action of this chapter is composed of the attempted "renderings" of this same text by different characters, beginning with Ahab, made mad by his encounter with Moby-Dick, and ending with Pip, made mad by his experience as castaway. Throughout the chapter, Ishmael emphasizes that these characters are themselves being observed as they attempt to "read" the doubloon; as each reader leaves, another, who was watching him, takes his place, to be observed reading in turn. The chapter unfolds as a series of differing interpretations—underscoring the limits of man's attempts to make meaning of the "signs" of his world.

Ahab reads each and every image on the doubloon as representing Ahab himself: "all are Ahab; and this round gold is but the image of the rounder globe, which, like a magician's glass, to each and every man in turn but mirrors back his own mysterious self" (332). Ahab identifies the round gold doubloon with the rounder globe—recalling once again his metaphor on the quarterdeck—and mixes this metaphor with another image: the rounder globe is also now "like a magician's glass." The globe is figured as one great mirror, in which man, seeking out meaning in the world, sees only his own reflection. Ahab acknowledges his own egotism; he is a character fully self-aware in this sense—aware of his egotism, but also of the view that all men are likewise egotistical, whether they are aware of the fact or not.

Starbuck is the second to attempt to read the doubloon, initiating his own reading by observing Ahab's act of reading: "The old man seems to read Belshazzar's awful writing" (333). Starbuck's reading reveals his own inner character, demonstrating the very point made by Ahab: each and every man, as he attempts to interpret the world around him, ends up seeing his own reflection. Starbuck's opening observation expresses his conventional, religious point of view: "Belshazaar's awful writing" alludes to the Book of Daniel, and Daniel's famous interpretation of the mysterious "writing on the wall" as a portent of doom. In the original story, the writing on the wall as interpreted by Daniel foretells the fall of Belshazzar's empire. Yet significant as well to "The Doubloon" chapter's broader representation of the interdependence of qualitative signification and quantitative valuation is the mysterious language of that writing on the wall in the biblical story: *Mene, Tekel, and Parsin*. These were the ancient Aramaic names for measures of currency; it was these names for monetary value which Daniel interprets, in ways other than their monetary significations, to decipher the writing on the wall as a prophecy of doom.

Starbuck's rendering of the doubloon ultimately "mirrors back his own mysterious self," as he interprets the doubloon's images through the terms of Christian allegory. The three mountain peaks "almost seem the Trinity," and the space between them the "vale of Death"—the "Valley of Death" from the 23rd Psalm: "Yea, though I walk through the valley of the shadow of death, I will fear no evil; For thou art with me; Thy rod and thy staff, they comfort me." Following the 23rd Psalm, Starbuck interprets the image of the Sun as the symbol for God, shining over the valley of the shadow of death, "over all our gloom, the sun of Righteousness still shines a beacon and a hope." Yet Starbuck's bravery, "while great in the face of natural, brute dangers, is one that quails in the face of more spiritual terrors" (103). And here his courage fails him: extending his allegory, he sees that the sun, however it may serve as a beacon and a hope, must set every night: it does not remain a steadfast fixture. His courage failing him, Starbuck stops when he reaches this logical conclusion to his own allegorical reading; looking away for fear that "Truth [will] shake me falsely" (333).

The next to read the text that is the doubloon is Stubb. Like Starbuck, Stubb begins by observing those who preceded him in reading the doubloon, and likewise announces his own act as an interpretation: "Let me read it once" (333). Indeed, it is through Stubb's voice that Melville will most forcefully link the concepts of signification and valuation. Throughout his comic rendering, Stubb puns on the biblical terms "signs and wonders": "Signs and wonders, eh? Pity if there is nothing wonderful in signs, and significant in wonders!" (334). Stubb's comic play on the paired terms is also significant to the broader discursive universe within which this chapter is situated. In this period, as the Union crisis escalated and as both Garrisonian abolitionists and proslavery politicians were calling for secession and the division of the Union into free-soil North and slaveholding South, the language of the slavery debates and the Union crisis repeatedly drew on the language of biblical doom. Reformers, religious leaders, and politicians repeatedly pointed to historical events—slave revolts or market collapses (such as the Panic of 1837)—as so many signs of a fallen generation, and portents of its impending demise. Preachers and politicians alike invoked biblical stories—such as the story of Belshazzar's "awful writing," or of wicked King Ahab—as lessons for their own day. As invoked in the comic voice of Stubb, "signs and wonders" serves in this context as Melville's engagement with his contemporaries' hyperbolic, biblical language of corruption and degeneration. The biblical "signs and wonders" most directly relevant to the chapter's representation of the hidden meanings of the doubloon as the white whale's talisman and as a portent of doom come from Matthew 12. The Pharisees, hearing of Jesus's performance of "wonders," whisper: "This fellow doth not cast out devils, but by Beelzebub the prince of devils. And Jesus knew their thoughts, and said unto them, 'Every Kingdom divided against itself is brought to desolation; and every city or house divided against itself shall not stand" (Matthew 12.24–25). Continuing to doubt Jesus's claim to be the son of God, the Pharisees ask him for a sign:

> "Master, we would see a sign from thee." But he answered and said unto them, "An evil and adulterous generation seeketh after a sign; and there shall no sign be given to it, but the sign of the prophet Jonas: For as Jonas was three days and three nights in the whale's belly; so shall the Son of

man be three days and three nights in the heart of the earth." (Matthew 12.38–40)

Stubb, holding little respect for religion or authority, uses the paired terms "signs and wonders" jokingly throughout; and it is through Stubb that Melville mixes the lofty language of the sacred with the profane language of the common sailor. If "signs and wonders" allude to the ways in which man attempts to prophecy the future, Stubb mixes this language of prophecy with the language of the almanac, that mundane book used by farmers and households throughout the United States as a predictor of the weather.

Melville does not give Queequeg's interpretation of the doubloon. Rather, Queequeg's character-function here is to underscore the chapter's representation of the doubloon as a text to be read, yet whose reading is limited by the perspective of the reader. This connection is made through Stubb's remarks upon observing Queequeg's scene of reading: "he's comparing notes!" The tattoos on Queequeg's body are themselves texts, yet written in the signs of a language no one on the ship can understand. As Ahab exclaims later, "when one morning turning away from surveying poor Queequeg," he remarks on the indecipherable language of Queequeg's tattoos: "Oh, devilish tantalization of the gods!" (367). When Stubb jokingly suggests Queequeg is comparing notes, he draws a parallel between the tattooed body of Queequeg as a text and the doubloon, as a likewise mysterious, indecipherable text.

"The Doubloon" famously concludes with Pip, whose reading is introduced by Stubb recalling the accidental abandonment of Pip, and expressing regret over his own involvement in it: "poor boy! Would he had died, or I" (335). Stubb's regret recalls "The Castaway" chapter's quantitative conception of value, the universal equivalent which governs man as "a money-making animal" (321), whereby the oil of whales sold on the Nantucket market can be exchanged for slaves in Alabama. Pip's reading, however, does not attempt to interpret the text of the doubloon; rather, it is an interpretation of all the others' attempts to read the doubloon, and of the significance of the doubloon's new status as the white whale's talisman: "I look, you look, he looks; we look, ye look, they look" (335). Pip's mad language only seems nonsensical. As Ishmael suggested at the close of "The Castaway" chapter: "He saw God's foot upon the treadle of the loom, and spoke it; and therefore his shipmates called him mad. So man's insanity is heaven's sense; and wandering from all mortal reason, man comes at last to that celestial thought, which, to reason, is absurd and frantic; and weal or woe, feels then uncompromised, indifferent as his God" (321–22). Stubb and the rest of the crew think Pip mad, just as Starbuck thinks Ahab mad, while Ahab considers himself "demoniac... madness maddened!" (143), and Stubb can't bear to be reminded of his own role, however accidental, in making Pip so. Yet Melville will use the language of mad Pip's seemingly nonsensical speech to reflect on the series of readings that have constituted the action of this chapter.

In Pip, Melville links the visions of madness and the visions of prophecy, through their shared language of metaphor, the very premise of signification as interpretation, of making signs of wonders. When Pip says "And I, you, and he; and we, ye, and they, are all bats" (335), he refers to each and all of them looking at the doubloon, but being blind as bats—unable to see. Likewise, when Pip calls himself a "crow" it makes no literal sense, but it does make metaphorical sense. As we learned in "The Mast-Head," the lookout at the top of the masthead often sat in a rigging called, in the seaman's language, the "crow's-nest"—so called for its resemblance to the nest at the tops of high trees, and for the bird's-eye view it provided, overlooking the ship and across the horizon. Pip's "pine tree" is the mainmast, and Pip is a crow, "especially when... stand[ing] a'top of this pine tree" (355). Pip is figured here as that character who has the view from the masthead—the bird's-eye view of the present proceedings and of the events looming on the horizon. In ancient myth and contemporary folklore, the crow was the dark bird of omen, portending naught but ill. Even in the comic minstrel song "Old King Crow," whose lines Pip sings at the end of his rendering, the crow is both the classic trickster figure ("he's the blackest thief I know"), sly, unreadable and uncatchable; and a figure of likely trouble. Pip extends this metaphor—the mast as a pine tree—to make his final, elliptical prediction: just as with that wedding ring—a symbol of the bonds of promise—found deep in the pine tree cut down by his father, so too will they find the doubloon, still attached to this pine tree, the mainmast, "in the resurrection, when they come to fish up this old mast" (335). All this will happen, according to Pip, for their mad desire for "the gold, the precious, precious, gold!," the talisman of the white whale, the "monomaniac incarnation" (156) of the market.

Through Pip, Melville concludes the chapter with a formal symmetry. Ahab—made mad after his "almost fatal encounter" with the white whale, and thought mad by Starbuck because of his monomaniac obsession with Moby-Dick—was the first to be observed in his attempt to read the doubloon. Here, at the chapter's conclusion, Pip—made mad by his abandonment during the hunt for whales—speaks, in his own metaphoric language, the impending doom of the *Pequod*. According to the folk joke, unscrew your navel, and your bottom falls out. In this metaphor, the doubloon nailed to the mast is the navel of the body of the *Pequod*, and "they are all on fire to unscrew it" (335). They are all on fire to "unscrew it" in the metaphorical sense, to interpret its meaning; but they are also all on fire to unscrew it in the literal sense: the doubloon will be removed from the mast and given to whoever first sights Moby-Dick. Once that happens, the *Pequod*'s bottom will fall out, and the ship will sink. Yet again, as Pip avers, "if it stays here, that is ugly, too, for when aught's nailed to the mast it's a sign that things grow desperate" (335). "The Doubloon" thus concludes with Pip's invocation of that very meaning raised by Ahab on the quarterdeck, when he initiated the transvaluation of the doubloon into a "sign and wonder" by striking the mast.

"If I Shall Touch That Workman's Arm with Some Ethereal Light"

While Ishmael the storyteller repeatedly abstracts beyond Ahab's individual hunt, seeing it as representative of a universal struggle of modern man, Melville the writer reminds us throughout *Moby-Dick* of the very specific historical circumstances that created Ahab's monomania: the Nantucket market. Melville returns to these historical circumstances in "The Symphony" (chapter 132), when he stages the last extended dialogue between Ahab and Starbuck. In this private dialogue immediately preceding the concluding "Chase" chapters of the novel, Ahab reveals to Starbuck more of himself than he has to any of the crew:

> On such a day . . . I struck my first whale—a boy-harpooneer of eighteen! Forty—forty—forty years ago!—ago! Forty years of continuous whaling! forty years of privation, and peril, and storm-time! forty years on the pitiless sea! for forty years has Ahab forsaken the peaceful land, for forty years to make war on the horrors of the deep! Aye and yes, Starbuck, out of those forty years I have not spent three ashore. When I think of this life I have led; the desolation of solitude it has been; the masoned, walled-town of a Captain's exclusiveness, which admits but small entrance to any sympathy from the green country without—oh, weariness! heaviness! Guinea-coast slavery of solitary command! (405)

"Forty years" serves as the refrain in Ahab's lament, emphasizing that Ahab has spent his entire adult life in this business of whaling; and identifying this lifelong time at sea with the exile of the Israelites, wandering forty years in the wilderness. Ahab acknowledges these thoughts as previously "only half-suspected: not so keenly known to me before" (405). Depicted as a moment of both recognition and regret, Ahab's reflections on his life spent chasing whales lead him to see himself as a fool: "what a forty years' fool—fool—old fool, has old Ahab been!" (405). With Ahab's revelations to Starbuck—who had declared on the quarterdeck, "I am game for . . . the jaws of Death . . . if it fairly comes in the way of the business we follow" (139)—Melville reminds us once again of the historical origins of Ahab's madness: the business they follow. Ahab is the "demoniac" side of that antebellum American ideal of the independent, self-reliant man; the ideal of absolute solitude now identified with "the desolation of solitude . . . the masoned, walled-town of a Captain's exclusiveness," with little possibility for human "sympathy" (405). After forty long years, Ahab understands the mastery of "solitary command" as the deepest of slavery.

The dialogue between Ahab and Starbuck in "The Symphony" chapter follows a structure directly parallel to that of their opening debate on the stage of "The Quarter-Deck." If the quarterdeck scene initiated Ahab's quest, over Starbuck's objections, "The Symphony" offers Ahab the opportunity, through the sympathy of Starbuck, to turn back. In their quarterdeck debate, Ahab called for Starbuck to "come closer" to him so that Ahab might instruct him in the "little lower layer" (139) of meaning, and the antagonism of their opposing wills was figured as a confrontation of gazes: "Take off thine eye!" Ahab yelled, "more intolerable than fiends' glarings is a doltish stare!" (140). Their first confrontation ended with Starbuck's "silence" and "downcast eyes" (140), Starbuck's averted glance indicating his defeat, the "abasement of poor Starbuck's fortitude" (103) in the face of those "more spiritual terrors, which sometime menace you from the concentrating brow of an enraged and mighty man" (103). Whereas their quarterdeck debate was a public rhetorical battle, however, their dialogue in "The Symphony" is a private exchange of sentiments, a scene of intimate "sympathy" (405). As on the quarterdeck, Ahab again asks Starbuck to "come closer" to him, but here it as a gesture of sympathetic identification: "Close! Stand close to me, Starbuck; let me look into a human eye; it is better than to gaze into sea or sky; better than to gaze upon God" (406). If on the quarterdeck the meeting of eyes marked a confrontation of opposing wills, here in

"The Symphony" it is the site of sympathy, in the original sense of "fellow-feeling, fellow-suffering," the imaginary identification of self and other: "By the green land; by the hearth-stone! this is the magic glass, man; I see my wife and my child in thine eye. No, no; stay on board, on board!—lower not when I do; when branded Ahab gives chase to Moby Dick. That hazard shall not be thine. No, no! not with the far away home I see in that eye!" (406).[28] Seeing his own wife and child in Starbuck's eyes, Ahab sees in Starbuck an alternate version of his own younger self, before the "forty, forty years" of "weariness! Heaviness! Guinea-coast slavery of solitary command" have transformed Ahab, making him "more a demon than a man" (405). In this moment of sympathetic identification, Ahab appeals to Starbuck to not lower for the chase, wishing to save Starbuck from Ahab's own fate.

Melville extends the identification of these two men as Starbuck responds in kind to Ahab's sympathy: "Oh, my Captain! my Captain! noble soul! grand old heart, after all! why should any one give chase to that hated fish! Away with me! let us fly these deadly waters! let us home! Wife and child, too, are Starbuck's—wife and child of his brotherly, sisterly, play-fellow-youth; even as thine, sir, are the wife and child of thy loving, longing, paternal old age!" (406). As Starbuck pursues this sympathetic identification to dissuade Ahab from his hunt, however, Ahab ceases to listen: "But Ahab's glance was averted; like a blighted fruit tree he shook, and cast his last, cindered apple to the soil" (406). If their debate in "The Quarter-Deck" chapter ended with Starbuck's "downcast eyes," in "The Symphony" it is Ahab who looks away, his averted glance marking the end to their moment of sympathy, and the return of Ahab to his "masoned, walled-town of a Captain's exclusiveness."

The scene shifts from outward-looking dialogue to Ahab's inward-looking soliloquy, a soliloquy that again parallels Ahab's speech on the quarterdeck. Ahab had announced his grand ambition on the quarterdeck "with the hammer uplifted in one hand" (138), and he had declared to Starbuck: "Talk not to me of blasphemy, man; I'd strike the sun if it insulted me. For could the sun do that, then could I do the other; since there is ever a sort of fair play herein. . . . But not my master, man, is even that fair play. Who's over me? Truth hath no confines" (140). Now, in this moment of intimacy, Ahab wonders aloud:

> What is it, what nameless, inscrutable, unearthly thing . . . commands me; that against all natural lovings and longings, I keep so pushing. . . . Is Ahab,

Ahab? Is it I, God, or who, that lifts this arm? But if the great sun move not of himself, but is as an errand-boy in heaven; ... how then can this one small heart beat; this one small brain think thoughts; unless God does that beating, does that thinking, does that living, and not I. (406–7)

On the quarterdeck, Ahab's arm wielding the hammer and striking the mast was identified with Ahab's defiant will, setting aside the question of the white whale's "inscrutable" agency (140). Here at the onset of "his disastrous set of sun" (103), the emblematic image of Ahab's will is refigured, as Ahab questions who "lifts this arm" (406). Likewise, if the sun over the quarterdeck was the symbol of everything that Ahab denied stood over his mortal powers, it now serves as an analogy for Ahab's lack of agency, Ahab's sense that some "nameless, inscrutable, unearthly thing ... [some] hidden lord and master, and cruel, remorseless emperor commands" him (407).

While Ahab, with averted glance, wonders aloud of his own powerlessness to stop hunting Moby-Dick, Starbuck leaves his side: "But blanched to a corpse's hue with despair, the Mate had stolen away" (407). The chapter completes its representation of this failure of sympathy—the degree of Ahab's alienation from his fellow man and the depths of his "Guinea-coast slavery of solitary command" (405)—with Ahab, failing to see Starbuck, crossing "the deck to gaze over on the other side" (407). Looking now into that other "magic glass" the sea, Ahab "started at two reflected, fixed eyes in the water," belonging not to himself but to Fedallah, identified throughout the novel as Ahab's otherworldly shadow and the fire-eating embodiment of his unalterable fate.

The Flag of Ahab

At the close of *Moby-Dick*, Melville returns to the upraised arm clutching a hammer, that image through which Ahab's monomaniacal hunt was first identified with his strike against the market, and against the whale as its "agent or principal," and links it to another image drawn from the iconography of class struggle, the red flag. Just as it was Starbuck who first recognized the meaning implied by Ahab's striking of the mast on the quarterdeck, it is Starbuck, in "The Chase—Third Day," who first draws attention to the red flag nailed to the mainmast: "Masthead there! ... mark well the whale!—Ho! again!—drive off that hawk! see! he pecks—he tears the vane'—pointing to the red flag flying at the main-truck—'Ha! he soars away with it!—Where's the old man now? sees't thou that sight, oh Ahab!—shudder, shudder!" (422). Ahab does not hear Starbuck, but soon sees for himself: "And now marking that the vane or flag was gone from the main-mast-head, he shouted to Tashtego, who had just gained that perch, to descend again for another flag, and a hammer and nails, and so nail it to the mast" (423).

Like the "strike," the red flag's meaning as a symbol of defiance had its origins in the nautical history of sailors' revolts. Originally, a red flag was "displayed as a sign of battle-readiness or defiance" when two ships met. As Ephraim Chambers described in his *Cyclopedia* of 1728, "The red flag is the Signal of Defiance and Battle."[29] The red flag became identified with political revolt during the "Terror" of the French Revolution. Thomas Carlyle cited this appropriation of the image by revolutionaries in his history of *The French Revolution* (1837):

> Sieur Motier [Lafayette], with Municipals in scarf, with blue National Patrollism, rank after rank, to the clang of drums; wending resolutely to the Champ-de-Mars; Mayor Bailly, with elongated visage, bearing, as in sad duty bound, the *Drapeau Rouge* [Red Flag]. Howl of angry derision rises in treble and bass from a hundred thousand throats, at the sight of Martial Law; which nevertheless, waving its Red sanguinary flag, advances there, from the Gros-Caillou Entrance; advances, drumming and waving towards the Altar of the Fatherland [where the petition had been set up].[30]

Carlyle's imaginary historical observer takes a critical view of the red flag, aligning its symbolism with "Martial Law" and the "sanguinary" excesses of radical revolution. The red flag as a symbol of political revolt was likewise raised during the Great Mutiny of the *Nore* in 1797. Melville would recall this history when he wrote of the Great Mutiny in *Billy Budd*:

> It was the summer of 1797.... The [Nore mutiny] is known, and without exaggeration in the epithet, as "the Great Mutiny." It was indeed a demonstration more menacing to England than the contemporary manifestoes and conquering and proselytizing armies of the French Directory. To the British Empire the Nore Mutiny was what a strike in the fire brigade would be to London threatened by general arson.... *that* was the time when at the mastheads of the three-deckers and seventy-fours moored in [England's] own roadstead... the bluejackets, to be numbered by thousands, ran up with huzzas the British colors with the union and cross wiped out; by that

cancellation transmuting the flag of founded law and freedom defined, into the enemy's red meteor of unbridled and unbounded revolt. (112)

Establishing the historical setting for the plot of *Billy Budd*, Melville explicitly likens mutiny to the labor "strike," and identifies "the Red flag," as sign of "the spirit animating the men" (113), with both sailors' revolts and the broader revolutionary ferment at the turn of the century: it was the summer of 1797.

The sailors' red flag of defiance had become fully identified with political revolution by the mid-nineteenth century, with workers throughout Europe raising the red flag during the revolutions of 1848.

Walt Whitman incorporated this symbolism of the red flag into "Resurgemus," his 1850 poem on those 1848 revolutions:

> Yet behind all, lo, a Shape,
> Vague as the night, draped interminably,
> Head, front and form, in scarlet folds,
> Whose face and eyes none may see,
> Out of its robes only this,
> The red robes, lifted by the arm,
> One finger pointed high over the top,
> Like the head of a snake appears.[31]

In "Resurgemus," one of the pre-1855 poems incorporated into *Leaves of Grass*, this vague figure in red looms over the scene of defeated revolutionaries and "martyrs that hang from the gibbets" (134), pointing toward the future resurgence of revolution.

Melville returns to this image of the red flag throughout the action of "The Chase—Third Day." As Moby-Dick bears down on the *Pequod*: "Meantime, for that one beholding instant, Tashtego's mast-head hammer remained suspended in his hand; and the red flag, half-wrapping him as with a plaid, then streamed itself straight out from him, as his own forward-flowing heart" (425). Melville here directly links the red flag to the workman's arm wielding a hammer, that image Ishmael invoked as emblematic of the "democratic dignity" he as artist aspired to depict, and that Melville identified with Ahab's "strike" in "The Quarter-Deck" chapter. Even as the *Pequod* is sinking, Ahab calls upon Tashtego to nail his banner to the mast, to persist in their collective defiance of the whale: "What ho, Tashtego! let me hear thy hammer. Oh! ye three unsurrendered spires of mine; thou uncracked keel ... death-glorious ship! must ye then perish, and without me?" (426). Ahab's appeal to Tashtego, to nail the red flag to the mast, is Ahab's last appeal to his crew before he commits his own final act: "let me then tow to pieces, while still chasing thee, though tied to thee, thou damned whale! *Thus*, I give up the spear!" (426). Ahab's final act in *Moby-Dick* refigures his first act in "The Quarter-Deck": Ahab strikes at Moby-Dick just as he had struck the mast and the doubloon, "the white whale's talisman" (332). In the novel's last image of Ahab, Melville thus links the red flag of revolt to Ahab's defiance: in the face of his certain death, Ahab remains committed to the truth of "the living act, the undoubted deed" (140), and continues to strike.

Melville combines these two images of class struggle in the final image of "The Chase—Third Day," and identifies them both with the figure of defiant Ahab. As the last whelming waters pour over the *Pequod*, "at that instant, a red arm and a hammer hovered backwardly uplifted in the open air, in the act of nailing the flag faster and yet faster to the subsiding spar" (426). With a sky-hawk's

> broad fluttering wing [caught] between the hammer and the wood ... the submerged savage beneath, in his death-grasp, kept his hammer frozen there; and so the bird of heaven, with archangelic shrieks, and his imperial beak thrust upwards, and his whole captive form folded in the flag of Ahab, went down with his ship, which, like Satan, would not sink to hell till she had dragged a living part of heaven along with her, and helmeted herself with it. (426–27)

This is not literally Ahab's arm, but the symbolic image is his, for the crew had now become Ahab's "arms and ... legs" (423). The "frenzies of the chase" for Moby-Dick have transformed them from a crew of "*Isolatoes*" (107), a multitude of individual agents, into one: "They were one man, not thirty. For as the one ship that held them all; though it was put together of all contrasting things ... even so, all the individualities of the crew, this man's valor, that man's fear; guilt and guiltlessness, all varieties were welded into oneness" (415). They were "welded into oneness" just as their oaths "had been welded" (152) together on the quarterdeck. Like "that great Leviathan, called a Commonwealth or State," they are "but an artificial man" "by art ... created" (10). Tashtego's upraised arm stands in for the collective arm of this "oneness," as it persists in defiance.

Ahab is a "representative man" in that he embodies the dark contradictions of the modern citizen as split subject, divided into private and public selves. Ahab rails against the division of the individual into private interests and public law, into inner personality and the mask of persona. Thus in "The Candles," as all the crew interpret the burning lightning-rod ends of the ship's three masts as an omen—and as Ishmael suggests it is "God's burning finger . . . laid on the ship; . . . His 'Mene, Mene, Tekel, Upharsin' . . . woven into the shrouds and the cordage" (381), Ahab articulates his "defiance" (382) as an insistence on the undivided self: "In the midst of the personified impersonal, a personality stands here" (382). Against the freedom defined by the market's fiction of contract among self-interested competing individuals, Ahab offered the crew a unifying, communal covenant. This unifying appeal is what resonated with Ishmael: "I, Ishmael, was one of that crew; my shouts had gone up with the rest; my oath had been welded with theirs" (152). It is through the collective ritual of the oath itself that "I, Ishmael" became one with the crew. Ishmael pointedly frames the chapter "Moby-Dick" with this narrative fact. Though the primary focus of "Moby-Dick" is the meaning of the white whale to Ahab, Ishmael opens and closes the chapter with reflections on that "mad oath" sworn by the crew during "The Quarter-Deck" scene, forging a new bond to replace the market contract rejected by Ahab:

> How it was that they so aboundingly responded to the old man's ire—by what evil magic their souls were possessed, that at times his hate seemed almost theirs; the White Whale as much their insufferable foe as his; how all this came to be—what the White Whale was to them, or how to their unconscious understandings, also, in some dim, unsuspected way, he might have seemed the gliding great demon of the seas of life,—all this to explain, would be to dive deeper than Ishmael can go. (158)

Reflecting on the enthusiastic assent of the crew to Ahab's appeal, Ishmael imagines the crew's response as an imaginary identification: "his hate seemed almost theirs." While Ishmael asserts that the explanations for the crew's "aboundingly" enthusiastic response to Ahab's appeal—which he calls a form of "possession," a loss of individual will in the moment of collective sympathetic identification—lie deeper than Ishmael can dive, his reflections on their individual and collective bonds remind us of the distinction between coercion and consent central to the meaning of Ahab's appeal on the quarterdeck, and central to Ishmael's artistic vision of Ahab's fatal hunt for Moby-Dick as a form of tragic resistance, a Promethean fidelity to his strike.

Conclusion. The Labors of Emancipation
Founded Law and Freedom Defined

After Emancipation, Melville looked back on the long nineteenth century, to trace the ambiguities of modern freedom and the rule of law to that moment with which *Bonds of Citizenship* began, the Age of Revolution. Like Douglass's "man from another country," who looked beyond the forms of law to the history of labor struggles that made possible their founding, Melville in *Billy Budd, Sailor (An Inside Narrative)* (1888?–91) tells a suppressed story of this age, recovering the histories of slavery and servitude inhering in the revolutionary reconstitution of citizenship.

Throughout *Billy Budd*, Melville reminds us of the class of men whose story he tells: "Passion, and passion in its profoundest, is not a thing demanding a palatial stage whereon to play its part. Down among the groundlings, the beggars and rakers of the garbage, profound passion is enacted."[1] As the inside narrative of "how it fared with the Handsome Sailor during the year of the Great Mutiny" (167), *Billy Budd* is a story of these bondsmen; and of the revolutionary threat posed by them as a class. Immediately after introducing Billy Budd, Melville emphasizes that historical context through which his inside narrative must be read:

> It was the summer of 1797. In the April of that year had occurred the commotion at Spithead followed in May by a second and yet more serious outbreak in the fleet at the Nore. The latter is known, and without exaggeration in the epithet, as "the Great Mutiny." . . . To the British Empire the Nore Mutiny was what a strike in the fire brigade would be to London threatened by general arson. (112)

Melville's comparison of the mutiny and the strike is not a mere analogy. The two are different not in kind but in scale: where the strike is a danger to the capital threatened by arson, the mutiny is a danger to the whole of the empire threatened by revolution. This comparison of their dangers emphasizes, furthermore, that mutiny itself was a labor protest. It recalls that historical meaning of the labor "strike" discussed in the last chapter of this study, locating its origins in the seamen's act of striking mast to announce their mutinous intentions. Framing Billy's story with this specter of labor mutiny, Melville also historicizes the symbols of their revolt. Indeed, he traces the origins of Ahab's red flag of defiance to the eruption of seamen's revolts against the impressment of their labor: "at the mastheads of the three-deckers and seventy-fours... the bluejackets, to be numbered by thousands, ran up with huzzas the British colors with the union and cross wiped out; by that cancellation transmuting the flag of founded law and freedom defined, into the enemy's red meteor of unbridled and unbounded revolt" (112). Thus striking the masts, the seamen appropriated the symbols of their rulers: wiping out the colors of the union and cross leaves only the red, transforming the "flag of founded law and freedom defined" into the symbol of their own defiance of that law.

In describing these symbolic acts, Melville emphasizes another point elaborated throughout *Bonds of Citizenship*, that official histories suppress these facts: "Such an episode in the Island's grand naval story her naval historians naturally abridge, one of them (William James) candidly acknowledging that fain would he pass it over did not 'impartiality forbid fastidiousness.' And yet his mention is less a narration than a reference, having to do hardly at all with details. Nor are these readily to be found in the libraries" (112). *Billy Budd* is a recovery of this lost history of class struggle, acknowledged as event but denied historical narration.

Despite its aversion to providing details or narrative form to the Spithead and Nore mutinies, James's *Naval History of Great Britain* acknowledged their origins in the seamen's protest refusal of their labor: "The spirit of mutiny had taken deep root in the breasts of the seamen.... It appears that... Lord Howe... received sundry petitions, as from the seamen at Portsmouth, all praying an advance of wages," and listing complaints regarding their working conditions. Receiving no answer, the seamen "could only attribute the silence of Lord Howe to a disregard of their complaints," and so refused "to obey Lord Bridport's signal to prepare for sea."[2] And although James's *History* intends to provide only a brief account, its sketch cannot avoid repeated references to those red flags raised throughout the mutiny: "On the return of the offended delegates to their respective ships, those of the Royal-George . . . immediately hoisted the preconcerted signal of the red or bloody flag; a signal which, owing to its usual sanguinary import, alarmed all the well-disposed in the fleet."[3] James emphasizes here the shared understanding of the flag's "sanguinary import," as signaling the start of the seamen's labor strike. Likewise, James later records that the seamen "struck the flag" of their masters, replacing it with their own: "the mutineers struck Vice-admiral Buckner's flag, hoisting, in its stead, that dreadful emblem of mutiny, the red or bloody flag"; and that the beginning of the end to the Great Mutiny was signaled when "the red flag had disappeared from every ship's mast-head."[4] Read from the perspective of the bondsman, against the author's intentions, the *Naval History* thus records for the future historian the origins of modern political radicalism's symbol of working-class defiance in the seamen's "dreadful emblem of mutiny." This was the historical context, of mutinous labor protests during "the summer of 1797" (112), which Melville recovers when, framing the inside narrative of *Billy Budd*, he depicts "the Red Flag" as sign of "the spirit animating the men" (113).

Billy Budd himself is literally a man from another country—a foundling, without known origins—and the narrative stages his subjection to "the flag of founded law and freedom defined" (112). Melville introduces Billy through the scene of labor impressment, his "arbitrary enlistment into the *Bellipotent*" (112). Billy begins the narrative "free in the double sense";[5] the scene of impressment emphasizes the limits of such nominal freedom. Likewise, when Melville introduces John Claggart and the rumors surrounding his enlistment, Melville takes Claggart's mysterious origins as occasion to historicize impressment as a form of "arbitrary" labor coercion: "not only were press-gangs notoriously abroad both afloat and ashore, but there was little or no secret about another matter, namely, that the London police were at liberty to capture any able-bodied suspect, any questionable fellow at large, and summarily ship him to the dockyard or fleet" (120). Much of the press-gang's quota of forced laborers "would be eked out by drafts culled directly from the jails" (121). As with his recovery of the red flag's origins, in such moments of historicization Melville also comments on the difficulty of "proving or disproving" (121) these facts, because they are rarely written into official history. They are suppressed, subaltern histories: "Such sanctioned irregularities, which for obvious reasons the government would hardly think to parade at the time and which consequently, and as affecting the least influential class of mankind, have all but dropped into oblivion" (121). Melville again ties the active suppression of these histories to the interests of the state, and to the material fact that the subjects of this labor coercion were "the least influential class of mankind" (121).

It is this coercive labor exploitation that Claggart recalls when he brings to Captain Vere his accusations against Billy: "he had seen enough to convince him that at least one sailor aboard was a dangerous character in a ship mustering some who not only had taken a guilty part in the late serious troubles, but others also who, like the man in question, had entered His Majesty's service under another form than enlistment" (140). Recognizing the reference in Claggart's euphemism, Vere demands: "Be direct, man; say *impressed men*" (140). Significantly, while Vere insists here that Claggart speak directly by naming the thing to which he refers—impressment, and those bound-yet-free laborers whose discontent might be organized by "a dangerous character"—when Claggart alludes to mutiny itself, Vere stops him from speaking the name:

> "God forbid, your honor, that the *Bellipotent*'s should be the experience of the——"
>
> "Never mind that!" here peremptorily broke in the superior, his face altering with anger, instinctively divining the ship that the other was about to name, one in which the Nore Mutiny had assumed a singularly tragical character that for a time jeopardized the life of its commander. (140)

The historical reality of mutiny is literally unspeakable here; the memory of recent events must be repressed, even as they continue to determine events in the "ever-present now."[6]

In readings focusing on Vere's judgment and the debated justice of Billy's execution, Billy assumes the role of victim, sacrificed to man-made law; and the narrative agents of the plot are the accuser Claggart, and the judge Vere.[7] Against this view, Melville emphasizes Billy Budd's agency, using Billy's own words: "I am sorry that he is dead," Billy says during his trial, "I did not mean to kill him. Could I have used my tongue I would not have struck him. But he foully lied to my face and in presence of my captain, and I had to say something, and I could only say it with a blow, God help me!" (150) Although Billy is innocent of conspiracy to mutiny, he is not merely the passive victim of Claggart's accusations, or of Vere's judgment. While Billy "did not mean to kill him," he did intend to strike Claggart; Billy's act was not involuntary. Because of his stutter, that "vocal defect" erupting "under sudden provocation of strong heart-feeling" (111), Billy could not use his tongue. Unable to speak with words, he spoke with his blow at Claggart: "I had to say something, and I could only say it with a blow." In one of the few direct representations of Billy Budd's voice in the narrative, Billy claims his intentions and his agency, the free will motivating his act. When it comes to the deed that matters "in the year of the Great Mutiny," Billy Budd is in fact a "dangerous character," and like all hereditary bondsmen who would be free, he himself strikes the blow.

Free in the Double Sense

In writing this history of the transformations of modern citizenship, recovering the role of the bondsman in the dialectic of race and class, *Bonds of Citizenship* has also advanced an alternative understanding of American literary history. It is this perspective on the bonds of labor that apprehended in Ahab's declaration—"If man will strike, strike through the mask! How can the prisoner reach outside except by thrusting through the wall?"—direct invocation of both the letter and the spirit of those lines so frequently proclaimed by Douglass: "Hereditary bondsmen! know ye not, / Who would be free, themselves must strike the blow?"[8] It is a hermeneutic, I have argued, attuned to the "little lower layer" beyond phenomenal forms of appearance; one that continually looks to the historical-material ground underlying the ambiguous forms of the law.

As we have seen, Douglass originally applied this hermeneutic to the Constitution itself, to recover the essential spirit of that founding law. When the original compact was broken by secession, Douglass continued to draw on this perspective, to argue that this "revolutionary crisis" would become a war for abolition, despite the federal government's intentions.[9]

Abraham Lincoln began his First Inaugural Address by speaking to the "apprehension . . . among the people of the Southern States" that the accession of his administration endangered "their property, and their peace, and personal security."[10] In a disavowal of antislavery views Douglass called "wholly discreditable to the head and heart of Mr. Lincoln,"[11] the new president reiterated his position of noninterference with slavery: "I have no purpose, directly or indirectly, to interfere with the institution of slavery in the States where it exists. I believe I have no lawful right to do so, and I have no inclination to do so." Addressing the nation after seven states had already seceded, Lincoln continued to insist upon his intention to respect the rights of slaveholders, by citing that shared interpretation of the Constitution's "original intention" to do so in the "fugitive slave clause": "It is scarcely questioned that this provision was intended by those who made it for the reclaiming of what we call fugitive slaves; and the intention of the lawgiver is the law."[12] In his editorial entitled "The Inaugural Address," Douglass employed that critique of "original intent" he had elaborated since publishing his "Change of Opinion" a decade prior to the election of "our first modern anti-slavery President": "Well, suppose we grant it in this case, that the intention of the law-maker is the law.... Who made the Constitution? The preamble to the Constitution answers that question. 'We, the people, do ordain and establish this Constitution.' The people then, made the law."[13] Lincoln's claim that "the intention of the lawgiver is the law" not only identified the spirit of the law with supposed original intentions; it located sovereignty in the ruling elite who wrote the law, describing them in terms of sovereign authorship and authority, as "the lawgiver." In contrast, Douglass's perspective—that of the "man from another country"—located authority in the text of the law, and sovereignty in "the people."

And from this same perspective Douglass saw that all questions of original intentions—of the constitutional framers, of southern secessionists, of disunion abolitionists, or of Lincoln's Republican Party—would soon no longer matter; they would be overtaken by historical events. The ambiguity of the word would be overruled by "the living act, the undoubted deed."[14] It was the contingency of historical events, Douglass argued, that pushed Lincoln to issue the Emancipation Proclamation, and the nation to cross an irreversible threshold, despite the original intentions of the war for the Union: "The careful, and we think, the slothful deliberation which he has observed in reaching this obvious policy, is a guarantee against retraction. But even if the temper and the spirit of the President himself were other than what they were, events greater than the President, events which have slowly wrung this proclamation from him may be relied upon to carry him forward in the same direction."[15] Douglass likewise emphasized that the force of events would push the meaning of the Emancipation Proclamation beyond the explicit limits of its wording. "It was not a proclamation of 'liberty throughout all the land, unto all the inhabitants thereof,' such as we had hoped it would be," Douglass observed, for "[its] operation was confined within certain geographical and military lines. It only abolished slavery where it did not exist, and left it intact where it did exist."[16] Yet, as we have seen, Douglass had developed a reading practice that could find utopian possibilities within the narrow limits of codified law. Despite these words of "discriminations and reservations," Douglass asserted: "For my own part, I took the proclamation, first and last, for a little more than it purported, and saw in its spirit a life and power beyond its letter." As I have argued throughout *Bonds of Citizenship*, in the Age of Emancipation the spirit of the law became the object of ongoing struggle over the signification of the letter.

As I have also argued, this perspective on the law and its letters was grounded in a materialist understanding of the interdependence of slave and free labor in the definition of freedom. From the outset of the slaveholders' rebellion, Douglass argued that slave emancipation must come because labor was key to winning the war: "The slaveholders have not hesitated to employ the sable arms of the Negroes at the South in erecting the fortifications which silenced the guns of Fort Sumter. . . . They have no scruples against employing the Negroes to exterminate freedom. . . . They work with spade and barrow with them, and will stand with them on the field of battle, shoulder to shoulder, to shoot down the troops of the U.S. Government. . . . Every consideration of justice, humanity, and sound policy confirms the wisdom of calling upon black men just now to take up arms in behalf of their country."[17] And when the contingencies of war pushed Lincoln's administration to heed Douglass's call for the formation of black regiments, Douglass again emphasized the decisive role of black laborers. In "Men of Color, to Arms!," Douglass recalled his early appeals for their deployment in the war: "Only a moderate share of sagacity was needed to see that the arm of the slave was the best defense against the arm of the slaveholder. Hence with every reverse to the national arms, with every exulting shout of victory raised by the slaveholding rebels, I have implored the imperiled nation to unchain against her foes, her powerful black hand."[18] Yet, asserting again the contingency of history, Douglass insisted that it was not the time to criticize the tardiness of Lincoln's policy: "Stop not now to complain that it was not heeded sooner. . . . This is not the time to discuss this question. Leave it to the future. When the war is over, the country is saved, peace is established, and the black man's rights are secured, as they will be, history with an impartial hand will dispose of that and sundry other questions."[19] Recalling his perspective on the diachronic movement of history, a perspective that has guided the historical study and the reading practice of *Bonds of Citizenship*, Douglass emphasized that such interpretive debates would be decided in the future, once freedom was won. In the war for Emancipation in the "ever-present now," the deed took priority over the word: "Action! Action! not criticism, is the plain duty of this hour. Words are only useful as they stimulate to blows. The office of speech now is only to point out when, where, and how to strike to the best advantage."[20] This view led directly to Douglass's invocation of those resonant words whose universalist appeal he had cited in *My Bondage and My Freedom*: "'Who would be free themselves must strike the blow.' 'Better die free, than to live slaves.'"[21] If before the Civil War Douglass invoked these words to characterize his resistance to the slave-breaker, a resistance whose spirit made him "a freeman in *fact* though ... a slave in *form*,"[22] in the midst of that war which Douglass knew to be "essentially an abolition war," Douglass now linked the spirit of these words to the collective labors of emancipation.[23]

After Emancipation, Douglass looked back to characterize the "vast changes" of this era: "Though slavery was abolished, the wrongs of my people were not ended. Though they were not slaves, they were not yet quite free. No man can be truly free whose liberty is dependent upon the thought, feeling, and action of others, and who has himself no means in his own hands for guarding, protecting, defending and maintaining that liberty."[24] Recalling the distinction between form and fact, letter and spirit, Douglass articulated that understanding of nominal freedom whose legal and social limits have also been traced throughout *Bonds of Citizenship*. Freedom, radical antislavery and labor activists long argued, remained merely nominal without the means in one's "own hands" to exercise and to protect it. The freedman was "free from the individual master, but the slave of society. He had neither money, nor property, nor friends. He was free from the old plantation, but he had nothing but the dusty road under his feet. He was free from the old quarter that once gave him shelter, but a slave to the rains of summer and ... frosts of winter."[25] Douglass learned this lesson in the precariousness of nominal freedom during his own "apprenticeship life," while still enslaved, in the world of free labor. Describing the "privilege of hiring [his] time," Douglass used the language of the labor contract: "I was to be allowed all my time; to make all bargains for work; to find my own employment, and to collect my own wages; and, in return for this liberty, I was required, or obliged, to pay him three dollars at the end of each week, and to board and clothe myself, and buy my own calking tools."[26] In this arrangement between master and slave, the slave in form would behave in fact as a free laborer, and so was likewise subject to that same world of necessity which led labor activists to liken their condition to slavery: it was "a lash and a driver, far more efficient than any I had before known." Under this "hard bargain," Douglass concluded, "I endured all the evils of being a slave, and yet suffered all the care and anxiety of a responsible freeman."[27] *Bonds of Citizenship* began with the figure Douglass describes here, the figure of the bondsman. As we have seen, it served since the eighteenth century as the metaphor and model for practical emancipation, and the assimilation of the formerly enslaved into the social and civic life of the nation; the passage from "abject serfdom to absolute citizenship."[28] After the "Abolition War," Douglass used this same figure to describe the recently emancipated, in order to illuminate the persisting difference between nominal liberty and its substantive realization, between the proclamation of freedom and the practice of freedom.[29] If the formerly enslaved were now "free in the double sense," they remained bound to this figure, to the letter and the spirit of its history. Such is the long career of the bondsman.

Notes

NOTES TO INTRODUCTION

1. Frederick Douglass, "Letter to C. H. Chase," *North Star,* 9 February 1849, in *The Life and Writings of Frederick Douglass,* ed. Philip S. Foner (New York: International, 1950), 1: 352–53.

2. Frederick Douglass, "The Address of the Southern Delegates in Congress to their Constituents; or, the Address of John C. Calhoun and Forty Other Thieves," *North Star,* 9 February 1849, in *The Life and Writings of Frederick Douglass,* ed. Philip S. Foner (New York: International , 1950), 1: 354–55.

3. Ibid., 1: 355.

4. Ibid., 1: 356–57, emphasis in original.

5. Ibid., 1: 354.

6. Ibid., 1: 355.

7. Ibid., 1: 356.

8. In "What to the Slave Is the Fourth of July?," Douglass declares: "The existence of slavery in this country brands your republicanism as a sham, your humanity as a base pretense, and your Christianity as a lie. It destroys your moral power abroad.... [It] makes your name a hissing, and a by-word to a mocking earth" ("What to the Slave Is the Fourth of July?: An Address Delivered in Rochester, New York, on 5 July 1852," in *The Frederick Douglass Papers, Series One: Speeches, Debates and Interviews,* ed. John W. Blassingame, vol. 2, *1847–54* [New Haven: Yale University Press, 1982], 383).

9. Douglass, "Address of the Southern Delegates," 1: 356.

10. Ibid.

11. On the "culture of constitutionalism," see Joyce Appleby, "The American Heritage: The Heirs and the Disinherited," *Journal of American History* 74, no. 3 (December 1987): 798–813.

12. Douglass, "Address of the Southern Delegates," 1: 356.

13. Eric Foner, *Free Soil, Free Labor, Free Men: The Ideology of the Republican Party before the Civil War* (New York: Oxford University Press, 1995), 75.

14. Prigg v. Pennsylvania, 41 U.S. 539 (1842), 612–13. In this case, the Supreme Court ruled against the Commonwealth of Pennsylvania and in favor of Edward Prigg, a Maryland slave catcher hired by slave owner Margaret Ashmore to recapture her "fugitive from

labor" Margaret Morgan. The Court also struck down as unconstitutional Pennsylvania's 1826 personal liberty law, "An act to give effect to the provisions of the constitution of the United States relative to fugitives from labor, for the protection of free people of color, and prevent kidnapping." The Court held that while states were not required to enforce the 1793 federal Fugitive Slave Act, they could not enact laws overriding it.

15. Frederick Douglass, "The Constitution of the United States: Is It Pro-Slavery or Anti-Slavery?," in *The Life and Writings of Frederick Douglas*, ed. Philip S. Foner (New York: International, 1950), 2: 476; Karl Marx, *Capital: A Critique of Political Economy*, vol. 1 (New York: Penguin, 1990), 127, hereafter cited in the chapter text as *Capital* 1.

16. Louis Althusser and Etienne Balibar, *Reading Capital*, trans. Ben Brewster (London: Verso, 1997), 227.

17. Ibid, emphasis in original.

18. Ibid., 229, emphasis in original. For a related historical analysis of the "ambiguous identities" of race and class, see Etienne Balibar and Immanuel Wallerstein, *Race, Nation, Class: Ambiguous Identities* (London: Verso, 1991), esp. chaps. 3–5.

19. On the trace as the sign of the absent presence of a discourse, see Jacques Derrida, *Of Grammatology* (Baltimore: Johns Hopkins University Press, 1976), esp. chap. 2. On the *trace* and the relation between political discourse and deconstruction, see Gayatri Chakravorty Spivak, "Feminism and Critical Theory," in *In Other Worlds: Essays in Cultural Politics* (New York: Routledge, 1988), 77–94; and "Feminism and Deconstruction, Again: Negotiations," in *Outside in the Teaching Machine* (New York: Routledge, 1993), 121–40.

20. Barbara Fields, "Ideology and Race in American History," in *Region, Race, and Reconstruction: Essays in Honor of C. Vann Woodward*, ed. J. Morgan Kousser and James McPherson (New York: Oxford University Press, 1982), 143–77.

21. Robert J. Steinfeld, *The Invention of Free Labor: The Employment Relation in English and American Law and Culture, 1350–1870* (Chapel Hill: University of North Carolina Press, 1991), 10.

22. William Wiecek, *The Sources of Antislavery Constitutionalism in America* (Ithaca, NY, and London: Cornell University Press, 1977), 78.

23. James Madison, *The Debates in the Federal Convention of 1787 Which Framed the Constitution of the United States of America: Reported by James Madison, a Delegate from the State of Virginia*, ed. Gaillard Hunt and James Brown Scott (Buffalo, NY: Prometheus, 1987), 2: 481.

24. Ibid., 2: 487.

25. Etienne Balibar, "Subjection and Subjectivation," in *Supposing the Subject*, ed. Joan Copjec (London: Verso 1994), 9–10. Balibar's thesis asserts two historical "breaks." The first of these can be described briefly as having been accomplished with the transition from Aristotle to Augustine. In contrast to Aristotle's conception of ancient "man as a citizen, that is, a being 'naturally' and 'normally' a politès, but only in a given sphere of activity, the 'public' sphere of reciprocity and equality with his fellow men," there emerges, marking this threshold, the medieval "figure of the inner subject . . . who confronts a transcendental law, both theological and political, religious (therefore also moral) or imperial

(monarchical)—because he hears it, because in order to be able to hear it, he has to be called by it" (9). The result of this first historical break is the emergence of a unified category of subjection: "the subject, for the first time bearing that name in the political field where (he) is subjected to the sovereign, the lord, ultimately the Lord God, in the metaphysical field necessarily subjects himself to himself" (10). Most relevant to our present discussion is the second historical break of Balibar's thesis, as it is that very moment revisited by Douglass's "man from another country."

26. Ibid., 11–12.
27. Ibid.
28. Ibid., 12.
29. Steinfeld, *Invention of Free Labor*, 138.
30. Fredric Jameson, "The Vanishing Mediator; or, Max Weber as Storyteller," in *Ideologies of Theory* (Minneapolis: University of Minnesota Press, 1988), 2: 3–34.
31. Ibid., 2: 25.
32. Ibid., 2: 23. Jameson's narrative analysis supplements Claude Levi-Strauss's formalization of the deep structure of myth with the semantic rectangle of A. J. Greimas. Whereas the Levi-Strauss formula could claim to deal with diachrony, or, in other words, with the *irreversible* character of narrative and historical change, Greimas's "relatively static and logical scheme is . . . able to demonstrate, what is absent from Levi-Strauss' formula . . . the hypothesis of some central mediatory figure or institution that can account for the passage from one temporal and historical state to another" (2: 22).
33. Ibid., 2: 23.
34. Ibid., 2: 25. The passage from feudalism to capitalism described in Jameson's account does not involve, as Slavoj Žižek asserts, an "inversion" of the determinative relation between the economic "base" (or infrastructure) and the ideological superstructure (Žižek, *For They Know Not What They Do: Enjoyment as a Political Factor* [London and New York: Verso, 1996], 182). The central point of the theory of the vanishing mediator is not to "invert" the topology of base and superstructure (itself a caricature of the Marxist conception of social totality); such an inversion would remain bound to the false problems of cause and effect, and, indeed, to the expressive (idealist) and economistic (or "vulgar Marxist") models of social totality which the concept was supposed to counter. Rather, "in both Weber and Marx, the *superstructure* may be said to find its essential function in the *mediation* of *changes in the infrastructure* . . . and to understand it in this way, as a 'vanishing mediator,' is to escape the false problems of priority or of cause and effect in which both vulgar Marxist and the idealist positions imprison us" ("Vanishing Mediator" 25, emphasis added). The theory of the vanishing mediator thus maintains the Marxist claim for the "ultimately determining instance" of the economic, while registering the significance of the *ideology of form*. Essential to any critical deployment of the concept of the vanishing mediator, therefore, is this understanding of its function in the particular historical narrative under analysis or revision. In Weber's story, Protestantism serves as a mediating form, through which one dominant historical "content" is transformed into another. The concept of the vanishing mediator should be read as a corollary to Jameson's

wider-ranging claims for interpretation in *The Political Unconscious*—that is, as operative on that ultimate semantic horizon or "final enlargement of the analytical frame," which conceives of "history . . . in its vastest sense of the sequence of the modes of production, and the succession and destiny of the various human social formations" (*The Political Unconscious: Narrative as a Socially Symbolic Act* [Ithaca: Cornell University Press, 1994], 88; 75). In the context of any revisionary literary history such as that proposed by the present study, to recover the connection between the vanishing mediator and the political unconscious is to emphasize the former's narrative function in the latter's broader intervention in the debates over "synchronic" versions of historicism and the question of historical determination. Recovering this connection between the vanishing mediator as narrative concept and the hermeneutic of the political unconscious situates those phenomena described by Weber in *The Protestant Ethic and the Spirit of Capitalism* in that object of study constructed by this final analytic horizon, the bourgeois cultural revolution itself, "in which the values and the discourses, the habits and the daily space, of the ancient regime were systematically dismantled so that in their place could be set the new conceptualities, habits and life forms, and value systems of a capitalist market society" (*Political Unconscious* 96). It was in the context of analyzing Weber's narrative of this process that the dialectical concept of the vanishing mediator first emerged. Recognizing that "every 'social formation,' every historically existing society, has consisted in the structural coexistence of several modes of production," cultural revolution designates "that moment in which the coexistence of various modes of production becomes visibly antagonistic, their contradictions moving to the very center of political, social, and historical life" (95). In this final horizon of cultural revolution, the individual text is "restructured as a field of force in which the dynamics of sign systems of several distinct modes of production can be registered and apprehended. These dynamics—the newly constituted 'text' of our third horizon—make up what can be called the *ideology of form*" (98). What will be especially relevant for the present study's analyses of cultural forms, and of the legal forms of appearance "registered and apprehended" within their respective fields of force, is the understanding that on this horizon of analysis, "'form' is apprehended as content" (99), and not merely or even primarily as the expression of a particular work's social content.

35. The Constitution refers to "citizens" (each time without definition) in three sections delineating the criteria for holding office; and in one section on the reach of the Supreme Court. Article I, § 2: "No Person shall be a Representative who shall not have attained to the Age of twenty-five Years, and been seven years a Citizen of the United States." Article I, § 3: "No Person shall be a Senator who shall not have attained to the Age of thirty Years, and been nine Years a Citizen of the United States." Article II, § 1: "No person except a natural born Citizen, or a Citizen of the United States, at the time of the Adoption of this Constitution, shall be eligible to the Office of President." Article III, § 2: "The judicial Power shall extend to all Cases, in Law and Equity, arising under this Constitution, the Laws of the United States and Treaties made, or which shall be made, under their Authority; . . . to Controversies between two or more States;—between a State and Citizens of another State;—Between Citizens of different States;—between Citizens of the same

State claiming Lands under Grants of different States, and between a State, or the Citizens thereof, and foreign States, Citizens or Subjects" (*The Constitution of the United States and Related Documents*, ed. Martin Shapiro [Northbrook, IL: AHM, 1973]).

36. James Kettner, *The Development of American Citizenship, 1608–1870* (Chapel Hill: University of North Carolina Press, 1978), 345. Deak Nabers explores the legal and literary background to the Fourteenth Amendment in *Victory of Law: The Fourteenth Amendment, the Civil War, and American Literature, 1852-1867* (Baltimore: Johns Hopkins University Press, 2006). For Nabers, "the great achievement of that amendment was precisely its capacity to fuse moral, aesthetic, and technical orders of law" (16). For a more critical view of the Fourteenth Amendment's achievements, see Saidiya V. Hartman, *Scenes of Subjection: Terror, Slavery, and Self-Making in Nineteenth-Century America* (New York: Oxford University Press, 1997), esp. chap. 6.

37. The narrowest interpretation of this clause, now the settled one, was decided by the Court in Paul v. Virginia 75 U.S. (8 Wall) 168, 180 (1869):

> It was undoubtedly the object of the clause in question to place the citizens of each State upon the same footing with citizens of other States, so far as the advantages resulting from citizenship in those States are concerned. It relieves them from the disabilities of alienage in other States; it inhibits discriminating legislation against them by other States; it gives them the right of free ingress into other States, and egress from them; it insures to them in other States the same freedom possessed by the citizens of those States in the acquisition and enjoyment of property, and in the pursuit of happiness; and it secures to them in other States the equal protection of their laws.

38. U.S. Const. art. IV, § 2.

39. James Madison, *The Debates in the Federal Convention of 1787*, 2: 487.

40. 1 Stat. 302 (1793).

41. Edlie Wong explores this conceptualization of freedom as free mobility in her illuminating study of freedom suits and the culture of travel. Wong argues that "travelling slaves challenged, even more profoundly than did the fugitive, the cultural logic of slavery and freedom" (Wong, *Neither Fugitive nor Free: Atlantic Slavery, Freedom Suits, and the Legal Culture of Travel* [New York and London: NYU Press, 2009], 2). For an analysis of the long nineteenth century history and legacy of the figure of the fugitive slave as errant property, see Stephen M. Best, *The Fugitive's Properties: Law and the Poetics of Possession* (Chicago and London: University of Chicago Press, 2004).

42. *Constitution of the United States and Related Documents*, ed. Shapiro, 2, emphasis added.

43. Don E. Fehrenbacher, *The Dred Scott Case: Its Significance in American Law and Politics* (New York: Oxford University Press, 1978), 193; Barbara Fields, "Slavery, Race, and Ideology in the United States of America," *New Left Review* 181 (1990): 99.

44. This is the argument, following David Brion Davis, of Barbara Fields (see Fields, "Slavery, Race, and Ideology" 102).

45. U.S. Const. art. I, § 2.

46. U.S. Const. art. I, § 9.

47. *The Federalist No. 42* (James Madison): "It were doubtless to be wished that the power of prohibiting the importation of slaves had not been postponed until the year 1808, or rather that it had suffered to have immediate operation. But it is not difficult to account either for this restriction on the general government, or for the manner in which the whole clause is expressed.... Attempts have been made to pervert this clause into an objection against the Constitution by representing it on one side as a criminal toleration of an illicit practice, and on another as calculated to prevent voluntary and beneficial emigrations from Europe to America" (*The Federalist Papers*, ed. Clinton Rossiter [New York: Penguin, 1961], 266–67).

48. Luther Martin, "The Genuine Information, delivered to the Legislature of Maryland, relative to the Proceedings of the General Convention, held at Philadelphia, in 1787," in *Secret Proceedings and Debates of the Convention to Form the U.S. Constitution*, ed. Robert Yates (1821; repr., Birmingham, AL: Southern University Press, 1987), 63.

49. Douglass, *Life and Writings*, 1: 355–57.

50. *Debates and Proceedings in the Congress of the United States*, 5th Cong. (1797–98). See Gallatin, 1979, Baldwin, 1978–79 from the *Debates*, 5C. See also James Morton Smith, *Freedom's Fetters: The Alien and Sedition Laws and American Civil Liberties* (Ithaca, NY: Cornell University Press, 1956), 79–81. This semantic debate also reveals the extent to which "original intent" was perceived as central to later debates over the legal form of citizenship.

51. "The Constitution and Slavery," *North Star*, 16 March 1849, in *Life and Writings of Frederick Douglass*, ed. Philip S. Foner, 1: 361.

52. Ibid.

53. Ernest Mandel and Etienne Balibar discuss the significance of this qualitative transformation in the relations of production (see Mandel's introduction to the appendix to *Capital* 1: 943–47; and Balibar, *Reading Capital* 236–43).

54. J. Hector St. John Crèvecœur, *Letters from an American Farmer*, ed. Susan Manning (Oxford: Oxford University Press, 1998), 44.

55. Benjamin Franklin, *Autobiography and Other Writings*, ed. Ormond Seavey (Oxford and New York: Oxford University Press, 1993), 23.

56. Christopher Tomlins, *Law, Labor, and Ideology in the Early American Republic* (Cambridge: Cambridge University Press, 1993), 21. On the novel and nationalism, see Benedict Anderson, *Imagined Communities: Reflections on the Origin and Spread of Nationalism* (London: Verso, 1991), 9–65.

57. Charles Sellers, *The Market Revolution: Jacksonian America, 1815–1846* (New York: Oxford University Press, 1991).

NOTES TO CHAPTER 1

1. *The Federalist No. 54*, in *The Federalist Papers*, ed. Clinton Rossiter (New York: Penguin, 1961), 339. Further references to *The Federalist Papers* are to this edition and are cited parenthetically in the chapter text as *FP*. Historians have established that *Federalist No. 54* was written by James Madison, but I use the collective "Publius" because the authorship of individual papers was kept secret during the ratification debates.

2. Wendell Phillips, ed., *The Constitution: A Pro-Slavery Compact; Selections from the Madison Papers* (New York: Negro Universities Press, 1969), 24. (Originally published in 1844 by the American Anti-Slavery Society.)

3. The question of "the true principle of representation" was raised by William Patterson, who opposed the three-fifths representation, and proposed instead the New Jersey Plan for a unicameral legislature with equal representation from each state (see "Madison's Notes," quoted in Phillips, *A Pro-Slavery Compact*, 15).

4. As James Madison insisted, "the States were divided into interests not by their difference or size, but by other circumstances; the most material of which resulted partly from climate, but principally from their having or not having slaves. These two causes concurred in forming the great division of interests in the United States. It did not lie between the large and small States. It lay between the Northern and Southern" ("Madison's Notes," in Phillips, *A Pro-Slavery Compact*, 14). Madison's assessment of the fundamental division of interests among the states would be cited throughout the antebellum debates of the Union crisis, becoming the dominant understanding of the Constitution as a "national compromise" by the 1840s.

5. New Jersey delegate William Patterson opposed the "combined rules of numbers and wealth" and the inclusion of slaves by citing the "true principle of representation" (Extract from "Debates in the Federal Convention" of 1787, for the formation of the Constitution of the United States, in Phillips, *A Pro-Slavery Compact*, 15).

6. In the antebellum period, antislavery forces would focus on the "fugitive slave clause" as the provision that nationalized what previously had been recognized as a local institution of the slaveholding states. Modern commentators have likewise focused on this clause as the most representative of the Constitution's slavery-sanctioning "original intent." During the 1787 convention, however, this "slave clause" was not the most debated. In fact, what Douglass's "man from another country" would call the fugitive-from-labor provision was added late in those secret proceedings, with very little debate, and, as we have seen, this clause was conceived and understood as equally applicable to runaway indentured servants and apprentices, those persons "voluntarily" bound to service. The most serious confrontation over constitutional protections of slaveholding interests was occasioned by the debate over whether slaves should be included in the apportionment clause and its calculus of political representation (see Paul Finkelman, *Slavery and the Founders: Race and Liberty in the Age of Jefferson* [New York: M. E. Sharpe, 2001], 10, 32).

7. For the ambivalent role of legal forms as "expressing and codifying, the 'economic' reality which each mode of production defines in its own way, and yet simultaneously

masking it," see Louis Althusser and Etienne Balibar, *Reading Capital*, trans. Ben Brewster (London: Verso, 1997), 229. For the relation between slavery and eighteenth-century legal definitions of freedom, see David Brion Davis, *The Problem of Slavery in the Age of Revolution, 1770–1823* (New York and Oxford: Oxford University Press, 1999). For the debates over practicable emancipation and "the problem of freedom" in the British West Indies, see Thomas C. Holt, *The Problem of Freedom: Race, Labor, and Politics in Jamaica and Britain, 1832–1938* (Baltimore and London: Johns Hopkins University Press, 1992), esp. chap. 1.

8. "Extracts from Madison's Report of Debates in the Congress of the Confederation," in Phillips, *A Pro-Slavery Compact*, 13. The report continues: "Mr. [James] Wilson (of Pennsylvania) said he would sacrifice his opinion on this compromise" (13).

9. Finkelman, *Slavery and the Founders*, 13.

10. In his analysis of Justice Roger Taney's misreading of the clause in *Dred Scott v. Sanford* (1857), Stephen Best observes: "As measures of value and wealth, the focal points for taxation and representation, slaves were no more treated as property than were free persons. The clause only incorporated a differential estimate of the slave's wealth-producing capacity as a person—reflecting, by that estimate, the widespread and largely accurate belief, long championed by utilitarian political economists such as Adam Smith, 'in the relative inefficiency of slave labor' as against free labor" (Best, *Fugitive's Properties: Law and the Poetics of Possession* [Chicago: University of Chicago Press, 2004], 80). The three-fifths ratio was a compromise over what James Madison (writing as Publius in *The Federalist No. 54*) described as the "mixed character" of the slave under slave law: regarded primarily as chattel property, yet also as "moral person." The wording of the clause gives the misleading impression that the rule of representation preceded taxation. In fact, slaves were included in the rule of representation because it had been agreed first that they must be included in the rule of taxation. For the ruling class of the new nation, however, there could be no taxation without representation.

11. "Extracts from Debates in the Congress of Confederation, preserved by Thomas Jefferson, 1776," in *A Pro-Slavery Compact*, 10.

12. Ibid.

13. Ibid.

14. Ibid., 11.

15. Ibid.

16. Ibid.

17. See Adam Smith, *An Inquiry into the Nature and Causes of the Wealth of Nations* (London: George Routledge and Sons, 1776), 301–2.

18. "Extracts from Madison's Report of Debates in the Congress of the Confederation," in *A Pro-Slavery Compact*, 12.

19. Ibid., 13.

20. For an illuminating analysis of this debate over "wear and tear" costs of labor reproduction and relative labor productivity in the British West Indian context, see Seymour Drescher, "Free Labor and Slave Labor," in *Terms of Labor: Slavery, Serfdom, and Free Labor*, ed. Stanley L. Engerman (Stanford: Stanford University Press, 1999), 50–86.

21. Phillips, *A Pro-Slavery Compact*, 13.

22. Paul Finkelman points out that James Wilson proposed the ratio for the apportionment of representation (Article I, § 2) in the 1787 Federal Convention. Yet to appreciate fully the political-economic history of this "compromise," we should note as well that Wilson took this ratio from the taxation debates of 1783, and that in the 1783 debates, the ratio was first proposed by James Madison. Wilson was initially opposed to taxing slave laborers less than free laborers, but "said he would sacrifice his opinion on this compromise" (Phillips, *A Pro-Slavery Compact*, 13).

23. For the practical implications of the three-fifths clause on the rise of the slave power, see Garry Wills, *"Negro President": Jefferson and the Slave Power* (Boston and New York: Houghton-Mifflin, 2003).

24. Phillips, *A Pro-Slavery Compact*, 16, emphasis in original

25. Ibid.

26. Ibid.

27. Ibid., 17.

28. Ibid., 15.

29. Ibid.

30. Ibid., 18.

31. Ibid., 17.

32. Ibid., 18.

33. Ibid., 16.

34. Ibid., 19.

35. Ibid., 18–20.

36. Ibid., 17.

37. Ibid., 10.

38. Ibid., 32.

39. J. Hector St. John Crèvecœur, *Letters from an American Farmer* (Oxford: Oxford Classics, 1994), 43. Further references to this text are to this edition and are cited in the chapter text as *Letters*.

40. Benedict Anderson, *Imagined Communities: Reflections on the Origin and Spread of Nationalism* (London: Verso, 1991), 9–36.

41. Luther Martin, "The Genuine Information," in *Secret Proceedings and Debates of the Convention to Form the U.S. Constitution*, ed. Robert Yates (1821; repr., Birmingham, AL: Southern University Press, 1987), 63.

42. Madison elaborates this analogy in *The Federalist No. 10*, in *The Federalist Papers*, ed. Rossiter, 77–84.

43. Raymond Williams, *Keywords: A Vocabulary of Culture and Society* (New York: Oxford University Press, 1983), 234.

44. Ibid., 235.

45. Pierre Bourdieu, "The Forms of Capital," in *The Handbook of Theory and Research for the Sociology of Education*, ed. John G. Richardson (New York: Greenwood, 1983), 241–58.

46. Williams, *Keywords*, 235.

47. Benjamin Franklin, *Autobiography and Other Writings*, ed. Ormond Seavey (Oxford: Oxford University Press, 1993), 14. All citations to Franklin are from this edition and are cited in the chapter text as Franklin.

48. See Christopher Looby, *Voicing America: Language, Literary Form, and the Origins of the United States* (Chicago: University of Chicago Press, 1996), 114–15; and Michael Warner, *The Letters of the Republic: Publication and the Public Sphere in Eighteenth-Century America* (Cambridge: Harvard University Press, 1990), 76–77.

49. David Waldstreicher focuses on the political economic ground of Franklin's self-representation in *Runaway America: Benjamin Franklin, Slavery, and the American Revolution* (New York: Hill and Wang, 2004). Waldstreicher takes for granted the conception of indentured servants and apprentices as "unfree" (6) like slaves, and thus likewise describes Franklin as "unfree" (6) and "not—a free man" (3). This modern equation of the unfreedom of slavery and indentured servitude, "however, depends upon a particular scheme of understandings that ignores the characteristics indentured servitude shares with free labor—contractual freedom, limited term, compensation—and that classifies it with slavery because of the legal compulsion both involve" (Robert J. Steinfeld, *The Invention of Free Labor: The Employment Relation in English and American Law and Culture, 1350–1870* [Chapel Hill: University of North Carolina Press, 1991], 10). As we have seen, the framers likewise distinguished between the indentured servant as bound-yet-free labor and the absolute unfreedom of chattel slavery.

50. John Locke, *An Essay Concerning Human Understanding*, ed. Alexander Campbell Fraser (New York: Dover, 1959), 350 (bk. 2, chap. 21, para. 54).

51. Ibid., 345.

52. Ibid.

53. John Locke, *Second Treatise of Government*, ed. C. B. MacPherson (Indianapolis: Hackett, 1980), 70.

54. Ibid., my emphasis.

55. Ibid., 78.

56. Christopher Looby argues that Franklin's text addressed those of the post-Revolutionary era "who were less equal than others [and] consequently impatient and frustrated"; and "taught such people the virtue of patience in the face of such deferral" of the Revolution's promise of equality: "it taught the necessity of frugality and diligence at a time when, for instance, the poor were wondering why, now that British authority had been removed, their condition was substantially unchanged" (*Voicing America*, 131).

57. Martin, "The Genuine Information," 63.

58. Houston Baker, *Blues, Ideology, and Afro-American Literature: A Vernacular Theory* (Chicago: University of Chicago Press, 1984), 36.

59. Ibid., 37.

60. David Kazanjian offers a different corrective to Baker's argument in *The Colonizing Trick: National Culture and Imperial Citizenship in Early America* (Minneapolis: University of Minnesota Press, 2003). Kazanjian suggests that "Baker's failure to consider how

Equiano narrates his mercantile encounters with mercantil*ism*—a political-economic system that helped to form nation-states—thus mirrors his failure to consider the *Narrative* . . . as a text about the interdependent emergence of nation and race" (48).

61. James Madison, *The Federalist No. 54*, in *The Federalist Papers*, ed. Rossiter, 337.

62. William Blackstone, *Commentaries on the Laws of England* (Oxford, 1765), 1: 123, quoted in Davis, *Problem of Slavery in the Age of Revolution*, 473. Davis points out that in the third edition (1768–69), Blackstone revised the sentence to read: "falls under the protection of the laws, and so far becomes a freeman; though the master's right to his service may probably continue" (485).

63. *Somerset v. Stewart* (R. v. Knowles, ex parte Somerset) (1772) 20 State Tr 1 (1772). The most cited lines of the ruling declare: "The state of slavery is of such a nature, that it is incapable of being introduced on any reasons, moral or political; but only positive law, which preserves its force long after the reasons, occasion, and time itself from whence it was created, is erased from memory: it's so odious, that nothing can be suffered to support it, but positive law. Whatever inconveniences, therefore, may follow from a decision, I cannot say this case is allowed or approved by the law of England; and therefore the black must be discharged."

64. Olaudah Equiano, *The Interesting Narrative and Other Writings*, ed. Vincent Carretta (New York: Penguin, 2003), 163. All references to *Interesting Narrative* are to this edition and are cited in the chapter text as Equiano.

65. David Barclay, "Advice to Servants," broadside, Friends House, quoted in Davis, *Problem of Slavery in the Age of Revolution*, 252.

66. For more on the advised characteristics of the good servant, see Sharon V. Salinger, *"To Serve Well and Faithfully": Labor and Indentured Servants in Pennsylvania, 1682–1800* (New York: Cambridge University Press, 1987).

67. Baker, *Blues*, 36.

68. Pierre Bourdieu, "The Forms of Capital," 241–58.

69. In *The Crisis of the Sugar Colonies* (1802), James Stephen addressed the transition from slave labor to free labor by focusing on the cultivation of foresight in the formerly enslaved: "Man is naturally indolent, and impatient of bodily restraint. Though spurred by his hopes and fears into activity, and often to the most ardent exertions, he is with difficulty bent to the yoke of uniform and persevering labour. The suggestions of foresight however are very powerful impulses, especially when seconded by habit. . . . When we bow to the golden scepter of reason, obedience has many facilities, and its pains many mitigations" (*The Crisis of the Sugar Colonies; or, An Enquiry into the Objects and Probable Effects of the French Expedition to the West Indies; And their Connection to the Interests of the British Empire* [London: J. Hatchard, 1802], 48–49).

70. Anthony Benezet, *Some Historical Account of Guinea . . . With an inquiry into the rise and progress of the slave-trade, its nature, and lamentable effects* (London: Frank Cass, 1968), 116. (Originally published in Philadelphia, 1771; 2nd ed., London, 1788.)

71. Ibid.

72. Ibid.

73. Ibid., 117, emphasis added.

74. Davis, *Problem of Slavery in the Age of Revolution*, 242.

75. Benezet, *Some Historical Account of Guinea*, 118.

76. Cugoano, *Thoughts and Sentiments on the Evil and Wicked Traffic of the Slavery and Commerce of the Human Species, Humbly Submitted to the Inhabitants of Great Britain, by Ottobah Cugoano, a Native of Africa*, in *Pioneers of the Black Atlantic: Five Slave Narratives from the Enlightenment, 1772–1815*, ed. Henry Louis Gates Jr. and William L. Andrews (Washington, DC: Basic Civitas, 1998), 169.

77. Richard B. Morris, *Government and Labor in Early America* (New York: Octagon, 1965), 363–65.

78. Cugoano, *Thoughts and Sentiments*, 170.

79. "Letter from Granville Sharp," quoted by Benjamin Rush, "An Address Upon Slave-Keeping" (1773), in *The Selected Writings of Benjamin Rush*, ed. Dagobert D. Runes (New York: Philosophical Library, 1947), 14.

80. Thomas Holt notes that later proposals for emancipation in the British West Indies looked to *coartación* as a model: "The planters were encouraged to move with all deliberate speed to prepare their slaves to join a free labor force. Slaves should be given religious instruction; marriages and families should be protected; physical coercion, especially whipping, should be controlled if not abolished; and manumission should be encouraged. Consciously copying the Spanish system of *coartación*, the Colonial Office sought to achieve a gradual emancipation by enabling individual slaves to buy their freedom" (Holt, *The Problem of Freedom: Race, Labor, and Politics in Jamaica and Britain, 1832–1938* [Baltimore: Johns Hopkins University Press, 1992], 18). Holt does not draw a connection between Sharp's discussion of *coartación* as an exemplary model of gradual emancipation and these proposals later advanced by the Colonial Office. For the role of punishment in the apprenticeship period of gradual emancipation, see Diana Patton, *No Bond but the Law: Punishment, Race, and Gender in Jamaican State Formation, 1780-1870* (Durham: Duke University Press, 2004).

81. The central concern of debates over practicable emancipation in the British West Indies was continuity in sugar production levels, which depended upon the transformation of an enslaved population to one of "free labor" (see Seymour Drescher, "Free Labor vs. Slave Labor: The British and Caribbean Cases," in *Terms of Labor: Slavery, Serfdom, and Free Labor*, ed. Stanley Engerman [Stanford: Stanford University Press, 1999], 50–86). For an illuminating analysis of such gradualist emancipation schemes and the conceptions of "need" and "value" in assimilation, see Thomas Holt, "'An Empire over the Mind': Emancipation, Race, and Ideology in the British West Indies and the American South," in *Region, Race, and Reconstruction*, ed. J. Morgan Kousser and James M. McPherson (Oxford: Oxford University Press, 1982), 283–313.

82. Joseph Fichtelberg, "Word between Worlds: The Economy of Equiano's Narrative," *American Literary History* 5 (1993): 471.

83. Philip Gould, *Barbaric Traffic: Commerce and Antislavery in the Eighteenth-Century Atlantic World* (Cambridge: Harvard University Press, 2003), 142.

84. "Letter from Granville Sharp," in *Selected Writings of Benjamin Rush*, 14.

85. Cugoano, *Thoughts and Sentiments*, 112–13, emphasis added.
86. Ibid., 113.
87. *Oxford English Dictionary*, 2nd ed., s.v. "consideration."
88. Franco Moretti, *The Way of the World: The Bildungsroman in European Culture* (London: Verso, 1987).

NOTES TO CHAPTER 2

1. Ian Watt, *The Rise of the Novel: Studies in Defoe, Richardson, and Fielding* (Berkeley: University of California Press, 1957), 31.
2. Ibid. Watt further equates the jury and the novel: "The narrative method whereby the novel embodies this circumstantial view of life may be called its formal realism; formal because the term realism does not here refer to any specific literary doctrine or purpose, but only to a set of narrative procedures which are so commonly found together in the novel and so rarely in other literary genres, that they may be regarded as typical of the form itself" (32).
3. David Thomas Konig, "Legal Fictions and the Rule(s) of Law: The Jeffersonian Critique of Common-Law Adjudication," in *The Many Legalities of Early America*, ed. Christopher L. Tomlins and Bruce H. Mann (Chapel Hill: University of North Carolina Press, 2001), 101.
4. Ibid., 99, citing Giles Jacob, *A Law Grammar; or Rudiments of the Law . . .*, 4th ed. (London, 1767), 199.
5. John Cowell, *A Law Dictionary; or, The Interpreter of Words and Terms . . .* (London, 1727), cited in Konig, "Legal Fictions," 101.
6. Blackstone, cited in Konig, "Legal Fictions," 102.
7. Watt, *Rise of the Novel*, 32.
8. Michael McKeon, *The Origins of the English Novel, 1600–1740* (Baltimore: Johns Hopkins University Press, 1987), 35. McKeon adds: "The feudal system of ordeal, which is justified by the assumption that divine will and righteousness are immanent in human affairs, is now replaced by inquest, testimony, witnesses, documentary evidence, and the possibility of appeal—strictly human mechanisms that bespeak the commitment to the faithful re-creation of past events in their historical factuality" (35).
9. Ibid., 36.
10. On the development of "reasonable doubt," see Theodore Waldman, "Origins of the Legal Doctrine of Reasonable Doubt," *Journal of the History of Ideas* 20, no. 3 (June–September 1959): 299–316.
11. Douglas Lane Patey, *Probability and Literary Form: Philosophic Theory and Literary Practice in the Augustan Age* (New York: Cambridge University Press, 1984), 138.
12. Richard Blackmore, *Essays on Several Subjects* (1716), 24, quoted in Patey, *Probability and Literary Form*, 138.
13. Charles Brockden Brown, *Arthur Mervyn; or Memoirs of the Year 1793*, ed. Sydney J. Krause (Kent: Kent State University Press, 1980), 3. Subsequent references are cited by page number in the chapter text.

14. Brown's prediction that the yellow fever outbreak of 1793 would "probably form an aera" in Philadelphia history proved true, as Mathew Carey noted in his 1830 introduction to the fifth and final edition of his widely popular history of the 1793 Philadelphia plague, *A Short Account of the Malignant Fever*: "The novel of *Arthur Mervyn*, by C. B Brown, gives a vivid and terrifying picture, probably not too highly coloured, of the horrors of that period" (see Carey's *A Short Account of the Malignant Fever which prevailed in Philadelphia, in the year 1793: with a statement of the proceedings that took place on the subject, in different parts of the United States* [Philadelphia: Clark and Raser, 1830]). Carey, one of the Committee of Health formed in response to the epidemic, first published the *Short Account* on 13 November 1793, immediately after the crisis had passed. Carey is quoted in Norman S. Grabo, "Historical Essay," in *Arthur Mervyn*, 451. According to Grabo, by 1830 "Charles Brockden Brown's fame was inseparable from his picture of that gruesome summer of 1793" (449).

15. "Walstein's School of History," in *The Rhapsodist, and Other Uncollected Writings by Charles Brockden Brown*, ed. Harry R. Warfel (New York: Scholars' Facsimiles and Reprints, 1943), 149. (Originally published in *Monthly Magazine and American Review* 1 [1799].)

16. Ibid.

17. Here we can see one point of emergence in that conceptual shift in modernity, which Franco Moretti has argued found its fullest expression in the nineteenth century:

> What constitutes [youth] as symbolic form is no longer a "spatial" determination, as in the case of Renaissance perspective, but rather a temporal one. This is not surprising, since the nineteenth century, under the pressure of modernity, had first of all to reorganize its conception of change—which too often, from the time of the French Revolution, had appeared as a meaningless and thus threatening reality.... This accounts for the centrality of history in nineteenth-century culture ... and for the centrality of narrative within the domain of literature. Narrative and history, in fact, do not retreat before the onslaught of events, but demonstrate the possibility of giving them order and meaning. Furthermore, they suggest that reality's meaning is now to be grasped solely in its historico-diachronic dimension. Not only are there no 'meaningless' events; there can be meaning only through events" (Franco Moretti, *The Way of the World: The Bildungsroman in European Culture* [London: Verso, 1987], 6).

18. Mathew Carey, *A Short Account of the Malignant Fever, lately prevalent in Philadelphia: with a statement of the proceedings that took place on the subject, in different parts of the United States*, 4th ed. (Philadelphia: Mathew Carey, 1794), 58. For Carey's summary of the various city resolutions barring citizens, ships, and goods from Philadelphia, see 47–58 (chaps. 10–11).

19. "Free workers in the double sense that they neither form part of the means of production themselves, as would be the case with slaves, serfs, etc., nor do they own the means of production.... The free workers are therefore free from, unencumbered by, any means of production of their own" (Marx, *Capital* 1: 874).

20. Mieke Bal, *Narratology: Introduction to the Theory of Narrative*, 2nd ed. (Toronto: University of Toronto Press, 1997), 52.

21. Ibid., 60.

22. Ibid., 52.

23. The two best contenders for the "first" American novel, William Hill Brown's *The Power of Sympathy*, and Hannah Webster Foster's *The Coquette*, both follow the epistolary form. Neither novel, however, contains any frame narrative for its letters. It is important to note also that Charles Brockden Brown was aware of other narrative strategies; he employed several different ones in his major novels. As Brown writes in his "Advertisement" to *Wieland* (1798), for example, the entire "narrative is addressed, in an epistolary form, by The Lady whose story it contains" (Charles Brockden Brown, *"Wieland" and "Memoirs of Carwin the Biloquist,"* ed. Jay Fleigelman [New York: Penguin, 1991], 4).

The fictional introduction letter to *Ormond* (1799) describes the narrative as a "biographical sketch"; this novel thus proceeds in a third-person narration. Both *Edgar Huntly* (1799) and *Carwin, the Biloquist* (1803–5), the magazine sequel to *Wieland*, are titled *Memoirs*; accordingly, they are told as first-person narrations. Finally, while the major novels assume different narrating devices (letters, memoirs, biographies and histories), they all follow the procedure initiated with *Arthur Mervyn*, and foregrounded as its structuring principle: the embedded narrative of various testimonies. While *Wieland* was Brown's first published novel, textual historians speculate that *Arthur Mervyn* was most likely the "Philadelphia novel" he began as early as 1795 (Norman S. Grabo, "Historical Essay," in *Arthur Mervyn* [Kent: Kent State University Press, 1980], 450).

24. Anderson, *Imaginary*, 24–25.

25. Katie Trumpener, *Bardic Nationalism: The Romantic Novel and the British Empire* (Princeton: Princeton University Press, 1997), 164. For the relation between "imagined communities" and theories of contagion, see Pricilla Wald, *Contagious: Cultures, Carriers, and the Outbreak Narrative* (Durham: Duke University Press, 2008).

26. Ibid.

27. Michael Warner, *The Letters of the Republic: Publication and the Public Sphere in Eighteenth-Century America* (Cambridge: Harvard University Press, 1990), 169. See also Trish Loughran, *The Republic in Print: Print Culture in the Age of U.S. Nation-Building, 1770-1870* (New York: Columbia University Press, 2007).

28. Ibid., 166.

29. Ibid., 166, 169.

30. Christopher Looby, *Voicing America: Language, Literary Form, and the Origins of the United States* (Chicago: University of Chicago Press, 1996), 5.

31. Ibid.

32. McKeon, *Origins of the English Novel, 1600–1740*. McKeon emphasizes the importance of developments in legal history as "perhaps the most striking evidence of the growth and effects of literacy. It is in post-Conquest England ... that royal writs become central in property litigations, and writing becomes the normal mode of conducting legal

business. These developments are intimately related to the contemporary rationalization of the idea of judicial trial" (35).

33. On the culture of rhetorical performance, see Jay Fliegelman, *Declaring Independence: Jefferson, Natural Language, and the Culture of Performance* (Stanford: Stanford University Press, 1993).

34. John Locke, *An Essay Concerning Human Understanding*, ed. John W. Yolton (New York: Dutton, 1978), 247.

35. Ibid., 247–48.

36. Brown, "Walstein's School," 152.

37. Barbara Shapiro, *Beyond Reasonable Doubt and Probable Cause: Historical Perspectives on the Anglo-American Law of Evidence* (Berkeley and Los Angeles: University of California Press, 1991), 27–29. On the predominance of Scottish Enlightenment thought in early America, see Richard B. Sher and Jeffrey R. Smitten, eds., *Scotland and America in the Age of Enlightenment* (Princeton: Princeton University Press, 1990). On the relation between liberalism and the development of moral philosophy, see Mary Poovey, *A History of the Modern Fact: Problems of Knowledge in the Sciences of Wealth and Society* (Chicago: University of Chicago Press, 1998), esp. chap. 4, "Experimental Moral Philosophy and the Problems of Liberal Governmentality."

38. Wilson draws from Thomas Reid's writings throughout his *Lectures on Law*. For the influence of Scottish Common Sense on Anglo-American legal theory, see Shannon C. Stimson, "A Jury of the Country": Common Sense Philosophy and the Jurisprudence of James Wilson," in *Scotland and America in the Age of Enlightenment*, ed. Richard B. Sher and Jeffrey R. Smitten (Princeton: Princeton University Press, 1990), 193–208.

39. James Wilson, *The Works of James Wilson*, ed. Robert Green McCloskey, 2 vols. (Cambridge: Belknap Press of Harvard University Press, 1967), 2: 395.

40. Emphasizing the connections "among things actually existing," Wilson asserts the greater importance of such contingent truths. While "in point of authority, demonstrative evidence is superiour; moral evidence is superiour in point of importance. By the former, the understanding is enlightened, and many of the elegant and useful arts are improved. By the latter, society is supported; and the usual but indispensable affairs of life are regulated" (ibid., 2: 396).

41. Ibid., emphasis added.

42. For an account of the development of the concept of "moral certainty," see Shapiro, *Beyond Reasonable Doubt*, esp. chap. 1.

43. The legal writing of James Wilson, the republic's first major legal theorist, is an index of the transition in Anglo-American legal thought, moving as it does between a continuing reliance on English common law and a recurring critique of the common law tradition (as represented by Coke and Blackstone).

44. Barbara Shapiro, *A Culture of Fact: England, 1550–1720* (Ithaca: Cornell University Press, 2000), 10. Shapiro suggests that it was the "widespread experience and familiarity with legal institutions and the language of fact and methods of fact determination," along

with the "confidence in juries" to ascertain the truth of the fact "that made 'fact' so easily transportable to a variety of nonlegal contexts" (9–10).

45. Ibid., 11.

46. See ibid., chap. 1, "Facts and the Law." On the distinction between the "vera" of a historical account and its "veritas," see McKeon, *Origins of the English Novel,* 36. Discussing the shifts in historiography, McKeon argues that the "canonical truth of Scriptures is still, in the twelfth century, the unique standard of spiritual and historical truth against which all other writings are understood to be relatively less veracious. The *vera,* the "facts," of a history are relevant but subordinate to its *veritas,* or "truth," and in cases of apparent conflict the pure abstraction is superior to the concrete attribute" (36). Following Lennard Davis, Robert Mayer, Michael McKeon, and others, I proceed from the historical understanding that what came to be called "the novel" arose in relation to broader epistemological concerns regarding historical truth and questions of veracity. While these literary historians differ in their specific claims regarding the novel's origins, most agree with Shapiro's claim that the procedures to obtain acceptable degrees of certainty originated in the legal sphere, and were subsequently carried over into the discourses of natural science, history, and, later, "fictive" literature such as the novel (see Lennard J. Davis, *Factual Fictions: The Origins of the English Novel* [Philadelphia: University of Pennsylvania Press, 1996]; and Robert Mayer, *History and the English Novel: Matters of Fact from Bacon to Defoe* [Cambridge: Cambridge University Press, 1997]).

47. This basic distinction remains in the law books today: see Henry Campbell Black, M.A., *Black's Law Dictionary: Definitions of the Terms and Phrases of American and English Jurisprudence, Ancient and Modern,* 4th ed. (St. Paul: West, 1968), 706. Put simply, the jury weighs the evidence, deciding their truth, while the court judge makes the legal decisions, applying the law to the verdict of the jury.

48. Wilson, *Works,* 2: 505.

49. Ibid., 2: 503.

50. Ibid., 2: 395. Wilson cites instead the "scientific distinction" of the civil law theorists. For the influence of the civil law on American jurisprudence, see Peter Stein, "The Attraction of the Civil Law in Post-Revolutionary America," *Virginia Law Review* 52, no. 3 (April 1966): 403–34.

51. Ibid., 395.

52. Christopher Looby argues that in his *Lectures,* Wilson "patiently constructs" an "edifice of epistemological certitude," an edifice "undercut" and deconstructed by Brown in his novel *Wieland* (Looby, *Voicing America,* 192).

53. Wilson, *Works,* 1: 396, emphasis added.

54. Ibid., 2: 529.

55. Wilson concludes the lecture entitled "Juries" by reinforcing the connection between the jury trial and republican citizenship: "With regard to the law in criminal cases, every citizen, in a government such as ours, should endeavor to acquire a reasonable knowledge of its principles and rules, for the direction of his conduct, when he is called to obey, when he is called to answer, and when he is called to judge. On questions of law, his

deficiencies will be supplied by the professional directions of the judges, whose duty and whose business it is professionally to direct him" (2: 549).

56. Ibid., 2: 503.

57. Ibid., 2: 547.

58. Ibid., 2: 505–6, emphasis added.

59. Ibid., 1: 398.

60. Ibid., 1: 383

61. Shapiro, *Culture of Fact*, 8.

62. Locke, *Essay*, 259. Locke writes that "In the testimony of others is to be considered: 1) The number. 2) The integrity. 3) the skill of the witness. 4) The design of the author, where it is a testimony out of a book. 5) The consistency of the parts, and circumstances of the relation. 6) Contrary testimonies" (259).

63. Geoffrey Gilbert, *The Law of Evidence: By a Late Learned Judge* (London: Henry Lintot, 1756), 5. Classifying the "several Sorts of Testimony" into "Written" and "Unwritten," Gilbert emphasizes that "the Balance of Probability is certainly on the . . . Side [of written testimony], for the Testimony of an honest Man, however fortified with the Solemnities of an Oath, is yet liable to the Imperfections of Memory" (5–6).

64. John Locke, *Essay Concerning Human Understanding*, ed. John W. Yulton (New York: Dutton, 1961); see bk. 4, chap. 15, sec. 4.

65. Cited in Wilson, *Works*, 1: 382.

66. Ibid., 1: 383

67. Ibid.

68. Ibid.

69. Thomas Reid, *Inquiry into the Human Mind*, in *The Works of Thomas Reid*, ed. Sir William Hamilton, vol. 1, 7th ed. (Edinburgh: MacLachlan and Stewart, 1872). Reid argued that men have a "propensity to speak truth, and to use the signs of language to so as to convey our real sentiments," which he called the "the principle of veracity." The "counterpart" to this "original principle," and likewise "implanted in us by the Supreme Being, is a disposition to confide in the veracity of others," which he called "the principle of credulity" (Reid, *Works*, 1: 196).

70. Wilson, *Works*, 1: 383.

71. Ibid.

72. Michael Dalton, *The Country Justice* (London, 1635 edition), 297, cited in Shapiro, *Beyond Reasonable Doubt*, 190. Dalton's book was the most "widely distributed handbook of the seventeenth century, in both England and the American colonies. It conveyed the law and practice of the English criminal process to lawyers and nonlawyers alike for several generations. Although originally a nonofficial handbook for the justices, it became virtually an official legal document which later authorities such as Sir Mathew Hale would cite as legal authority" (*Beyond Reasonable Doubt*, 132). Shapiro adds, "Dalton's Country Justice was purchased by the General Courts of Virginia and Massachusetts" and was circulated throughout the colonies and, later, the early republic (309 n. 175).

73. See Shapiro, *Culture of Fact*, 16–17.

74. Sir Mathew Hale, *The History of the Common Law of England*, ed. Charles M. Gray (Chicago, 1971), 164, cited in Shapiro, *Beyond Reasonable Doubt*, 195.

75. Hale, *History of the Common Law*, 164, cited in Shapiro, *Beyond Reasonable Doubt*, 195.

76. Shapiro, *Beyond Reasonable Doubt*, 195.

77. Wilson, *Works*, 1: 370. For "degrees of assent" and the scale of probability, see Locke, *Essay*, 250. According to Locke, most knowledge could only be considered "probable knowledge": "most of the propositions we think, reason, discourse, nay, act upon, are such as we cannot have undoubted knowledge of their truth" (250). This did not mean that all was uncertain, however, for "some of them border so near upon certainty that we make no doubt about them; but assent to them as firmly, and act, according to that assent, as resolutely as if they were infallibly demonstrated, and that our knowledge of them was perfect and certain" (250). Locke elaborated a scale of probability: "But there being degrees herein, from the very neighborhood of certainty and demonstration quite down to improbability and unlikeliness, even to the confines of impossibility; and also degrees of assent from full assurance and confidence quite down to conjecture, doubt, and distrust" (250).

78. Wilson, *Works*, 1: 370–71.

79. Daniel Defoe, *Robinson Crusoe*, ed. Michael Shinagel (New York: Norton, 1994), 149.

80. Wilson, *Works*, 1: 379–80.

81. Ibid., 1: 386.

82. As Ian Watt points out in the *Rise of the Novel*, "Modern realism ... begins from the position that truth can be discovered by the individual through his senses: it has its origins in Descartes and Locke, and received its first full formulation by Thomas Reid in the middle of the eighteenth century" (12).

83. Reid, *Inquiry*, 1: 117.

84. Ibid., 1: 195.

85. Ibid.

86. Celeste Langan has argued with respect to the modern subject of Romanticism: "Argument by analogy thus stands as the logic—and the methodology—of the liberal subject" (*Romantic Vagrancy: Wordsworth and the Simulation of Freedom* [New York: Cambridge University Press, 1995], 15).

87. Wilson, *Works*, 1: 379.

88. Reid, *Inquiry*, 1: 118.

89. Ibid., 1: 379, emphasis added.

90. Ibid.

91. Brown's representations of the debates over testimonial credibility drew from the law's conceptualization of natural language—especially its valorization of natural signs in the trial of testimony, such as the "different looks and features of the countenance." Brown's novels were committed to exploring philosophies of evidence. Anglo-American philosophies of evidence—exemplified here, because synthesized by, Wilson's *Lectures on Law*—provided the ideational field from which early American writers engaged in such

thought projects necessarily drew. Engaged as they were with this evidentiary aesthetic, early American novels like those of Brown thus elaborated, within the still-developing genre, the law's epistemological forms because these were the forms of fact-finding most readily available. These epistemological forms must be understood as used by the legal sphere because they were the broader cultural dominant; not the dominant because they were legal.

92. Wilson, *Works*, 1: 380.

93. Fliegelman, *Declaring Independence*, 87.

94. On cultural and social capital, see Bourdieu, "The Forms of Capital," 241–58. For a literary historical account of Charles Brockden Brown's "experiments in character" in *Arthur Mervyn*, see Samuel Otter, *Philadelphia Stories: America's Literature of Race and Freedom* (New York: Oxford University Press, 2010) 25-70.

95. Wilson, *Works*, 1: 380.

96. Cathy Davidson, *Revolution and the Word: The Rise of the Novel in America* (New York: Oxford University Press, 1986), 240; Michael Warner, *Letters of the Republic*, 167. While comparing the novel to a trial, both Davidson and Warner argue that the novel's narrative replaces the law itself. In Davidson's view, "the extended metaphoric trial becomes possible only because a more literal one is subverted in the novel" (240). Warner, who follows Davidson in this view, argues further that Mervyn's disclosure, which Warner sees as "identical with the novel's narration—operates in lieu of the law" (167).

97. Brown's early apprenticeship in law, as well as his expressed disdain for the rhetoric of lawyers, is well known. Both Davidson (in *Revolution and the Word*) and Looby (in *Voicing America*) provide useful biographical information on this topic. Brown had both theoretical and practical knowledge of legal procedures; his familiarity with the early American legal tradition appears in several of his novels.

98. Wilson, *Works*, 1: 396.

99. Emory Elliot, "Narrative Unity and Moral Resolution in *Arthur Mervyn*," in *Critical Essays on Charles Brockden Brown,* ed. Bernard Rosenthal (Boston: G. K. Hall, 1981), 142–63. In his "character analysis" of Arthur Mervyn, Elliot argues that we should be suspicious of Mervyn's character and virtue. For Elliot, to "see Mervyn as an innocent rewarded and thereby to ignore the elements of the con man in his character is to miss the novel's ironies and comic dimension." Warner Berthoff and Michael Davitt Bell share this ironic reading of Mervyn (see Berthoff, introduction to *Arthur Mervyn* [New York: Holt, Rinehart and Winston, 1962], xviii; and Bell, *The Development of American Romance* [Chicago: University of Chicago Press, 1980], 56–59).

100. Michael Warner points out that such ironic readings are based on a "liberal aesthetic of authorial craft" (*Letters of the Republic*, 155).

101. Warner's reading of the novel relies on the identification of the author, Brown, with his novel's main protagonist, Arthur Mervyn. Thus when Mervyn's character is represented as skilled in the use of the pen, Warner can say that "for Brown, literacy correlates with personality structures" (*Letters of the Republic*, 155). Identifying Mervyn the "virtuous" scrivener with Brown the writer of republican virtue, Warner argues that

Brown "certainly thinks that letters promote the kind of vigilant thinking exemplified by Mervyn" (156).

102. Until the very end of the novel's first chapter, Mervyn's words appear as reported speech; not until he is called to the "disclosure" of his acquaintance with the villain Thomas Welbeck are Mervyn's words presented (within the frame of Dr. Stevens's narration) as spoken by Arthur himself, in the first person.

103. Michael Dalton, *The Country Justice* (London, 1635 edition), 297, cited in Shapiro, *Beyond Reasonable Doubt*, 190.

104. Shapiro, *Beyond Reasonable Doubt*, 190, emphasis added.

105. Ibid. Shapiro cites Richard Chamberlain's, *The Complete Justice* (London, 1681), 449, as exemplary of this migration of criteria from the law of examination to the law of evidence (and witness credibility).

106. See Shapiro, *Culture of Fact*, 16–17.

107. Wilson, *Works*, 1: 386.

108. On the ideal of republican "virtue," see J. G. A. Pocock, *The Machiavellian Moment: Florentine Political Thought and the Atlantic Republican Tradition* (Princeton: Princeton University Press, 1975), esp. 513–34, chap. 15.

109. See Patey's discussion of verisimilitude and probability in chapter 3, "Vraisamblance, probability, and opinion," in *Probability*, 77–83.

110. Ibid., 86.

111. James Beattie, *Essays: On Poetry and Music, as They Affect the Mind* (1776), 3rd ed. (London, 1779), 200, cited in Patey, *Probability*, 86–87.

112. Wilson, *Works*, 1: 386.

113. Ibid., 1: 229.

114. Alexander Welsh, *Strong Representations: Narrative and Circumstantial Evidence in England* (Baltimore: Johns Hopkins University Press, 1992).

115. In his *Considerations on the nature and extent of the Legislative Authority of the British Parliament* (1774), James Wilson articulated the shared view of the framers that only those with an unqualified free "will of their own" should be allowed to participate in political representation: "All those are excluded from voting, whose poverty is such, that they cannot live independent, and must therefore be subject to the undue influence of their superiors. Such are supposed to have no will of their own: and it is judged improper that they should vote in the representation of a free state" (*Considerations*, in *The Works of the Honourable James Wilson*, ed. Bird Wilson (Philadelphia: Lorenzo Press, printed for Bronson and Chauncey, 1804), 209.

NOTES TO CHAPTER 3

1. Sacvan Bercovitch, "The Problem of Ideology in American Literary History," *Critical Inquiry* 12, no. 4 (Summer 1986): 631–53. Bercovitch expands on this influential argument in *The Rites of Assent: Transformations in the Symbolic Construction of America* (New York: Routledge, 1993), 353–76. Bercovitch argues: "To the extent that Douglass denounces

American society, it is for not being true to its own principles, for failing to comply in practice with a social order that is utopian in theory: reasonable, moral, and spiritually as well as economically just" (371).

2. On the culture of constitutionalism, see Joyce Appleby, "The American Heritage: The Heirs and the Disinherited," *Journal of American History* 74, no. 3 (December 1987): 798–813.

3. Eric Foner, *Free Soil, Free Labor, Free Men: The Ideology of the Republican Party before the Civil War* (New York: Oxford University Press, 1995), 75.

4. Ibid.

5. Frederick Douglass, "The Address of the Southern Delegates in Congress to their Constituents; or, the Address of John C. Calhoun and Forty Other Thieves," *North Star*, 9 February 1849, in *The Life and Writings of Frederick Douglass*, ed. Philip S. Foner (New York: International, 1950), 1: 355, emphasis in original.

6. Ibid., 1: 354.

7. Frederick Douglass, "Change of Opinion Announced," *North Star*, 15 May 1851, reprinted in *Liberator*, 23 May 1851, in *The Life and Writings of Frederick Douglass*, ed. Philip S. Foner (New York: International, 1950), 2: 155–56.

8. Ibid., 156, emphasis added.

9. Ibid, emphasis in original.

10. Ibid.

11. "Addresses Delivered in Cincinnati, Ohio, 11–13 April 1854," in *The Frederick Douglass Papers, Series One: Speeches, Debates and Interviews*, ed. John W. Blassingame, vol. 2, *1847–54* (New Haven: Yale University Press, 1982), 473.

12. "The Constitution of the United States: Is It Pro-Slavery or Anti-Slavery?," speech delivered in Glasgow, Scotland (March 26, 1860), in *Life and Writings of Frederick Douglass*, 2: 469.

13. Ibid.

14. Ibid. Douglass also emphasizes that "the debates in the convention that framed the Constitution . . . were not published until more than a quarter of a century after the presentation and adoption of the Constitution. These debates were purposely kept out of view, in order that the people should adopt, not the secret motives or unexpressed intentions of any body, but the simple text of the paper itself. Those debates form no part of the original agreement" (469).

15. Ibid., 2: 475.

16. "Addresses Delivered in Cincinnati, Ohio, 11–13 April 1854," in *Frederick Douglass Papers*, ser. 1, 2: 474.

17. "The Constitution of the United States: Is It Pro-Slavery or Anti-Slavery?," 2: 475–76.

18. Houston Baker, *Blues, Ideology, and Afro-American Literature: A Vernacular Theory* (Chicago: University of Chicago Press, 1984).

19. On the "American 1848," see Michael Paul Rogin, *Subversive Genealogy: The Politics and Art of Herman Melville* (Berkeley: University of California Press, 1985), 102–51. The "American 1848" is Rogin's name for the "crisis over slavery from the Mexican peace treaty in 1848 through the passage of the 1850 Compromise and the enforcement of its fugitive slave provisions in 1851" (103).

20. *Secret Proceedings and Debates of the Convention Assembled at Philadelphia, in the Year 1787, For the Purpose of Forming the Constitution of the United States of America; From the Notes Taken by the Late Robert Yates, Esq., Chief Justice of New York, and Copied by Jon Lansing, Jun. Esq., Late Chancellor of that State, Members of that Convention; Including the "Genuine Information," Laid before the Legislature of Maryland, by Luther Martin, Esq., then Attorney General of that State, and a Member of the Same Convention; also, Other Historical Documents Relative to the Federal Compact of the North American Union* (Albany: Printed by Websters and Skinners, 1821). The *Secret Proceedings* was published again by different printers in 1839 and 1844.

21. James Madison, *The Debates in the Federal Convention of 1787, which framed the Constitution of the United States of America; Reported by James Madison, a delegate from the State of Virginia*, ed. Gaillard Hunt and James Brown Scott (New York: Oxford University Press, 1920).

22. *Prigg v. Pennsylvania*, 41 U.S. 539 (1842).

23. Gary B. Nash and Jean R. Soderlund, *Freedom by Degrees: Emancipation in Pennsylvania and Its Aftermath* (New York: Oxford University Press, 1991), 198–201.

24. Don E. Fehrenbacher, *The Dred Scott Case: Its Significance in American Law and Politics* (New York: Oxford University Press, 1978), 45. Gregg Crane discusses Taney's *Dred Scott* Opinion in *Race, Citizenship, and Law in American Literature* (Cambridge: Cambridge University Press, 2002), 148–52. Like many modern commentators, Crane confuses the antebellum usages of the terms "strict construction" and "original intent." Crane thus asserts that "Taney's historical approach is ostensibly justified by his strict constructionist hermeneutic, an interpretive approach that reads the Constitution as one would a code, simply putting the lawmakers' will and intent into effect" (Crane 150). As I discuss in my introduction and at greater length in this chapter 3, this understanding is not historically accurate. It was actually the radical antislavery constitutionalists who argued for "strict construction," against the dominant "original intent" hermeneutic of judges Story and Taney.

25. *Prigg v. Pennsylvania* 41 U.S. 539 at 565.

26. Joseph Story, *Commentaries on the Constitution of the United States; with a Preliminary Review of the Constitutional History of the Colonies and States before the Adoption of the Constitution* (New York: De Capo Press, 1970), 3: 676–77. Unabridged republication of first edition published in Boston in 1833.

27. Ibid., 2: 108, 111–14. In his *Commentaries*, Story explained the meaning of the slave clauses as compromises by examining *The Federalist Papers* and *Eliot's Debates*. Story relied most on the arguments made by James Madison, and his readings incorporate Madison's language to describe the slave. For example, in Story's explanation of the three-fifths clause, he uses Madison's arguments from *The Federalist No. 54*: "The federal constitution should, therefore, view them in the mixed character of persons and property, which was in fact their true character" (*Commentaries*, 2: 109).

28. *Prigg v. Pennsylvania* 41 U.S. 539 at 612.

29. Robert Cover, *Justice Accused: Antislavery and the Judicial Process* (New Haven: Yale University Press, 1975), 168.

30. *Prigg v. Pennsylvania* 41 U.S. 539 at 612.

31. Ibid.

32. Ibid.

33. Ibid.

34. Fehrenbacher, *Dred Scott Case*, 44.

35. Ibid.

36. David Walker, "Walker's Appeal, in Four Articles, together with a Preamble, to the Colored Citizens of the World," in *Walker's Appeal and Garnet's Address*, by David Walker and Henry Highland Garnet (1848; Salem, NH: Ayer, 1994), 40–41.

37. William Goodell refers to "the color commonly supposed to be the badge of the slave" in his *Views of American Constitutional Law, in Its Bearing upon American Slavery; Second Edition: Revised with Additions* (Utica, NY: Lawson and Chaplin, 1845), 26.

38. Walker, "Walker's Appeal," 40.

39. Fehrenbacher, *Dred Scott Case*, 42.

40. Joseph Story, *A Familiar Exposition of the Constitution of the United States* (Lake Bluff, IL: Regnery Gateway, 1986). In the preface, Story says the "present Work is designed, not only for private reading, but as a textbook for the highest classes in our Common Schools and Academies. It is also adapted to the use of those, who are more advanced, and have left school, after having passed through the common branches of education" (15).

41. Cover, *Justice Accused*, 168.

42. "Address of the Executive Committee of the American Anti-Slavery Society," in Wendell Phillips, *The Constitution: A Pro-Slavery Compact; Selections from the Madison Papers* (New York: Negro Universities Press, 1969), 96. (Originally published in 1844 by the American Anti-Slavery Society.)

43. Lysander Spooner, *The Unconstitutionality of Slavery* (1860; repr., New York: Burt Franklin, 1965), 284.

44. The Garrisonian view of the Constitution's slavery-sanctioning intentions was so close to that of the slaveholders that the proslavery Alabama politician John Campbell suggested in an 1847 letter to John C. Calhoun that Phillips's *A Pro-Slavery Compact* was "an able pamphlet... which we might circulate to great advantage excluding a few paragraphs" (quoted in William M. Wiecek, *The Sources of Antislavery Constitutionalism, 1760–1848* [Ithaca, NY: Cornell University Press, 1977], 240).

45. Robert Cover discusses both at length in *Justice Accused*. See also Eric Foner, *Free Soil, Free Labor, Free Men*, esp. chap. 3, "Salmon P. Chase: The Constitution and the Slave Power." Chase, credited with articulating the political program of the Liberty Party, the Free Soil Party, and later, the Republican Party platform of Abraham Lincoln, would later serve as U.S. Treasury secretary under Lincoln, and as chief justice of the Supreme Court. For discussions of the radical antislavery constitutionalists, see Gregg Crane, *Race, Citizenship, and Law*, 107–26; and Deak Nabers, *Victory of Law: The Fourteenth Amendment, The Civil War, and American Literature, 1852–1867* (Baltimore: Johns Hopkins University Press, 2006), 132–72. Crane, relying on William Wiecek's summary of the radical antislavery constitutionalists' views, discusses them very briefly as part of his argument that

Frederick Douglass's shift to their position was governed by his commitment to higher law reasoning, and "moral perception" (Crane 113). Crane's study is exemplary of the critical attempt to insert Douglass (and other antebellum writers) into dominant historical narratives of higher law interpretations of the Constitution. Crane argues that Douglass's constitutional hermeneutic "begin[s] from a leap of faith that liberty and justice are the genius of American law" (115). It is also exemplary of another tendency, within traditional Law and Literature studies of race in American literature, of reproducing the critical dichotomy between text and context, wherein context means a social history inclusive of race and its representations, and text means the literary or legal text in which race is represented. In reproducing this dichomoty, literary critics read for "race" in its already codified forms. Indeed, despite the presence of "race" and "citizenship" in its title, Crane's study does not address the developments or transformations of either category. Crane is more "concerned to delineate conceptions of the ethical basis of American law," and "a plausibly universal moral consensus about the terms of justice and citizenship" (6). Deak Nabers provides a more comprehensive analysis of Lysander Spooner and the radical antislavery constitutionalists in *Victory of Law*, although he does not discuss Frederick Douglass's relationship to them. Following Robert Cover, Nabers understands the radical antislavery constitutionalists' position as one grounded in natural law. Nabers supplements Cover's account with the argument that "Spooner's rules of construction incorporate his higher law into his positive law" (Nabers 141). For one of the best accounts of Douglass's transformations with respect to law and formal politics, see Robert S. Levine, *Martin Delany, Frederick Douglass, and the Politics of Representative Identity* (Chapel Hill: University of North Carolina Press, 1997), esp. 58–143.

46. Cover, *Justice Accused*, 155.

47. Ibid., 156.

48. Ibid.

49. William Goodell, *Slavery and Anti-Slavery; A History of the Great Struggle in Both Hemispheres, with a View of the Slavery Question in the United States* (New York: William Harned, 1852), 476; William M. Wiecek, *The Sources of Antislavery Constitutionalism, 1760–1848* (Ithaca, NY: Cornell University Press, 1977).

50. Cover claims that Phillips's *Review of Lysander Spooner's Essay* "not only destroyed Spooner's position, but argued persuasively for resignation by anti-slavery judges" (*Justice Accused*, 151). Both claims are incorrect: Phillips's *Review* did little to stop the influence of Spooner's argument, merely reasserting the positions Phillips had already presented in *The Constitution: A Pro-Slavery Compact*; and only one judge (Francis Jackson) was cited by the Garrisonians as resigning his position due to a principled moral opposition to serving under a slavery-sanctioning Constitution. Spooner's *Essay* was expanded and republished in newer editions through 1860 (the edition I use for reference in this chapter). A prominent example of the limited success of Phillips's *Review* on the influence of Goodell's and Spooner's arguments is Frederick Douglass himself: after publishing his "Change of Opinion" in May 1851, Douglass used his rhetorical skills to advocate this very position.

51. Spooner, *A Defense for Fugitive Slaves, against the Acts of Congress of February 12, 1793 and September 18, 1850*, in *Unconstitutionality of Slavery*, 283. Spooner pointedly refers to the laws not as fugitive slave laws, but as (unconstitutional) acts of Congress. In this activist pamphlet written in response to the 1850 Fugitive Slave Law, Spooner synthesizes the legal arguments for "strict construction" he had elaborated in *The Unconstitutionality of Slavery*, first published in 1845. *A Defense* appears in the appendix to the 1860 edition.

52. Spooner, *Unconstitutionality of Slavery*, 283.

53. Story, *Commentaries*, 2: 533–34.

54. Ibid., 2: 534.

55. Spooner, *Unconstitutionality of Slavery*, 283.

56. See Spooner, *Unconstitutionality of Slavery*, 155–236 (chap. 17, "Rules of Interpretation").

57. Ibid., 284.

58. Ibid.

59. Goodell, *Views of American Constitutional Law*, 24.

60. Spooner, *Unconstitutionality of Slavery*, 69.

61. Goodell, *Views of American Constitutional Law*, 24.

62. Ibid.

63. Spooner, *Unconstitutionality of Slavery*, 69–70.

64. Henry Highland Garnet, "An Address to the Slaves of the United States of America," in *Walker's Appeal*, 96.

65. Goodell, *Views of American Constitutional Law*, 25, emphasis in original.

66. Spooner, *Unconstitutionality of Slavery*, 69

67. James Madison, *The Federalist No. 54*, in *The Federalist Papers*, ed. Clinton Rossiter (New York: Penguin, 1961), 337. In his exposition of the fugitive clause in the *Commentaries*, Story quotes directly from Madison's description of the slave as having the "mixed character of persons and property" (*Commentaries*, 3: 109).

68. George M. Stroud, *A Sketch of the Laws Relating to Slavery in the Several States of the United States of America*, 2nd ed. (Philadelphia: Henry Longstreth, 1856), 39, 99, 287.

69. Goodell, *Views of American Constitutional Law*, 25.

70. Ibid.

71. Ibid., 26.

72. Ibid.

73. Ibid., emphasis in original. For a discussion of the circulation of the terms "badge of slavery" and "badge of servitude" as descriptive of "race" and "color" after the Civil War and Reconstruction, see Brook Thomas, *Civic Myths: A Law-and-Literature Approach to Citizenship* (Chapel Hill: University of North Carolina Press, 2007) 122–24; 221.

74. U.S. Const. art. IV, § 2.

75. Goodell, *Views of American Constitutional Law*, 76.

76. Ibid., 75–76. After the uncovering of the Denmark Vesey slave revolt plot in 1822, South Carolina passed the Negro Seaman's Act, which required "that free Negro employees on any vessel which might come into a South Carolina port be imprisoned until the

vessel should be ready to depart." If these black sailors did not leave with their ship, they could be enslaved and sold. Similar laws barring the immigration of free blacks and requiring the imprisonment of black seamen while their ships were at port were passed in North Carolina, Georgia, Louisiana, and Florida (see Philip M. Hamer, "Great Britain, the United States, and the Negro Seaman Acts, 1822–1848," *Journal of Southern History* 1 [February, 1935], 3–28). For a discussion of these laws in relation to the distribution of David Walker's *Appeal* by black and white sailors, see Peter P. Hinks, *To Awaken My Afflicted Brethren: David Walker and the Problem of Antebellum Slave Resistance* (State College: Pennsylvania State University Press, 1997), 134–52.

77. Goodell, *Views of American Constitutional Law*, 76.

78. Olaudah Equiano, *The Interesting Narrative and Other Writings*, ed. Vincent Carretta (New York: Penguin, 2003), 122; David Walker, "Walker's Appeal, In Four Articles, Together with a Preamble, to the Colored Citizens of the World," (1829), in *Walker's Appeal and Garnet's Address to the Slaves of the United States of America* (Salem, NH: Ayer, 1994), 40.

79. Spooner, *Unconstitutionality of Slavery*, 68.

80. Ibid.

81. Ibid., 23.

82. Cover, *Justice Accused*, 155.

83. Spooner, *Unconstitutionality of Slavery*, 68–69.

84. "A Defense for Fugitive Slaves, against the Act of Congress of February 12, 1793 and September 18, 1850. By Lysander Spooner." Included as "Appendix A" to the enlarged edition of Spooner's *Unconstitutionality of Slavery*, 279, 281, emphasis in original. Anticipating reference to the temporal limits to this indentured servitude, as opposed to the lifelong and hereditary bondage of chattel slavery, Spooner adds: "The addition, in the one case, of the words 'for a term of years,' does not alter the meaning; for it does not appear that, in the other case, they are 'held,' beyond a fixed term" (281).

85. Spooner, *Unconstitutionality of Slavery*, 68–69.

86. Ibid., 69

87. For the implications of "the trope of the trial" to the slavery debates and antebellum print culture, see Jeannine Marie DeLombard, *Slavery on Trial: Law, Abolitionism, and Print Culture* (Chapel Hill: University of North Carolina Press, 2007).

88. H. Jefferson Powell, "The Principles of '98: An Essay in Historical Retrieval," *Virginia Law Review* 80, no. 3 (1994): 721.

89. Goodell, *Views of American Constitutional Law*, 20, emphasis in original.

90. Ibid., 79

91. Spooner, *Unconstitutionality of Slavery*, 112. This figure of the constitutional bond found its way into Wendell Phillips's *Review of Lysander Spooner's Essay on the Unconstitutionality of Slavery; Reprinted from the "Anti-Slavery Standard," with Additions* (Boston: Andrews and Prentiss, 1847; repr., Freeport, NY: Books for Libraries Press, 1971), 33. Narrating the historical circumstances surrounding the three-fifths ratio in the representation clause in order to argue the original intentions of the clause, Phillips remarks: "The North he [Spooner] represents as ready to spurn any allusion to Slavery, and the South surely

would not willingly be shorn of her strength, unless it were so 'nominated in the bond.' If neither party wished it, how was such an interpretation foisted upon the text?" (33). Phillips's ironic employment of the phrase opposes the "strict construction" point that Goodell and Spooner used it to make. Phillips reads the language of the clause as "descriptive" of slavery, and "intended" to guarantee slavery (and thus indirectly "nominated in the bond"). This interpretation of the "original intention" of the contracting parties to the constitutional "bond of Union" was one Phillips and the Garrisonians shared with slavery's defenders.

92. Goodell, *Views of American Constitutional Law*, 21.

93. Ibid., 28, emphasis in original.

94. Spooner, *Unconstitutionality of Slavery*, 59, emphasis in original.

95. John Quincy Adams, "Address at North Bridgewater, Nov. 6, 1844," in Phillips, *A Pro-Slavery Compact*, 120, emphasis added.

96. Waldo E. Martin Jr., *The Mind of Frederick Douglass* (Chapel Hill: University of North Carolina Press, 1985), 39–40. Martin's account of Douglass's shift to antislavery constitutionalism and political abolitionism focuses on the biographical background to it and attends primarily to Douglass's relationship with the Garrisonians (36–40).

97. "Change of Opinion Announced," in *Life and Writings of Frederick Douglass*, 2: 156, emphasis in original.

98. "The Constitution of the United States: Is It Pro-Slavery or Anti-Slavery?," 2: 478.

99. *Narrative of the Life of Frederick Douglass, An American Slave, Written by Himself*, ed. William L. Andrews (New York: Norton, 1997), 29–30.

100. "The Constitution and Slavery," *North Star*, 16 March 1849, in *Life and Writings of Frederick Douglass*, 1: 361.

101. On modern "racial states" and the legislation of race, see David Theo Goldberg, *The Racial State* (Malden, MA: Blackwell, 2002), esp. 74–188. See also Charles W. Mills, *The Racial Contract* (Ithaca: Cornell University Press, 1997).

102. Frederick Douglass, *Life and Times of Frederick Douglass* (New York: Library of America, 1994), 705–6.

NOTES TO CHAPTER 4

1. "The Address of the Southern Delegates in Congress to their Constituents; or, the Address of John C. Calhoun and Forty Other Thieves," *North Star*, 9 February 1849, in *The Life and Writings of Frederick Douglass*, ed. Philip S. Foner (New York: International, 1950) 1: 354–55.

2. Robert Cover, who characterized the radical antislavery constitutionalists as "utopians" and dismissed them as "a handful of relatively unimportant antislavery thinkers," cites this Douglass speech, ignoring the fact that by the time Douglass delivered it he had joined the ranks of those utopians (*Justice Accused*, 156).

3. "What to the Slave Is the Fourth of July?: An Address Delivered in Rochester, New York, on 5 July 1852," in *The Frederick Douglass Papers, Series One: Speeches, Debates and*

Interviews, ed. John W. Blassingame, vol. 2, *1847–54* (New Haven: Yale University Press, 1982), 360.

4. Ibid.

5. Ibid, 2: 361–64, 365.

6. Ibid., 2: 368.

7. "The Constitution and Slavery," *North Star*, 16 March 1849, in *Life and Writings of Frederick Douglass*, 1: 361.

8. "What to the Slave Is the Fourth of July?," 2: 366.

9. Ibid., 2: 368.

10. Ibid., 2: 371, 383.

11. Ibid., 2: 384.

12. See *Macbeth*, 5.8.20–22.

13. "A Nation in the Midst of a Nation," in *Frederick Douglass Papers*, ser. 1, 2: 424.

14. Ibid., 2: 424–25.

15. Ibid., 2: 425.

16. Ibid., 2: 427.

17. Ibid.

18. "Slavery, Freedom, and the Kansas-Nebraska Act: An Address Delivered in Chicago, Illinois, on 30 October 1854," in *Frederick Douglass Papers*, ser. 1, 2: 539.

19. Ibid., 540.

20. See Stephen Best, *The Fugitive's Properties: Law and the Poetics of Possession* (Chicago: University of Chicago Press, 2004); and Ariela Gross, *Double Character: Slavery and Mastery in the Antebellum Southern Courtroom* (Princeton, NJ: Princeton University Press, 2000).

21. Eric J. Sundquist, *To Wake the Nations: Race in the Making of American Literature* (Cambridge: Belknap Press of Harvard University Press, 1993), 83. Sundquist provides a survey of the critical reassessments of *My Bondage and My Freedom* in relation to the 1845 *Narrative* in the first chapter of *To Wake the Nations*, as does Priscilla Wald in *Constituting Americans: Cultural Anxiety and Narrative Form* (Durham: Duke University Press, 1998), 75. Sundquist and Wald attend to Douglass's revised self-representation in *My Bondage and My Freedom*. Like many readers, they focus on Douglass's self-fashioning: questions of "authority" and "authorship" (Sundquist, *To Wake the Nations* 90) and Douglass's engagements "with the terms of his authorship" (Wald, *Constituting Americans*, 75). In *Slavery on Trial*, Jeannine DeLombard similarly focuses on Douglass's "self-fashioning" to describe the "radical revision in Douglass's public persona" as "a shift from a testimonial to a prosecutorial posture" (103). I am more concerned with how Douglass changed his self-representation to advance his radically transformed political views: his political abolitionism, antislavery constitutionalism, and his focus on labor exploitation in the slavery debates.

22. Sacvan Bercovitch, *The Rites of Assent: Transformations in the Symbolic Construction of America* (New York: Routledge, 1993), 353–76.

23. *My Bondage and My Freedom*, ed. John David Smith (New York: Penguin, 2003), 292. Subsequent references are cited parenthetically in the text as *MB*. If dominant

accounts ignore the changes in Douglass's politics, corrective accounts tend to personalize Douglass's "Change of Opinion," as primarily an outgrowth of Douglass's wish to be an independent activist, apart from Garrison as a "father" figure. Others have framed Douglass's political shift as a response to the patronizing "racism" of the Garrisonians (see Waldo E. Martin, *The Mind of Frederick Douglass* [Chapel Hill: University of North Carolina Press, 1984]; and John Stauffer, *The Black Hearts of Men: Radical Abolitionists and the Transformation of Race* [Cambridge: Harvard University Press, 2001]). Douglass himself suggested otherwise. Less than a year after his announced "change of opinion," Douglass closed "What, to the Slave, Is the Fourth of July?" (5 July 1852) by reiterating both his "radical change" of view and his continued admiration for Garrison. After summarizing the principal arguments of the political abolitionist interpretation of the Constitution as an antislavery document, Douglass ended the speech invoking the "fervent aspirations of William Lloyd Garrison," and quoting in full Garrison's 1845 poem "The Triumph of Freedom." Likewise, in the closing lines of his "Nation in the Midst of a Nation" speech (11 May 1853), Douglass declared: "I honor and respect Lewis Tappan. I love and revere William Lloyd Garrison; and may God have mercy on me when I refuse to strike a blow against Slavery, in connection with either of these gentlemen. I will work with either; and if the one discards me because I work with the other, the responsibility is not mine" (440).

24. Frederick Douglass, "The Claims of the Negro Ethnologically Considered: An Address, Before the Literary Societies at Western Reserve College, at Commencement, July 12, 1854," in *The Frederick Douglass Papers*, ser. 1, ed. John W. Blassingame, vol. 2, *1847–54* (New Haven: Yale University Press, 1982), 520.

25. Robert B. Stepto, *From behind the Veil: A Study of Afro-American Narrative* (Urbana: University of Illinois Press, 1979); William L. Andrews, *To Tell a Free Story: The First Century of Afro-American Autobiography, 1760–1865* (Urbana: University of Illinois Press, 1986), 216–39; Houston Baker, *The Journey Back: Issues in Black Literature and Criticism* (Chicago: University of Chicago Press, 1980); William S. McFeely, *Frederick Douglass* (New York: Norton, 1991); Sundquist, *To Wake the Nations*, 90; Wald, *Constituting Americans*, 75.

26. Deborah McDowell suggests that Douglass's comparison of his mother's features to the image of an Egyptian prince registers "emphatically the discursive priorities of masculinity and its gendered relation to the feminine" (199). McDowell's criticism of Douglass ignores the historical context to which Douglass pointedly alludes here: the rise of the racist ethnography of Samuel Morton, Louis Agassiz, Josiah Nott, and George Gliddon, and the contemporary debates over "racial" origins and African inferiority (see McDowell, "In the First Place: Making Frederick Douglass and the Afro-American Tradition," in *Critical Essays on Frederick Douglass*, ed. William L. Andrews [Boston: G. K. Hall, 1991], 192–214).

27. Douglass, "Claims of the Negro," in *Frederick Douglass Papers*, ser. 1, 2: 509, emphasis in original.

28. Ibid., 2: 503.

29. Ibid., 2: 503–4, emphasis in original.

30. Ibid., 2: 508.
31. Ibid.
32. Ibid., 2: 510.
33. Ibid.
34. Ibid., 2: 509.
35. Ibid., 2: 510.
36. McDowell, "In the First Place," 192–214; Wald, *Constituting Americans*, 80–83; Saidiya Hartman, *Scenes of Subjection: Terror, Slavery, and Self-Making in Nineteenth-Century America* (New York: Oxford University Press, 1997), 3. Hartman has called attention to the "casualness with which [such scenes] are circulated," and the ways in which "they reinforce the spectacular character of black suffering" (3). Wald observes that Douglass, in his depiction of the scene in *My Bondage and My Freedom*, "has replaced the eroticized language and familial subtext with a more sedate reportage," and "downplays the sexual and familial relationships among the scene's participants" (83).

37. Paul Gilroy, *The Black Atlantic: Modernity and Double Consciousness* (Cambridge: Harvard University Press, 1993), 64.

38. Ibid.

39. Ibid., 63.

40. Like those accounts which take the 1845 *Narrative of the Life* as representative, ignoring the "radical change in [Douglass's] opinions," feminist critiques of Douglass ignore the fact that in the decade between the two autobiographies, Douglass had worked directly with leading women antislavery activists, and participated in the first convention for women's rights, at Seneca Falls in 1848 (*My Bondage*, 292).

41. Ibid., 67.

42. Frederick Douglass, *Narrative of the Life of Frederick Douglass, an American Slave; Written by Himself* (New York: Norton, 1997), 15.

43. Byron, *Childe Harold*, 2.720–21.

44. Ibid., 2.722–25.

45. Henry Highland Garnet, "Address to the Slaves of the United States of America," in *Walker's Appeal and Garnet's Address* (Salem, NH: Arno Press, 1994), 93.

46. Ibid., 96.

47. Ibid. In his monumental study of the Civil War and Reconstruction, W. E. B. Du Bois describes the large-scale escape of slaves from their plantations as the turning point of the Civil War. Du Bois describes the slave's "removal" of their labor as a "general strike": "As soon, however, as it became clear that the Union armies would not or could not return fugitive slaves, and that the masters with all their fume and fury were uncertain of victory, the slave entered upon a general strike against slavery. . . . He ran away to the first place of safety and offered his services to the Federal Army. So that in this way it was really true that he served his former master and served the emancipating army; and it was also true that this withdrawal and bestowal of his labor decided the war" (Du Bois, *Black Reconstruction in America, 1860–1880* [New York: Free Press, 1992], 57, and 55–83 [chap. 4, "The General Strike"]).

48. Garnet, "Address to the Slaves of the United States of America," 94. For a discussion of the concept of "death as agency," see Gilroy, *The Black Atlantic*, 63.

49. Garnet, "Address to the Slaves of the United States of America," 89.

50. Ibid.

51. *Radical Reformer's Gazette*, 26 January 1833, 170, quoted in Paul Thomas Murphy, *Toward a Working-Class Canon: Literary Criticism in British Working-Class Periodicals, 1816–1858* (Columbus: Ohio State University Press, 1994), 142.

52. *The Life and Times of Frederick Douglass* (1893), in *Autobiographies*, ed. Henry Louis Gates Jr. (New York: Library of America, 1994), 682. The influence of this visit to Ireland on Douglass is discussed by P. J. Ferreira, "Frederick Douglass in Ireland: The Dublin Edition of His Narrative," *New Hibernian Review* 5, no. 1 (Spring 2001): 53–67. For the development of Douglass's literary nationalism in the context of the Americas, see Robert S. Levine, *Dislocating Race and Nation: Episodes in Nineteenth-Century American Literary Nationalism* (Chapel Hill: University of North Carolina Press, 2008), 179–236.

53. W. E. B. Du Bois, *The Souls of Black Folk*, ed. Henry Louis Gates Jr. and Terri Hume Oliver (New York: Norton, 1999), 154–64.

54. Douglass, "Reception Speech at Finsbury Chapel, Moorfields, England, 12 May 1846," in *My Bondage and My Freedom*, 301-2.

55. Ibid., 408.

56. David Roediger, *The Wages of Whiteness: Race and the Making of the American Working Class*, rev. ed. (London: Verso, 1999), 82.

57. Eric Foner, "Abolitionism and the Labor Movement," 76, cited in Roediger, *Wages of Whiteness*, 81.

58. Karl Marx, *Capital: A Critique of Political Economy*, vol. 1, trans. Ben Fowkes (New York: Penguin, 1990), 925, 729.

59. Roediger, *Wages of Whiteness*, 82.

60. Garnet, "Address to the Slaves of the United States of America," 96.

61. On the "year of the strikes," see Sean Wilentz, *Chants Democratic: New York City and the Rise of the American Working Class, 1788–1850* (New York: Oxford University Press, 1984), 286.

62. See Edward Magdol, *The Antislavery Rank and File: A Social Profile of the Abolitionists' Constituency* (New York: Greenwood, 1986).

63. George Fitzhugh, *Sociology for the South; or, the Failure of Free Society* (Richmond, VA: A. Morris, 1854), 86.

64. Ibid., 27–28.

65. Roediger, *Wages of Whiteness*, 11.

66. Fitzhugh, *Sociology*, 83–84.

NOTES TO CHAPTER 5

1. Sean Wilentz, *Chants Democratic: New York City and the Rise of the American Working Class, 1788–1850* (New York: Oxford University Press, 1984), 246, 345.

2. Herman Melville, *Moby-Dick*, Norton Critical Edition, 2nd ed., ed. Herschel Parker and Harrison Hayford (New York: Norton, 2002), 103. Subsequent references to *Moby-Dick* are cited parenthetically in the text by page number.

3. Likewise, the one hint of Ishmael's physical appearance is given, late in the novel, as a glimpse of his right arm: "The skeleton dimensions I shall now proceed to set down are copied verbatim from my right arm, where I had them tattooed; as in my wild wanderings at that period, there was no other secure way of preserving such valuable statistics." Ishmael is figured once again in the role of the literary artist, and the artist's body becomes "the blank page for a poem" (346).

4. Michael Paul Rogin, *Subversive Genealogy: The Politics and Art of Herman Melville* (Berkeley and Los Angeles: University of California Press, 1985), 108; Larry J. Reynolds, *European Revolutions and the American Literary Renaissance* (New Haven: Yale University Press, 1988) 119. Reynolds argues that "Melville provides a damning appraisal of the workingman" (118).

5. *Oxford English Dictionary*, 2nd ed., s.v. "strike."

6. Ibid.

7. George Dyer, *Complaints of the Poor People of England* (1793), v.24.a.

8. See Charles Sellers, *The Market Revolution: Jacksonian America, 1815–1846* (New York: Oxford University Press, 1991), 338; and Christopher L. Tomlins, *Law, Labor, and Ideology in the Early American Republic* (New York: Cambridge University Press, 1993), 185. For discussions of labor and nineteenth-century American literature, see Nicholas K. Bromell, *By the Sweat of the Brow: Labor in Antebellum America* (Chicago: University of Chicago Press, 1993); and Cindy Weinstein, *The Literature of Labor and the Labors of Literature: Allegory in Nineteenth-Century American Fiction* (Cambridge: Cambridge University Press, 1995).

9. Cited in Wilentz, *Chants Democratic*, 288.

10. Ralph Waldo Emerson, "The Transcendentalist," in *Nature and Selected Essays*, ed. Larzer Ziff (New York: Penguin, 2003), 247.

11. "Address of the Executive Committee of the American Anti-Slavery Society to the Friends of Emancipation in the United States, Boston, May 20, 1844," in Wendell Phillips, *The Constitution: A Pro-Slavery Compact; Selections from the Madison Papers* (New York: Negro Universities Press, 1969), 112.

12. See F. O. Matthiessen, *The American Renaissance: Art and Expression in the Age of Emerson and Whitman* (Cambridge: Harvard University Press, 1941); Rogin, *Subversive Genealogy*, 107–8; C. L. R. James, *Mariners, Renegades, and Castaways: The Story of Herman Melville and the World We Live In*. The complete text, with an introduction by Donald E. Pease (Hanover, NH: University Press of New England, 2001), 14–17; Brook Thomas, *Cross-Examinations of Law and Literature: Cooper, Hawthorne, Stowe, and Melville* (Cambridge: Cambridge University Press, 1987), 215–16; and Andrew Delbanco, *Melville: His World and Work* (New York: Knopf, 2005), 162–66. For a reading of *Moby Dick* as "Melville's

conservative response to the French Revolution," and of Ahab as a "manipulative" figure who "plays upon [the crew's] fear and greed," see Reynolds, *European Revolutions*, 118-121. For a discussion of Ahab in the context of Jacksonian individualism, see Wai-Chee Dimock, *Empire for Liberty: Melville and the Poetics of Individualism* (Princeton: Princeton University Press, 1989), 129–39. For a survey of the two opposing critical strands in critical readings of Ahab, as either romantic rebel or authoritarian dictator, see John Michael, *Identity and the Failure of America: From Thomas Jefferson to the War on Terror* (Minneapolis: University of Minnesota Press, 2008), 71–91. Although Michael critiques both of these opposed readings of Ahab, Michael accepts the understanding of Ahab as a figure of authoritarianism, and argues that Ahab's "glorious romanticism depends, in practice, on his authoritarian manipulation of the crew" (Michael 86). Both sides of this long-running critical debate over the meaning of Ahab's madness understand Ahab and Ishmael as opposed figures.

13. Rogin, *Subversive Genealogy*, 128.

14. Ibid., 108.

15. Herman Melville, *White-Jacket; or, The World in a Man-of-War* (Evanston, IL: Northwestern University Press, 2000), 23.

16. Samuel Otter, *Melville's Anatomies* (Berkeley and Los Angeles: University of California Press, 1999), 50–100.

17. *Billy Budd, Sailor; An Inside Narrative*, in *Melville's Short Novels*, ed. Dan McCall (New York: Norton, 2002), 105. Further references to *Billy Budd* are to this edition and are cited parenthetically in the chapter text by page number.

18. Sellers, *The Market Revolution*, 54.

19. Tomlins, *Law, Labor, and Ideology*, 208.

20. Commonwealth v. Hunt (1842), 45 Mass. 111, at 121. The case arose from a dispute between the Boston Society of Journeyman Bootmakers and one of its members, Jeremiah Horne, over a fine levied by the society against him for working beyond their agreed hours. Horne refused to pay the fine and was expelled from the society, and then was made liable to pay additional fines before rejoining. With Horne continuing to refuse to pay the fines, the society threatened Horne's employer, Isaac Wait, with a walkout strike (a collective refusal to work in his shop). After Wait dismissed Horne, Horne took his dispute to the county attorney, who took the matter before the grand jury and procured an indictment of "conspiracy" against the journeymen (see Tomlins, *Law, Labor, and Ideology*, 209–12; and Leonard Levy, *The Law of the Commonwealth and Chief Justice Shaw: The Evolution of American Law, 1830–1860* [New York: Harper and Row, 1957], 188–91).

21. *Commonwealth v. Hunt*, 45 Mass. 111, at 136.

22. Ibid. Shaw noted that the individual journeymen had not contracted with their employer, Isaac Wait, and so were not violating any laws with their threat of a walkout strike. According to Shaw, because the journeymen were not violating any contracts with their employer, neither the "purpose" nor the "means" of their association was criminal.

23. Jameson's supplement to Mikhail Bakhtin's formalist point is that "the normal form of the dialogical is essentially an antagonistic one, and that the dialogue of class struggle is one in which two opposing discourses fight it out within the general unity of a code"

(*The Political Unconscious: Narrative as a Socially Symbolic Act* [Ithaca: Cornell University Press, 1994], 84).

24. Donald E. Pease, *Visionary Compacts: American Renaissance Writings in Cultural Context* (Madison: University of Wisconsin Press, 1987), 236. For Pease, this scene of "cultural persuasion" emphasizes "the 'scenic' character of [Ahab's] separation from the crew" (240).

25. "Of all things the measure is Man, of the things that are, that they are, and of the things that are not, that they are not." (DK80b1). See Kathleen Freeman, *Ancilla to the Pre-Socratic Philosophers; A complete translation of the Fragments in Diels, Fragmente der Vorsokratiker* (Cambridge, MA: Harvard University Press, 1970), 125. See also, Plato, *Theaetetus*, translated with notes by John McDowell (Oxford: Clarendon Press, 1973) 16: "Socrates: Because he [Protagoras] says . . . that a man is the measure of all things: of those which are, that they are, of those which are not, that they are not" (151e–152a).

26. About the gods, I am not able to know whether they exist or do not exist, nor what they are like in form" (DK80b4). See Freeman, *Ancilla*, 126; and Plato, *Theaetetus*: "Socrates: Protagoras . . . will reply to those arguments like this: 'You trot out the gods, whom I exclude from my speaking and writing, not discussing whether there are any or not" (162e).

27. Joseph Story, *Commentaries on the Law of Agency*, 1st ed. (Boston: Little, Brown, 1839), 443, 451, cited in Morton J. Horwitz, *The Transformation of American Law, 1870–1960: The Crisis of Legal Orthodoxy* (New York: Oxford University Press, 1992), 40–41.

28. *Oxford English Dictionary*, 2nd ed., s.v. "sympathy."

29. Ibid., 3rd ed., "red flag."

30. Thomas Carlyle, *The French Revolution: A History* (New York: Modern Library, 2002), 408.

31. Walter Whitman, "Resurgemus," *New York Daily Tribune*, 21 June 1850, 3. Whitman included a revised version of the poem in the first edition of *Leaves of Grass* ("Europe: The 72d and 73d Years of These States" in *Leaves of Grass: The First (1855) Edition* [New York: Penguin, 1986], 134).

NOTES TO CONCLUSION

1. *Billy Budd, Sailor; An Inside Narrative*, in *Melville's Short Novels*, ed. Dan McCall (New York: Norton, 2002), 130.

2. William James, *The Naval History of Great Britain, from the Declaration of War by France in 1793, to the Accession of George IV* (London: Richard Bentley, 1837), 2: 23.

3. Ibid., 2: 25.

4. Ibid., 2: 64.

5. "Free workers in the double sense that they neither form part of the means of production themselves, as would be the case with slaves, serfs, etc., nor do they own the means of production" (Marx, *Capital* 1: 874).

6. Frederick Douglass, "The Constitution and Slavery," *North Star*, 16 March 1849, in *Life and Writings of Frederick Douglass*, ed. Philip S. Foner (New York: International, 1950), 1: 361.

7. Most interpretations of *Billy Budd* have focused on the theme of "justice," debating whether the novel is a "testament" of Melville's "acceptance" of law and social order or his "testament of resistance" to them. For a survey of this long-standing debate, see Harrison Hayford and Merton M. Sealts, eds., *Billy Budd, Sailor (An Inside Narrative), Reading Texts and Genetic Texts, edited from the Manuscript with Introduction and Notes* (Chicago: University of Chicago Press, 1982), 25–27; and Carolyn Karcher, *Shadow over the Promised Land: Slavery, Race, and Violence in Melville's America* (Baton Rouge: Louisiana State University Press, 1980). Emphasizing Captain Vere's role as judge, this debate turns the novel into Vere's story, "and his dilemma" (Cover, *Justice Accused*, 5) (see Cover, *Justice Accused*, 2–7; and Thomas, *Cross-Examinations of Law and Literature*, 201–23). In *Literary Criticisms of Law*, Guyora Binder and Robert Weisberg reiterate this shared view: "The tale's true protagonist is Captain Vere, an intellectual, who uses all his powers of language and reason to convince the ship's officers—and himself—that Billy's execution, though undeserved, is required by law and good order" (203). See Guyora Binder and Robert Weisberg, *Literary Criticisms of Law* (Princeton, NJ: Princeton University Press, 2000), 201–15. Although it does not mistake Vere for "the tale's true protagonist," Barbara Johnson's influential deconstructive reading of *Billy Budd* reinforced this interpretation of the story as one about "the act of judgment" (see Johnson, "Melville's Fist: The Execution of Billy Budd," in *The Critical Difference: Essays in the Contemporary Rhetoric of Reading* [Baltimore: Johns Hopkins University Press, 1985], 107).

8. Melville, *Moby-Dick*, 140; Douglass, *My Bondage and My Freedom*, 182.

9. "Sudden Revolution in Northern Sentiment," *Douglass' Monthly*, May 1861, in *Life and Writings of Frederick Douglass*, 3: 91.

10. Abraham Lincoln, "First Inaugural Address," in *The Collected Works of Abraham Lincoln*, ed. Roy P. Basler (New Brunswick, NJ: Rutgers University Press, 1959), 4: 262.

11. "The Inaugural Address," *Douglass' Monthly*, April 1861, in *Life and Writings of Frederick Douglass*, 3: 73.

12. Lincoln, "First Inaugural Address," 4: 263.

13. "The Inaugural Address," in *Life and Writings of Frederick Douglass*, 3: 77.

14. Melville, *Moby-Dick*, 140.

15. "Emancipation Proclaimed," *Douglass' Monthly*, October 1862, in *Life and Writings of Frederick Douglass*, 3: 274.

16. *Life and Times of Frederick Douglass*, in *Frederick Douglass: Autobiographies*, ed. Henry Louis Gates Jr. (New York: Library of America, 1994), 792.

17. "How to End the War," *Douglass' Monthly*, May 1861, in *Life and Writings of Frederick Douglass*, 3: 94–95.

18. "Men of Color, To Arms!" in *Life and Writings of Frederick Douglass*, 3: 317.

19. Ibid., 3: 317–18.

20. Ibid., 3: 318.

21. Ibid.

22. *My Bondage and My Freedom*, 181.

23. "The Reasons for Our Troubles," *Douglass' Monthly*, February 1862, in *Life and Writings of Frederick Douglass*, 3: 208.

24. *Life and Times of Frederick Douglass*, in *Frederick Douglass: Autobiographies*, 815.

25. Ibid.

26. *My Bondage and My Freedom*, 239.

27. Ibid., 239–40.

28. Douglass, "The Proclamation and a Negro Army," *Douglass' Monthly*, March 1863, in *Life and Writings of Frederick Douglass*, 3: 323.

29. Throughout the Civil War, Douglass called it an "Abolition War," despite Lincoln's insistence that it was a war intended to restore the Union (see "The Mission of the War," *New York Tribune*, 14 January, 1864, in *Life and Writings of Frederick Douglass*, 3: 386–403).

Index

abolitionists: African American, 128, 147, 161–63, 167; Garrisonian, 22–23, 107–10, 120–23, 127, 135, 139, 162, 190, 234n44; moderate political, 4, 108, 120–121, 136, 166; political, 22, 107–10, 113, 139–40, 162, 238n96; radical political, 113, 120–23, 127–29, 132, 145–46, 161, 166–68, 170–71, 208, 233n24, 234–35n45, 238n2, 239n21, 239–40n23
Adams, John, 26–27, 29, 32
Adams, John Quincy, 138
Agassiz, Louis, 152
Alien and Sedition crisis, 15
Allen, Richard, 114
Althusser, Louis, 7, 217–18n7
American Anti-Slavery Society, 122, 161, 175–76
American Convention for Promoting the Abolition of Slavery, 114
Anderson, Benedict, 71, 216n56
Andrews, William L., 240n25
Appeal to the Colored Citizens of the World (Walker), 119, 132, 236–37n76
Appleby, Joyce, 211n11, 232n2
apprenticeship: and assimilation, 20, 35, 37, 54, 147, 209, 222n81; and character, 38–39, 42–44, 46–48; and citizenship, 30, 35, 37, 106, 146; and *coartaciÓn*, 56, 222n80; and contract, 41–44; and fugitive labor clause, 5, 7, 16, 109, 111, 129–30, 132, 217n6; and slavery, 4–5, 7, 16, 30, 52, 166–67; and slave emancipation, 20, 48, 50, 52–55, 57, 61–62, 170–71. *See also* indentured servant; master and servant law
Arthur Mervyn, or, Memoirs of the Year 1793 (Brown): apprentice in, 20; Arthur Mervyn (character) as free laborer, 70, 106; assimilation in, 106; as *bildungsroman*, 71–72; chronotope in, 74–75; citizen in, 21, 70–71, 95, 99; evidence in, 87–89, 99–105; and jury trial, 94–95, 97–102; narrative form of, 71–73, 78–79, 93–95, 101, 104–6; nation in, 71–73; testimony in, 89–91, 93, 95–96, 101, 104–6
Articles of Confederation, 26
assimilation, 35–37, 48, 50, 54–55, 57, 106, 209
Autobiography of Benjamin Franklin (Franklin), 20, 39–44

Baker, Houston, 45, 112, 240n25
Bakhtin, Mikhail, 71, 244n23
Bal, Mieke, 70
Baldwin, Abraham, 15
Balibar, Etienne, 7, 9–10, 212–13n25
Bell, Michael Davitt, 230n99
Benezet, Anthony, 53–54, 57
Benjamin, Walter, 71
Bercovitch, Sacvan, 231–32n1, 239n22
Berthoff, Warner, 230n99
Best, Stephen M., 215n41, 218n10, 239n20
Billy Budd, Sailor; An Inside Narrative

(Melville), 178, 197–98, 201–5
Binder, Guyora, 246n7
Blackstone, William, 46, 64, 82, 221n62
Black Reconstruction in America (Du Bois), 169, 241n47
bondsman: as transition between slavery and freedom, 33, 209; as figure for slave and servant in Constitution, 7–9, 11, 112, 121; in *Billy Budd*, 201–203; in Byron, 161, 163; and slave personhood, 13–14, 25, 47, 130, 171; and property, 26; self-emancipation of, 160–63, 208; slave as, 112, 141, 162, 167, 209; as figure of working class, 163, 203, 205; as vanishing mediator of citizenship, 10–17, 25–26, 32. *See also* bound-yet-free labor
bound-yet-free labor, 16, 32, 204, 220n49. *See also* bondsman
Bourdieu, Pierre, 37, 230n94
Bromell, Nicholas K., 243n8
Brown, Charles Brockden, 20–21, 66, 75–76, 225n23
Brown, William Wells, 225n23
Byron, George Gordon, Lord, 160–63

Calhoun, John C., 2–3, 5, 16, 108–9, 115, 123, 234n44
Capital (Marx), 6–7, 17–19, 224n19
Carey, Matthew, 69, 74, 224n14
Carlyle, Thomas, 197
Champion of American Labor, 172
character: and citizenship, 37–39; and credibility, 71, 93, 97–98, 102, 106; private versus public, 35–39, 42–44, 56–59; and republican virtue, 70–71; and of slave and of servant, 47–52; as social capital, 38, 93; and testimony, 84, 87, 93–97
Chase, Salmon P., 4, 108, 120–21, 123
Childe Harold's Pilgrimage (Byron), 160
citizenship: African American, 114, 119–20, 131–32, 143, 145, 146; and Atlantic slave trade, 20, 32, 33, 45–48; and bondsman, 17, 32, 205; Constitution (U.S.), 11–12, 14, 214–15n35, 215n37; and democratic will, 30; Frederick Douglass's claims to, 143–46, 171; and Fourteenth Amendment, 11; and free labor, 6–9, 11, 30, 35, 169–71; and Fugitive Slave Clause, 5, 12, 109, 114, 119–20, 131–32; and immigrants, 14, 34–35; and indentured servants, 30; and jury trial, 82–83, 106, 131, 227–28n55; and nation, 11, 19, 72, 78; and the novel, 20–21, 66–68, 70–72, 94–95, 99, 106; and personhood, 11–12, 19, 131; and racial state, 25, 141; racialization of, 33, 119, 131; and representation, 24; republican, 21, 67, 70, 95, 99; and slave, 24, 30–31, 33; split subject of, 23, 36–38, 199; and subjectivation, 9, 141, 212–13n25; as subjectivity, 10, 14–15, 18–20, 22; and testimony, 21, 86–87, 94, 227n55; and three-fifths clause, 25, 29–32. *See also* Constitution (U.S.)
The Claims of the Negro Ethnologically Considered (Douglass), 146, 152–54, 157
Clay, Henry, 109
coartación, 55, 222n80
Commentaries on the Constitution of the United States (Story), 22, 115, 120, 124–26
Commentaries on the Laws of England (Blackstone), 46, 221n62
Commonwealth v. Hunt (1842), 179–80
Compromise of 1850, 2, 19, 22, 108–10, 142, 144, 232n19
Congress of Confederation (1776), 26
Considerations on the nature and extent of the Legislative Authority of the British Parliament (Wilson), 231n115
Constitution (U.S.): Article I, section 2 (Three-Fifths Clause), 12–14,

24–26, 27–29, 32, 45, 116–18, 137, 217n3, 218n10, 219n22, 233n27, 237–238n91; Article I, section 9 (Migration and Importation Clause), 14–15; Article IV, section 2 (Fugitive Labor Clause): 3–15, 24, 109–20, 123, 126–38, 170, 206, 217n6, 233n27, 236n67; as compromise, 5, 24–28, 31, 112–13, 116, 118, 120–21, 125, 138, 144, 217n4; as contract, 111–12, 120, 135–37, 143; Fourteenth Amendment, 11, 215n36. *See also* citizenship

The Constitution: A Pro-Slavery Compact (Phillips), 122, 237–238n91

The Constitution of Man (Combs), 155

The Constitution of the United States: Is it Pro-Slavery of Anti-Slavery? (Douglass), 1, 139–40

Constitutional hermeneutics: "original intent," 1–6, 8, 11, 14, 22, 32, 108–13, 115–17, 118, 120–21, 123–26, 132–39, 141, 143, 206, 216n50, 217n6, 233n24, 237–38n91; "strict construction," 2–3, 6, 16, 109–10, 112, 120–21, 123, 126–27, 129–30, 132–34, 136–38, 140–41, 233n24, 236n51, 237–38n91

contract: free labor, 17–18, 111, 179–81, 208; and immigrant, 34; indentured servitude and apprenticeship, 8, 41–44, 55, 129–30, 132, 244n22; and law, 21, 22, 23, 62, 129, 132, 183; as legal fiction, 167, 184, 200; and market, 181, 183–85, 200; and slavery 58–62, 128–30, 170–71 207–8; social, 42

Cover, Robert, 121–123, 235n50, 245–46n7

Crane, Gregg, 233n24, 234–35n45

Crania Americana (Morton), 154

Crèvecœur, J. Hector St. John de, 20, 33–39, 42, 46–47, 59

The Crisis of the Sugar Colonies (Stephen), 221n69

Cugoano, Ottobah, 20, 53, 54–55, 57, 60–61

Cursory Remarks upon the Rev. Mr. Ramsay's Essay (Tobin), 45

Dalton, Michael, 86, 96, 228n72
Davidson, Cathy, 95, 230n96
Davis, David Brion, 13, 217–18n7
Davis, Lennard J., 227n46
Debates in the Federal Convention of 1787 (Madison), 8, 32, 110, 113, 121
Debates in the Several State Conventions on the Adoption of the Federal Constitution (Eliot), 113, 121, 125
debt-bondage, 60–61, 129–30
"A Defense for Fugitive Slaves" (Spooner), 124–25, 133, 236n51, 237n84
Defoe, Daniel, 88, 91–92
Delbanco, Andrew, 243n12
DeLombard, Jeannine Marie, 237n87, 239n21
Derrida, Jacques, 212n19
Dimock, Wai-Chee, 243–42n12
Douglass, Frederick: on African Americans as "aliens" within U.S., 144–45; on Compromise of 1850, 144; and the Constitution (U.S.), 2–15, 107–20, 137–39, 143, 170, 206, 234–35n45; and citizenship, 143–146, 171, 209; and dialectic of race and class, 140, 169–70; on labor exploitation and slavery, 7, 16, 146, 167–68, 207; literary style of, 138; reading practices of, 2–4, 107–8; shift from Garrisonian position, 22–23, 138, 146; on slave genealogy,147–51; on slave literacy, 140; on race-consciousness, 145; on racial classification, 150–51; views on ethnography, 152, 154–57, 240n26; and women's rights movement, 241n40; *works*: "Addresses Delivered in Cincinnati, Ohio, 11–13 April 1854," 110; "The Address of Southern Delegates in Congress to their Constituents; or, the Address

of John C. Calhoun and Forty Other Thieves," 2–3, 4, 108–9, 123; "Change of Opinion Announced," 3, 108, 109, 122, 123, 138, 141, 142, 206, 239–40n23; "The Claims of the Negro Ethnologically Considered," 146, 152–54, 157; "The Constitution of the United States: Is it Pro-Slavery or Anti-Slavery?," 1, 139–40; "The Inaugural Address," 206; "Men of Color, To Arms!," 207–8. "A Nation in the Midst of a Nation," 144–45, 239–40n23; "Reception Speech at Finsbury Chapel, Moorfields, England, 12 May 1846," 164–65, 169; "What to the Slave is the Fourth of July?," 142–44, 211n8
Dred Scott v. Sanford, 115, 120, 218n10
Drescher, Seymour, 218n20, 222n81
Du Bois, W.E.B., 164, 169, 241n47

Eliot, Jonathan, 113
emancipation: and assimilation, 48, 50, 57–58; gradual, 20, 31, 55, 114; *coartación* as model of, 56, 222n80; immediate, 147, 162, 171; practical, 53–56; Proclamation, 206, 208–9
Emerson, Ralph Waldo, 175
Equiano, Olaudah, 19–20, 45–50, 57–62, 132
Essay Concerning Human Understanding (Locke), 40–41, 79, 84
Essays: On Poetry and Music (Beattie), 97–98
evidence, 79–82, 84–85, 87–89, 94, 102–103, 226n40

A Familiar Exposition of the Constitution of the United States (Story), 120, 234n40
Federalist Papers, 14, 24–26, 32–33, 36, 45, 113, 216n47
Fehrenbacher, Don E., 215n43, 233n24, 234n34, 234n39
Ferreira, P.J., 242n52

Fichtelberg, Joseph, 222n82
Fields, Barbara, 8, 212n20, 215n43
Finkelman, Paul, 217n6, 218n9, 219n22
Fish, Stanley, 245n26
Fliegelman, Jay, 92, 226n33
Foner, Eric, 4, 107–8, 234n45
Foster, Hannah Webster, 225n23
Franklin, Benjamin 20, 39–44, 220n49, 220n56
fugitive: criminal, 8, 10, 12, 70, 126, 134; servants and apprentices, 4, 8–10, 39, 44, 111, 126–27, 129–30, 132–35; slaves, 2–3, 48, 128–29
Fugitive Slave Act: of 1793, 12, 108, 113, 119; of 1850, 2, 4, 5, 9, 19, 108–9, 111

Garner, Margaret, 158
Garnet, Henry Highland, 128, 162–63, 167
Garrison, William Lloyd, 120, 122, 175–76
General Society of Mechanics and Tradesmen of the City of New York, 172–73
"The Genuine Information, delivered to the Legislature of Maryland, relative to the Proceedings of the General Convention held at Philadelphia in 1787" (Martin), 14
Gilbert, Sir Geoffrey, 82–86
Gilroy, Paul, 157–58
Gliddon, George 152, 154, 157
Goldberg, David Theo, 238n101
Goodell, William, 121, 122, 127–33, 135
Gould, Philip, 222n83
Gross, Ariela, 239n20

Hale, Matthew, 87
Hamer, Philip M., 236–37n76
Hartman, Saidiya V., 215n36, 241n36
Hinks, Peter P., 236–37n76
Holt, Thomas C., 217–18n7, 222n80, 222n81

immigrant, 14–15, 30, 33–36, 47, 144

indentured servant, 5, 7–8, 11, 13–14, 16, 20–21, 30, 34, 37, 55, 57, 109, 111, 126–27, 130, 132–34, 217n6, 220n49, 237n84. *See also* apprenticeship; master and servant law
An Inquiry into the Human Mind, on the Principles of Common Sense (Reid), 89–91
An Inquiry into the Nature and Causes of the Wealth of Nations (Smith), 28

James, C.L.R., 243n12
Jameson, Fredric, 10–11, 180, 213–14n34
Jefferson, Thomas, 108
Johnson, Barbara, 246n7

Karcher, Carolyn, 245–46n7
Kazanjian, David, 220–21n60
Konig, David Thomas, 223n3, n5, n6
Kettner, James, 215n36

labor: and abolitionism, 168–69, 207–208; bondage, 5, 8–9, 11–13, 16, 20, 25, 30, 35, 45–47, 109–11, 126, 130, 11; competition between free and slave, 167–68; and criminal conspiracy, 23, 179–80; differences between free and slave, 130, 132–134; discipline, models of, 54, 56; free, 17–19, 21, 27–29, 46–47, 50, 52, 54, 107, 112, 123, 129–30, 133, 146, 164–71, 204, 207, 221n69; organized, 172, 174–76, 179, 201–2, 207–8; productivity of, 57–58, 60; slave, 6–8, 10, 26–29, 32, 167; slave refusal of, in Garnet, 128, 162–163; strike, 176, 179–80, 198, 202–3; wage, 22, 56, 123, 129–30, 165–72, 174, 206, 208
Langan, Celeste, 229n86
law: and aesthetic judgment, 21, 91; epistemological forms of, 84, 86, 94, 99, 101; and forms of appearance, 6–7, 9, 84, 139; and history of literacy, 225n32;

intent of, 134–36; letter of, 109, 121, 133, 136, 141, 142–43, 205, 207–9; natural, 107–8, 122; positive, 46, 117, 129, 147 221n63, 234–235n45; and probability, 65, 79–80, 82, 87, 94, 99, 228n63; and print, 78; *res facta* and *res ley*, 80–81, 83, 86; and rules of evidence, 21, 80–82; and slave personhood, 31–32, 45–46, 127–28; slave's form of appearance in, 16, 24–26, 30–32; spirit of, 3–4, 22, 32, 121, 125–26, 135–36, 141, 144, 159, 206–7; and testimony, 86, 89, 91–92
Law of Evidence (Gilbert), 84–85, 228n63
Leaves of Grass (Whitman), 198, 245n31
Lectures on Law (Wilson), 21, 79–91
Letters from an American Farmer (Crèvecœur), 20, 33–39
Levine, Robert S., 234–35n45, 242n52
Levy, Leonard, 244n20
Life and Times of Frederick Douglass, 141, 163
Lincoln, Abraham, 108, 205–6
Locke, John, 40, 41–42, 79, 84–85
Looby, Christopher, 77–78, 220n56

Madison, James, 8–9, 26, 31–32, 45, 129, 216n47, 217n4
Magdol, Edward, 242n62
Mandel, Ernest, 216n53
Martin, Luther, 14–15, 34
Martin, Waldo E., 238n96, 239–40n23
Marx, Karl, 6–7, 10, 17–19, 167, 224n19
master and servant law, 4, 8, 12, 40, 44, 132, 184; and law of agency, 30, 60, 111, 127, 171, 182–85, 196. *See also* apprenticeship; indentured servant
Matthiessen, F.O., 243n12
Mayer, Robert, 227n46
McDowell, Deborah, 240n26, 241n36
McFeely, William S., 240n25
McKeon, Michael, 65, 225n32, 227n46
Melville, Herman, 23, 107, 172, 201

Michael, John, 244n12
Mills, Charles W., 238n101
Moby-Dick; or, the Whale (Melville): contract in, 179–81, 184, 181–84; labor in, 174, 184–85; labor strike in, 174–79, 180, 185; market in, 180–86, 193, 196; red flag in, 196–99; signs and signification in, 187–91; slave market in, 184–85, 191
Moretti, Franco, 223n88, 224n17
Morris, Gouverneur, 24, 30
Morris, Richard B., 222n77
Morton, Samuel, 152, 154, 157
My Bondage and My Freedom (Douglass): African American citizenship in, 144–45; African American print culture in, 161–62; labor in, 167–71; master-slave dialectic in, 148–51; racial classification in, 151–52, 154–57; representations of slave women in, 22, 151, 154, 157–60
Murphy, Paul Thomas, 242n51

Nabers, Deak, 215n36, 234–35n45
narrative: and dialogue form, 51–52, 58; embedded, 70–75, 94–96; as epistemological form, 93; and jury trial, 63–65, 69; testimony as, 21, 77–78, 101
Narrative of the Life of Frederick Douglass, 22–23, 109, 140–41, 145–46, 158, 160, 169
Nash, Gary B., 233n23
nation: and chronotope, 71–75; and Constitutional convention of 1787, 10–12, 14, 24–26
nationalism, 33–34, 71–74, 139, 142–145
Natural History of Man (Prichard), 151–57
Naval History of Great Britain (James), 202–3
Negro Seamen Act, South Carolina, 236–37n76
Nott, Josiah, 152, 154, 157
novel: and Atlantic slavery, 20; and chronotope, 71–72, 74–75; epistolary, 225n23; and formal realism, 63–64, 66, 223n2; and the law, 21, 63–65, 66, 75, 83, 89, 94, 101; and nationalism, 71–73; as trial, 64–65, 89, 70, 94–99, 102–3, 223n2, 230n96

O'Connell, Daniel, 163
Otis, James, 31
Otter, Samuel, 178, 230n94

Patey, Douglas Lane, 223n11, 231n109
Patterson, William, 29, 31, 217n5
Paul v. Virginia, 215n37
Pease, Donald E., 243n12, 245n24
personal liberty law, Pennsylvania (1826), 113–14
Phillips, Wendell, 22, 120–21, 138
Pocock, J.G.A., 231n108
Poovey, Mary, 226n37
Powell, H. Jefferson, 135
Prichard, James, 152–57
Prigg v. Pennsylvania: 5, 112, 113–20, 124, 127, 211–12n14; and the "badge of the slave," 119, 131; and extraterritoriality of slaveholder's rights of property, 119, 131–32; and "original intent," 133–34; and racialization, 119–20, 131
property: and character, 38–39, 46, 51–52, 61, 70, 129; chattel, 51–52, 61, 127–28; and citizenship, 30–32, 34, 37–39, 215n37; freehold, 38; labor as, 17, 24, 127; and slavery, 3, 5–7, 24, 26–32, 45–46, 61 112, 115–19, 126–28, 45–46, 57, 128–29,165, 205; and wage-labor, 17, 166–67, 208

race: in slavery debates, 2, 4, 22, 130–31; and ethnography, 152–56; and gender, 146, 151–52, 154–55, 157; and scientific racism, 150–54, 157; social construction of, 22, 150–57

racialization: of citizenship, 33, 119–20, 131; of slavery, 18, 150–51, 156–57
Radical Reformer's Gazette, 163
Reid, Thomas, 80, 89–91
Review of Lysander Spooner's Essay on the Unconstitutionality of Slavery (Phillips), 122
Reynolds, Larry J., 243n4, 243n12
Robinson Crusoe (Defoe), 88, 90–91
Roediger, David, 165, 169
Rogin, Michael, 174, 177, 232n19, 243n12
Rush, Benjamin, 53, 222n79

Salinger, Sharon V., 221n66
Second Treatise of Government (Locke), 41–42
Secret Proceedings and Debates of the Convention Assembled at Philadelphia, in the Year 1787, 113, 233n20
Sellers, Charles, 216n57, 243n8
Shapiro, Barbara, 84, 96
Sharp, Granville, 46, 53, 55–56
Shaw, Lemuel, 111, 115, 179–80
A Short Account of the Malignant Fever, lately prevalent in Philadelphia (Carey), 69
Sims Case, 111, 115
slavery: and citizenship, 24–25, 30, 32; in Constitution (U.S.), 1–3, 7–9, 14–16, 32, 121, 108, 233n27; and debt, 60–61, 129–30; emancipation and assimilation, 48–50, 52–54; and economics of emancipation, 57–62; and indentured servitude, 126–27; labor, 6–8, 10, 26–29, 32, 167; as metaphor for wage-labor, 165–69; and personhood, 6, 25, 27, 29–31, 47, 130, 132–33, 135, 140–41; and political economy, 25–28, 45; and political representation, 24–32; 120; and property, 27, 29–31, 45–46, 128–29; and taxation, 27–29, 31–32
Smith, Gerritt, 121, 162

Smith, James McCune, 147, 155, 161
Smith, James Morton, 216n50
Sociology for the South; or, the Failure of Free Society (Fitzhugh), 169–70
Soderlund, Jean R., 233n23
Some Historical Account of Guinea (Benezet), 53–54
Somerset v. Stewart, 46, 117, 221n63
Spivak, Gayatri Chakravorty, 212n19
Spooner, Lysander, 22, 122–27, 133–34, 136–37, 235n50
Statute of Artificers (1562), 55
Stauffer, John, 239–40n23
Stein, Peter, 227n50
Steinfeld, Robert, 8, 220n49
Stepto, Robert, 240n25
Stimson, Shannon C., 226n38
Story, Joseph, 5, 22, 115–18, 120, 124–26, 184, 234n40
strike, 174–76, 179–80, 241n47, 244n20
Stroud, George, 129
Sundquist, Eric J., 239n21, 240n25

Taney, Roger B., 115, 120
Tappan, Lewis, 239–40n23
testimony, 85–89, 96–98, 102–3
Thomas, Brook, 236, n73, 243n12
Thoughts and Sentiments on the Evil and Wicked Traffic of the Slavery and Commerce of the Human Species (Cugoano), 20, 54–55, 60–61
Tobin, James, 45
Tomlins, Christopher, 21, 243n8, 244n20
Trumpener, Katie, 74
Typee (Melville), 179
Types of Mankind (Gliddon and Nott), 152, 155–56

The Unconstitutionality of Slavery (Spooner), 22, 122, 126–27, 137–38

Vesey, Denmark, 162, 236n76

Views of American Constitutional Law (Goodell), 122–23, 127–31, 135–38, 234n37

Wald, Priscilla, 225n25, 239n21, 240n25, 241n36
Waldman, Theodore, 223n10
Waldstreicher, David, 220n49
Walker, David, 119, 132
Wallerstein, Immanuel, 212n18
Warner, Michael, 75, 95
Watt, Ian, 63–66, 229n82
Weber, Max, 10–11, 213–214n34
Webster, Daniel, 109
Weinstein, Cindy, 243n8
Weisberg, Robert, 246n7
Welsh, Alexander, 102–3

Wieland; or, the Transformation (Brown), 78, 225n23
Wilentz, Sean, 242n61, 243n1
Wills, Garry, 219n23
White-Jacket, or, the World in a Man-of-War (Melville), 177–78
Whitman, Walt, 198
Wiecek, William, 8, 234n44
Williams, Raymond, 219n43, 220n46
Wilson, James: 21, 27, 31, 79–91, 94, 99; on natural language, 88–93; on political representation and "free will," 231n115; on testimony, 96–98
Wong, Edlie L., 215n41
Working Man's Advocate, 172

Žižek, Slavoj, 213n34

About the Author

Hoang Gia Phan is Associate Professor of English at the University of Massachusetts, Amherst, where he teaches early American literature, nineteenth-century American literature, and African American literature.